Building Websites with VB.NET and DotNetNuke 3.0

Daniel N. Egan

D1561124

PUBLISHING

Building Websites with VB.NET and DotNetNuke 3.0

First edition: February 2005

Published by Packt Publishing Ltd.
32 Lincoln Road
Olton
Birmingham, B27 6PA, UK.

ISBN 1-904811-27-2

www.packtpub.com

Cover Design by www.visionwt.com

Credits

Author
Daniel N. Egan

Commissioning Editor
Douglas Paterson

Technical Reviewers
Dennis J Bottjer
K. Scott Allen
Colin Munford

Technical Editors*
Nanda Padmanabhan
Niranjan Jahagirdar

Proofreader
Chris Smith

Layout*
Niranjan Jahagirdar

Indexer*
Niranjan Jahagirdar

Cover Designer
Helen Wood

* Services provided by www.editorialindia.com

About the Author

Daniel N. Egan has, over the past seven years, held a variety of positions in the information technology and engineering fields. Currently, he is a System Development Specialist for Automated Data Processing's Southern California region working extensively in database applications and web development. Daniel is an MCP and MCSD. In addition to his development work, he teaches a VB.NET Certification course at California State University Fullerton and also serves on its .NET Advisory board. He is also the founder and chief author of Dot Net Doc (www.DotNetDoc.com), a .NET and DotNetNuke developer resource website built using the DotNetNuke framework. He has written numerous articles on DotNetNuke and the underlying architecture. He is the cofounder of the LA/Orange County DotNetNuke User Group.

I would like to thank Kirsten, my true love and best friend, for putting up with the many hours spent at the computer during this process. I love you with all my heart. I would also like to thank Douglas Paterson for all his generous help answering my never ending flood of questions, and keeping me on track to finish this book. Finally I would like to thank the technical reviewers, among others, for all of the time they spent helping me find the right things to say and exactly how to say them.

Table of contents

Introduction

DotNetNuke is a free, open-source evolution of Microsoft's celebrated ASP.NET reference implementation, the IBuySpy portal solution kit. DotNetNuke began life as a framework for constructing data-driven intranet and Internet portal applications, and has now developed into an advanced web content management system with tools to manage a dynamic and interactive data-driven website. The DotNetNuke portal framework allows you to quickly create a fully featured community-driven website, complete with standard modules, user registration, and integrated security. This free open-source application puts a staggering range of functionality into your hands, and, either by using it as is or by customizing it to your requirements, you are giving your projects a great head start.

Supported and tested by thousands of developers in the DotNetNuke community across the world, the DotNetNuke framework, on one hand, offers you the luxury of a well-tested and proven architecture, and on the other, the ability to manage your site through an easy web-based administration system.

The book is structured to help you understand, implement, and extend the DotNetNuke framework; it will take you inside DotNetNuke, allowing you to harness its power for easily creating your own websites.

What This Book Covers

Chapter 1 introduces DotNetNuke (DNN) and discusses the meaning and purpose of web portals, and the common aspects of successful web portals. It looks at different types of open-source web portals, and discusses why we selected DotNetNuke for this book. We then meet our fictional client Coffee Connections and, using user stories, gather the requirements needed to build this client's site.

In *Chapter 2* we see how to install a local version of DotNetNuke with Microsoft SQL Server, and cover setting the required permissions on your machine to run DNN properly. The chapter also covers the process of upgrading from previous versions of DotNetNuke.

In *Chapter 3* we cover users, roles, and pages. Users are the individuals who visit or administer your portal, and their power depends on the roles that they have been assigned. We discuss how each page of your portal can be administered differently, laying the foundation for the rest of the book. From defining users, to registration, to security roles, this chapter will help you to begin administering a DNN portal.

In *Chapter 4* we cover the standard modules that come pre-packaged with DotNetNuke. We cover their basic uses as well as situations they may be used in. You will use these modules to build your portal's content.

Chapter 5 introduces the administrative functions available to the host and admin logins. These are special logins that have access to all areas of your portal, and are used to secure your site and make changes to its content. This chapter takes you through the tools to make sure you are comfortable with all that is available to you.

Understanding the core architecture of DNN is essential if you want to extend the system or even modify the existing code. In *Chapter 6* we learn how the DotNetNuke framework builds the pages, and what are the major classes that drive it.

In *Chapter 7* we take the knowledge we learned in the last chapter and use it to build a custom module. You will learn everything you need to know to start building your own modules so you can extend the capabilities of your portal. We begin by setting up a private assembly project, which allows you to create your custom module outside the core project code while still giving you the ability to debug within the DotNetNuke project. After creating your user controls, you will create your data access and business logic layers, and finish by learning how to package your module for distribution.

Chapter 8 talks about skins. A skin is the outer layer of your site, and defines the look and feel of the portal. In this chapter we design a custom skin for the Coffee Connections site. You will learn the skills needed to skin both your portal and your module containers.

Chapter 9 shows you how to enhance your module with some of the modules that are available to you from the DotNetNuke community. From user forums, to e-Commerce, to security modules, this chapter will help you get the most out of your portal without having to create everything yourself.

When you finally have your portal the way you want it to look and function, you are ready to deploy it, and that is what *Chapter 10* shows you how to do. The chapter advises on what you should look for in a web host and helps to steer you clear of common deployment mistakes.

In *Chapter 11* we show you how to take advantage of one of the most exciting features of DotNetNuke: multiple portals. These are additional portals that use the same underlying database, but can contain different content. So instead of just having one website, you can create as many as you need using just one DotNetNuke installation. From parent portals to child portals, this chapter gives you the information necessary to create new portals from scratch or to use the new template structure built into the framework.

Chapter 12, the final chapter of the book, focuses back on the DotNetNuke developer. In this chapter we walk through the steps necessary to create a new provider for a RichTextBox control, improving on the FreeTextBox. The provider model is used extensively throughout DotNetNuke and allows you to have a "pluggable" architecture, giving you the freedom to add different tools while keeping the core code unchanged.

What You Need for Using This Book

This book has been written both for the beginner wanting to set up a website and also for ASP.NET developers with a grasp of VB.NET and access to Visual Studio .NET. No prior knowledge of DotNetNuke is assumed. To use this book, you need to have access to Visual Studio .NET Professional or higher.

This book uses the DotNetNuke open-source project available from http://www.DotNetNuke.com. To install and run DotNetNuke, you will need:

- The .NET framework
- One of Windows Server 2003, Windows 2000, or Windows XP operating systems
- An installation of SQL Server 2000

Conventions

In this book, you will find a number of styles of text that distinguish between different kinds of information. Here are some examples of these styles, and an explanation of their meaning.

There are three styles for code. Code words in text are shown as follows: "The GetPortalSettings method call will retrieve enough information to populate the PortalSettings object".

A block of code will be set as follows:

```
Public Shared Function GetCurrentPortalSettings() As PortalSettings
    Return CType(HttpContext.Current.Items("PortalSettings"), _
        PortalSettings)
End Function
```

When we wish to draw your attention to a particular part of a code block, the relevant lines or items will be made bold:

```
Public Shared Function GetCurrentPortalSettings() As PortalSettings
    Return CType(HttpContext.Current.Items("PortalSettings"), _
        PortalSettings)
End Function
```

New terms and **important words** are introduced in a bold-type font. Words that you see on the screen, in menus or dialog boxes for example, appear in our text like this: "clicking the Next button moves you to the next screen".

> Tips, suggestions, or important notes appear in a box like this.

Any command-line input and output is written as follows:

```
>xcopy /s *.* ..\stage
cd ..\stage
```

Reader Feedback

Feedback from our readers is always welcome. Let us know what you think about this book, what you liked or may have disliked. Reader feedback is important for us to develop titles that you really get the most out of.

To send us general feedback, simply drop an e-mail to feedback@packtpub.com, making sure to mention the book title in the subject of your message.

If there is a book that you need and would like to see us publish, please send us a note in the SUGGEST A TITLE form on www.packtpub.com or e-mail suggest@packtpub.com.

If there is a topic that you have expertise in and you are interested in either writing or contributing to a book, see our author guide on www.packtpub.com/authors.

Customer Support

Now that you are the proud owner of a Packt book, we have a number of things to help you to get the most from your purchase.

Downloading the Example Code for the Book

Visit http://www.packtpub.com/support, and select this book from the list of titles to download any example code or extra resources for this book. The files available for download will then be displayed.

> The downloadable files contain instructions on how to use them.

Errata

Although we have taken every care to ensure the accuracy of our contents, mistakes do happen. If you find a mistake in one of our books—maybe a mistake in text or code—we would be grateful if you could report this to us. By doing this you can save other readers from frustration, and also help to improve subsequent versions of this book.

If you find any errata, report them by visiting http://www.packtpub.com/support, selecting your book, clicking on the Submit Errata link, and entering the details of your errata. Once your errata have been verified, your submission will be accepted and the errata added to the list of existing errata. The existing errata can be viewed by selecting your title from http://www.packtpub.com/support.

Questions

You can contact us at questions@packtpub.com if you are having a problem with some aspect of the book, and we will do our best to address it.

1

What Is DotNetNuke?

From company intranets to mom and pop shops to local chapters of the 4H club, most organizations are looking to have a presence on the World Wide Web. Open-source web portals answer this demand by providing easy to install and use websites that are not only extremely functional but also free. Whether it is to sell services or to have a place to meet, web portals play an important part of communications on the Web.

In this chapter, we will first discuss what web portals are and what successful web portals have in common. We will explore different types of open-source web portals and discuss why we selected DotNetNuke for our project over other available portals. In addition, we will cover the benefits gained by using an established program as a framework and the benefits of DotNetNuke specifically. We will then introduce Coffee Connections, our fictional client. We will get a brief overview of Coffee Connections, determine the specific requirements for its website and gather the requirements using user stories. This will give you a general overview of what to expect from this book and how to best use it depending on your role and experience with web portals and Visual Basic .NET.

Open-Source Web Portals

So what does it actually mean to have a web portal? We begin the chapter with an explanation of what a portal is, and then go on to the features of a web portal and reasons for selecting open-source web portals.

What Is a Web Portal?

You have decided to start a portal and first need to find out what makes a web portal. Does throwing up a few web pages with links to different topics make it a web portal? A portal, in its most basic sense, aims to be an entry point to the World Wide Web. Portals will typically offer services such as search engines, links to useful pages, news, forums, and e-mail, all in an effort to draw users to their site. In most cases, portals provide these services free in the hope that users will make the site their home page or at least come back often. Successful examples include Yahoo! and MSN. These sites are horizontal portals because they typically attract a wide audience and primarily exist to produce advertising income for their owners. Other web portals may focus on a specific group of users or be part of a corporate intranet. They will most often concentrate on one particular subject, like gardening or sports. This type of portal is a vertical portal because they focus inward and cater to a more select group of people.

The type of portal you create depends on the target audience you are trying to attract. You may discover that the portal you create is a combination of both horizontal and vertical portals in order to address specific needs, while simultaneously giving a broader range of services to your visitors. Whatever type of portal you decide on, horizontal or vertical, they both will share certain key characteristics and functionality that guarantee users will return to your site.

Common Portal Features

What makes a great portal? Is it a free prize giveaway, local weather forecasts, or sports scores for the teams you watch? While this package of extras might attract some users, you will certainly miss a large group of people who have no interest in these offerings. There are as many web portals to choose from as programming languages they are written in. However, one thing is for certain: there are particular services your portal should incorporate in order for it to be successful and attract a wide audience.

- **A Gateway to the World Wide Web**: Web portals are the way we start our day. Most of us have set up our home page to one web portal or another and whether you start at MSN, Yahoo!, or Apple, you will notice some common features. Local weather forecasts, movie reviews, or even maps of your community are a few features that make the web portal feel comfortable and tailored for you. Like reading the morning newspaper with a cup of coffee, it gives you a sense of home. Web portals attempt to be the place where all of your browsing starts.

- **Content Management**: Content management has come a long way from the days of paper memos and sticky notes. Computers have done away with the overflowing file cabinets holding copies of every document that crossed our desks. Little did we realize that even though we would be solving one problem, another one would rise in its place. How many times have you searched your computer wondering where you saved the document your boss needs right now? Then once you find it, you need to make sure that it is the correct version. Alternatively, if you run a Soccer Club, how do you ensure that all of your players can get a copy of the league rules? One of the commonest uses for a web portal is content management. It allows users to have one place to upload, download, and search for a file that is important to them or their company. It also alleviates the problem of having more than one copy of a document. If the document is stored only in one location, you will always have the current copy.

- **Community Interaction**: People have always found a place to meet. From the malt shop on Main Street to your local church, people like to find others who have the same interests. This is one of the main drawing powers of a web portal. Whether you are a Christian looking for other Christians (`http://www.christianwebsite.com/`) or someone who is interested in **Person Digital Assistants (PDAs)** (`http://www.pdabuzz.com`) there is a web portal out there for you. Web portals offer different ways for users to communicate. Among these are discussion forums that allow you to either post a question or comment to a message board or comment on the posts of others. Chat rooms take this a step further with the ability to talk to one or more persons "live" and have your questions answered immediately.
One of the most interesting ways to express your opinions or communicate your ideas to others on a web portal is to use a **blog**. A blog (also know as a weblog) is sort of like a diary on the Web, except you don't lock it when you are done writing in it. Instead, you make all your thoughts and observations available to the world. These blogs range in topic from personal and comical (`http://weblog.herald.com/column/davebarry/`) to technical (`http://weblogs.asp.net/scottgu`) and in recent years, have exploded on the scene as the *de facto* way to communicate on the Internet. Most web portals will offer at least one of these ways to communicate.

- **Security & Administration**: Web portal security not only manages who can access particular sections of the site but enables administrators to access, add, and change content on the site. Most web portals use a **WYSIWYG** (what you see is what you get) style editor that allows users to add and edit content without needing to know programming or HTML. It is as simple as adding content to a text file. Having users authenticate with the portal allows you to tailor the site to individuals so that they can customize their experience.

Why DotNetNuke?

When the time comes to decide how you want to build your portal, you will have to make many decisions: Do I create my portal from scratch? If not, which web portal framework should I use? What type of hardware and software do I have available to me? Moreover, what is my skill level in any particular platform? In this section, we will discuss some of the better-known portals that are available.

For our portal, we have decided that it would be counter-productive to start from scratch. Instead, we will be using an already developed framework in designing our portal. We will have many options from which to select. We will discuss a few of our options and determine why we believe DotNetNuke fits us best.

PHP-Nuke

Most likely the grandfather of DotNetNuke (in name at least) is PHP-Nuke
(http://www.phpnuke.org). PHP-Nuke is a web portal that uses **PHP** (a recursive
acronym for **PHP: Hypertext Preprocessor**) pages to create dynamic web pages. You
can use it in a Windows environment but it is most comfortable in a Linux/Unix
environment. PHP is and open-source, HTML-embedded scripting language, which is an
alternative to Microsoft's **ASP (Active Server Pages)** the precursor to ASP.NET, which
is the programming language used in DotNetNuke. PHP-Nuke, like DotNetNuke, is a
modular system that comes with pre-built standard modules and allows you to enhance
the portal by creating custom modules. Since we will be using a Windows platform, and
are more comfortable using ASP.NET, this choice would not fit our needs.

Metadot

Metadot Portal Server is another open-source portal system available to those looking to
create a web portal. Metadot states that "its user friendly environment" allows non-
technical individuals to create powerful websites with just a "few clicks of the mouse".
Like PHP-Nuke, Metadot runs primarily on the Linux operating system, Apache web
server, and a MySQL database. It uses Perl as its scripting language. It also supports
Windows but is most comfortable in a Linux environment. For the same reasons as PHP-
Nuke, this framework will not fit our needs.

Rainbow

Similar to DotNetNuke, the Rainbow project is an open-source initiative to build a **CMS**
(content management system) based on the IBuySpy portal using Microsoft's ASP.NET.
In contrast to DotNetNuke, the Rainbow Project used the C# implementation of IBuySpy
as its starting point. It does run on Windows and uses ASP.NET, but our language of
choice for this project is VB.NET so we will rule our Rainbow.

DotNetNuke

So why did we select DotNetNuke as the web portal of choice for this book? Well here
are a few reasons for selecting DotNetNuke:

- **Open-source web portal written in VB.NET:** Since we wanted to focus on
building our web portal using the new VB.NET language, this was an
obvious choice. The original author of DotNetNuke (formerly IBuySpy
Workshop), Shaun Walker of Perpetual Motion Interactive Systems Inc.,
originally released DotNetNuke 1.0 as an open-source project in December
2002. This represented an expansion of the Portal Starter Kit, which
Microsoft released as a reference project for a best practices approach for
building ASP.NET applications. Since then DotNetNuke has evolved to
version 3.0 and the code base has grown from 10,000 to over 90,000 lines of

managed code and contains many feature enhancements over the original Starter Kit.

- **Utilizes the new ASP.NET version 2 Provider Model**: With the release of ASP.NET version 2 (Code-named Whidbey) Microsoft will be debuting a new provider pattern model. This enhances the ability to separate the data tier from the presentation tier and provides the ability to specify your choice of databases. The DotNetNuke framework comes pre-packaged with an SQL Data Provider (Microsoft's SQL Server or MSDE). You can also follow this model to create your own data provider or obtain one from a third-party vendor. There are already a Microsoft Access (outsourced in version 3.0), MySQL, and Oracle database providers available from BlueJacket Software (http://www.dnndp.com/) with many more on the way. In addition, the DotNetNuke framework also uses many of Microsoft's building-block services like the **Data Access Application Block** for .NET (http://msdn.microsoft.com/library/default.asp?url=/library/en-us/dnbda/html/daab-rm.asp) introduced by Microsoft in its Patterns and Practices articles.

- **Contains key portal features expected from a web portal**: DotNetNuke comes pre-packaged with modules that cover discussions, events, links, news feeds, contact, FAQs, announcements and more. This gives you the ability to spend your time working on specialized adaptations to your site.

- **Separates page layout, page content, and the application logic**: This allows you to have a designer who can manage the "look and feel" of the site, an administrator with no programming experience who can manage and change the content of the site, and a developer who can create custom functionality for the site.

- **Ability to "skin" your site**: Separating the data tier from the presentation tier brings us to one of the most exciting advancements in recent versions of DotNetNuke, skinning. DotNetNuke employs an advanced skinning solution that allows you to change the look and feel of your site. In this book, we will show you how to create your own custom skin, but you will also find many custom skins free on websites like eXtra Dimensions Design Group (http://www.xd.com.au/), NukedSkins (http://www.nukedskins.com/), and Snowcovered (http://www.snowcovered.com). These give you the ability to change the look and feel of your site without having to know anything about design, HTML, or programming.

- **Supports multiple portals**: Another advantage of using DotNetNuke as your web portal of choice is the fact that you can run multiple portals using one code base and one database. This means you can have different portals for different groups on the same site but still have the all of the information reside in one database. This gives you an advantage in the form of easy access to all portal information, *and* a central place to manage your hosting environment. The framework comes with numerous tools for banner advertising, site promotion, hosting, and affiliate management

- **Designed with an extensible framework**: You can extend the framework in a number of ways. You can modify the core architecture of the framework to achieve your desired results (we will discuss the pratfalls of doing this in later chapters) and design custom modules that "plug in" to the existing framework. This would be in addition to the pre-built modules that come with DotNetNuke. These basic modules give you a great starting point and allow you to get your site up and running quickly.

- **Mature portal framework**: As of the writing of this book, DotNetNuke is on version 3.0. It means that you will be using an application that has gone through its paces. It has been extensively tested and is widely used as a web portal application by thousands of existing users. What this affords you is stability. You can be comfortable knowing that thousands of websites already use the DotNetNuke framework for their web portal needs.

- **Active and robust community**: Community involvement and continuing product evolution are very important parts of any open-source project and DotNetNuke has both of these. The DotNetNuke support forum is one of the most active and dynamic community forums on the ASP.NET website. There are currently over 120,000 users registered on the DotNetNuke website. At the time of writing, the much-anticipated DotNetNuke version 3.0 had just been released, and has brought about a significant number of improvements over its previous releases. The core team continues to move forward, always striving towards a better product for the community.

- **Recognized by the Microsoft team as a best-practices application**: In March 2004 at the VSLive conference in San Francisco, the premiere conference for Visual Studio .NET Developers, DotNetNuke 2.0 was officially released, and showcased for the public. This gave DotNetNuke a great leg up in the open-source portal market and solidified its position as a leader in the field.

Benefits of Using an Established Program

Whether you are building a website to gather information about your soccer club or putting up a department website on your company's intranet, one thing is certain—to write your web portal from the ground up, you should plan on "coding" for a long time. Just deciding on the structure, design, and security of your site will take you months. After all this is complete, you will still need to test and debug. At this point, you still have not even begun to build the basic functionality of your web portal.

So why start from scratch when you have the ability to build on an existing structure? Just as you would not want to build your own operating system before building a program to run on it, using an existing architecture allows you to concentrate on enhancing and customizing the portal for your specific needs. If you are like me and use Visual Studio to do your development, then you already adhere to this concept. There is no need for you to create the basic building blocks of your application (forms, buttons, textboxes, etc.); instead you take the building blocks already there for you and assemble (and sometimes enhance) them to suit your needs.

The DotNetNuke Community

The DotNetNuke has one of the most active and dynamic support forums on the ASP.NET website and has over 120,000 users registered on the DotNetNuke website.

Core Team

The core team comprises individuals invited to join the team by Shaun Walker, whom they affectionately call the "Benevolent Dictator". Their invitations were based on their contributions and their never-ending support of others in the DotNetNuke forum. Each team member has a certain area of responsibility based on his or her abilities. From database functionality and module creation to skinning, they are the ones responsible for the continued advancement of the framework. However, not being a member of the core team does not mean that you cannot contribute to the project. There are many ways for you to help with the project. Many developers create custom modules they make freely available to the DotNetNuke community. Other developers create skins they freely distribute. Still others help answer the many questions in the DotNetNuke forum (http://www.asp.net/forums/showforum.aspx?forumid=90). You can also be a contributor to the core architecture. You are welcome to submit code improvements to extend, and/or expand the capabilities of DotNetNuke. These submissions will be evaluated by the core team and could possibly be added to the next version.

The DotNetNuke Discussion Forum

With well over 80,000 individual posts in the main DotNetNuke forum alone, it is one of the most active and attentive forums on the ASP.NET Forums website (http://www.asp.net/Forums/). Here you will find help for any issue you may be having in DotNetNuke.

The main forum is where you will find most of the action but there are also sub-forums covering topics such as Core Framework, Resources, Getting Started, and Custom Modules. You can search and view posts in any of the forums but will need to register if you want to post your own questions or reply to other users posts. The great thing about the forums is that you will find the core team hanging out there. Who better to ask questions about DotNetNuke than those who created it? However, do not be shy, if you know the answer to someone else's question feel free to post an answer. That is what the community is all about, people helping people through challenging situations.

The Bug Tracker

Like any application there are bound to be a few bugs that creep into the application now and then. To manage this occurrence, DotNetNuke core team uses a third-party bug tracking system called Gemini, by CounterSoft. The bug tracker is not for general questions or setup and configuration errors; questions of that nature should be posted in the discussion forum. You can view the status of current bugs at the Gemini site (`http://support.dotnetnuke.us`), but will not be able to add new bugs to the system. Reporting a bug is currently done by posting to the DotNetNuke forum. Follow the guidelines currently posted there (`http://www.asp.net/Forums/ShowPost.aspx?tabindex=1&PostID=752638`). To summarize; you need to first search the bug tracker to make sure that it has not already been reported. If you cannot find it in the system you will need to supply the forum with exactly what you did, what you expected to have happen, and what actually happened. Verified bugs will be assigned to core team members to track down and repair.

DotNetNuke Project Roadmap Team

If you want to find out what is in the works for future releases of DotNetNuke then you will want to check out the DotNetNuke Project Roadmap (`http://www.dotnetnuke.com/Default.aspx?tabid=616`). The main purpose of this document is as a communication vehicle to inform users and stakeholders of the project's direction. The Roadmap accomplishes this by using User Stories. User Stories are closely related to Use Cases with the exception that they take the view of a fictitious customer requesting an enhancement. The priority of the enhancements depends on both the availability of resources (core team) and the perceived demand for the feature.

The License Agreement

The license type used by the DotNetNuke project is a modified version of the BSD (Berkeley Software Distribution) license. As opposed to the more restrictive GPL (GNU General Public License) used by many other open-source projects, the BSD license is very permissive and imposes very few conditions on what a user can do with the software; this includes charging clients for binary distributions, with no obligation to include source code. If you have further questions on the specifics of the license agreement, you can find it in the documents folder of the DotNetNuke application or on the DotNetNuke website.

Coffee Connections

Wherever your travels take you, from sunny Long Beach, California to the cobblestone streets of Hamburg, Germany, chances are that there is a coffee shop nearby. Whether it is a Starbucks (located on just about every corner) or a local coffee shop tucked neatly in between all the antique stores on Main Street, they all have one thing in common. Coffee, right? Well yes, they do have coffee in common, but more importantly, they are places for people with shared interests to gather, relax, and enjoy their coffee while taking in the environment around them. Coffee shops offer a wide variety of services in addition to coffee, from WiFi to poetry readings to local bands; they keep people coming back by offering them more than just a cup o' joe.

But how do you find the coffee shops that have the type of atmosphere you are looking for? In addition, how do you locate them in your surrounding area? That's where Coffee Connections comes in; it is its desire to fill this void by creating a website where coffee lovers and coffee shop regulars can connect and search for coffee shops in their local area that cater to their specific needs. Coffee Connections has a vision to create a website that will bring this together and help promote coffee shops around the world. Users will be able to search for coffee shops by zip code, types of entertainment, amenities, or name. It will also allow its customers to purchase goods online and communicate with others through chat rooms and forums.

Determining Client Needs

In any project, it is important to determine the needs of the client before work begins on the project. When designing a business-driven solution for your client your options range from an extensive **Request for Proposal (RFP)** and case modeling, to user stories and **Microsoft Solutions Framework (MSF)**. To determine the needs and document the requirements of Coffee Connections we will use user stories.

We selected **User Stories** as our requirements collection method for two reasons. First, the DotNetNuke core team uses this method when building enhancements and upgrading the DotNetNuke framework. Thus using user stories will help to give you a better understanding of how the core team works, the processes team members follow, and how they accomplish these tasks in a short amount of time. Second, it is a very clean and concise way to determine the needs of your client. We will be able to determine the needs of Coffee Connections without the need for pages and pages of requirement documents.

What Is a User Story?

User stories were originally introduced as part of **Extreme Programming**. Extreme Programming is a type of software development based on simplicity, communication, and customer feedback. It is primarily used within small teams when it is important to develop software quickly while the environment and requirements of the program rapidly change. This fits the DotNetNuke project and the DotNetNuke core team well.

User stories provide a framework for the completion of a project by giving a well-designed description of a system and its major processes.

The individual stories, written by customers, are features they wish the program to possess. Since the user stories are written by the customer, they are written in the customer's terminology and without much technical jargon. The user stories are usually written on index cards and are approximately three sentences long. The limited space for detail forces the writer to be concise and get to the heart of the requirement. When it is time to implement the user story, the developer will sit down with the customer—in what is referred to as an iteration meeting—to go over particular details of each user story. Thus, an overview of a project is quickly conceptualized without the developer or customer being bogged down in minor details.

User stories also help in the creation of **acceptance tests**. Acceptance tests are specified tests performed by the user of a system to determine if the system is functioning correctly according to specifications the user presented at the beginning of the development process. This assures that the product performs as expected.

Advantages of Using User Stories

There are many different methods of defining requirements when building an application, so why use user stories? User stories fit well into **Rapid Application Development (RAD)** programming. Software and the computer industry in general change on a daily basis. The environment is fast moving and in order to compete in the marketplace it is important to have quick turn around for your product. User stories help to accomplish this in the following ways:

- **Stressing the importance of communication**: One of the central ideas behind user stories is the ability to have the users write down what exactly is expected from the product. This helps to promote communication by keeping the client involved in the design process.

- **Being easily understandable**: Since user stories are written by the customer and not by the developer, the developer won't have the problem of "talking over the head" of the customer. User stories help customers know exactly what they are getting because they personally write down what they want in terms that they understand.

- **Allowing for deferred details**: User stories help the customer as well as the developer understand the complete scope of a project without being bogged down by the details.

- **Focusing on project goals**: The success of your project depends less on creative coding strategies and more on whether you were able to meet the customer's goals. It is not what you think it should do but what the customer thinks it should do.

Coffee Connections User Stories

Below you will find the user stories for Coffee Connections. From these stories, we will use DotNetNuke to build the customer's website. The title of the card is followed by a short description of what is needed. Throughout the book, we will refer back to these as we continue to accomplish the project goals for Coffee Connections.

Title	Description
Web Store	Users will be able to purchase coffee and coffee-shop-related merchandise through the website.
Coffee Shop Search	Users will be able to find coffee shops in their area by searching a combination of zip code, coffee shop name, amenities, or atmosphere and rating.
Coffee Finder Additions	Users will be able to post coffee shops they find and give a description of the coffee shop for other users to see.
Coffee Shop Reviews	Users will have the ability to rate the coffee shops that are listed on the website.
Site Updates	Administrators will have the ability to modify the site content easily using a web-based interface.
Coffee Chat	Users will be able to chat with people from other coffee shops on the site.
Coffee Forum	Users will be able to post questions and replies in a Coffee Shop Forum.

When referring back to the user stories later in the book, we will use a card to compare and determine if we've met the customer's needs.

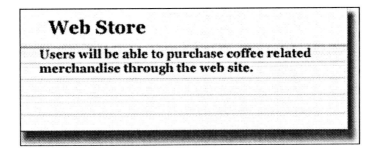

Web Store

Users will be able to purchase coffee related merchandise through the web site.

Summary

In this chapter, we have discussed the meaning and purpose of web portals, what successful web portals have in common, looked at different types of open-source web portals, and discussed why we selected DotNetNuke. We then met our fictional client Coffee Connections, and using user stories, gathered the requirements to build their site.

The next chapter will cover the always-enlightening task of installing the software. We will cover what we need to run DotNetNuke and describe the process of installing the framework.

2
Installing DotNetNuke

In previous versions of DotNetNuke (version 2.0), you had the ability to use Microsoft Access as your database when installing the application. While this functionality has not disappeared completely, it is no longer part of the core DotNetNuke framework. In this chapter, we will cover the steps necessary to set up a local copy of DotNetNuke by using Microsoft SQL Server. We will start by setting up a clean installation and then discuss how to upgrade from a previous instance of DotNetNuke. Finally, we will log in as an administrator and change the default passwords.

Installing DotNetNuke (Local Version)

Before you begin installing DotNetNuke, you will need to determine if you have the .NET Framework installed. The easiest way is to open up your browser and go to `http://www.asp.net/webmatrix/CheckDotNet.aspx?tabindex=0&tabid=1`. This website, which was set up to help those installing WebMatrix, will search your computer and let you know if you have the .NET Framework installed. If you need to install it, the site will direct you to where you can download the framework. For our examples, we will be using Windows XP Professional, IIS 5.1, and version 1.1 of the .NET Framework.

Clean Installation

If this is the first time you are installing DotNetNuke, or you do not want to upgrade from a previous version, then you will want to perform a clean installation. This means that you will have to build your DotNetNuke instance from scratch. This chapter will walk you through all the steps necessary to accomplish this task. If you wish to upgrade DotNetNuke from a previous version, please refer to the *Upgrading* section towards the end of the chapter.

Downloading the Code

Before we start installing our web portal, we need to download the source code. Go to the DotNetNuke website `http://www.DotNetNuke.com`. You will be required to register before you can download the code. This step is simple, just click on the Register link in the upper right-hand corner, and fill out the required information. Fill out a working e-mail address, as the registration process will send an e-mail that includes a verification code.

Once you receive the e-mail you may continue to the DotNetNuke site, log in, and download the code. You will find the DotNetNuke source by clicking on the Download the Code icon or by clicking on the Downloads tab. While the file is downloading, take time to explore what the DotNetNuke site has to offer. You will find information that will help you as you build your portal.

Once you have the source code downloaded from the site, you can double-click on the ZIP file to extract its contents. Where you extract the file is entirely up to you. Most of the documentation you come across will assume that you extract it to C:\DotNetNuke so for consistency's sake we will do the same.

Setting Up a Virtual Directory

After you unzip the files, you will need to set up a virtual directory in IIS. **IIS** stands for **Internet Information Services** and is the web server application that will run our web portal. If IIS is not already installed on your system, you can install it by going to Control Panel | Add Remove Programs | Add Remove Windows Components.

> For more information on installing and using IIS, http://www.IISFaq.com, (which utilizes the DotNetNuke framework for its portal) should suffice.

A virtual directory is a **friendly name**, also called an **alias**, that allows you to separate a physical folder from a web address and defines the application's boundaries. A virtual directory is needed if your files are not located in the home directory. The home directory for IIS is found at C:\Inetpub\wwwroot (if installed at the default location). The virtual directory, or alias name, is used by those accessing your website. It is the name they type in the browser to bring up your portal so select a simple name.

The following table shows examples of mapping between physical folders and virtual directories. As you can see, we will need to set up a virtual directory for DotNetNuke since its location is outside the home directory, in C:\DotNetNuke.

Physical Location	Alias	URL
C:\Inetpub\wwwroot	home directory (none)	http://localhost
\\AnotherServer\SomeFolder	Customers	http://localhost/Customers
C:\DotNetNuke	DotNetNuke	http://localhost/DotNetNuke

Physical Location	Alias	URL
`C:\Inetpub\wwwroot\My WebSite`	None	`http://localhost/MyWebSite`

There are two different ways of setting up the virtual directory.

Using Windows Explorer (the Easy Way)

If you are using Windows XP then the easiest way for you to set up you virtual directory is to go to `C:\DotNetNuke`, right-click on the folder, and select Sharing and Security.

This will open up the DotNetNuke Properties dialog. Click on the Web Sharing tab and select Share this folder.

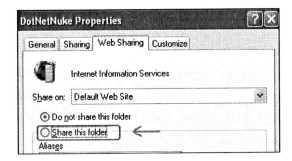

This will present you with the Edit Alias dialog box. The dialog box will default to the name of the folder it is in, so if you extracted your file to `C:\DotNetNuke`, then your virtual directory will be called DotNetNuke. Leave all the default permissions and click OK to save the settings.

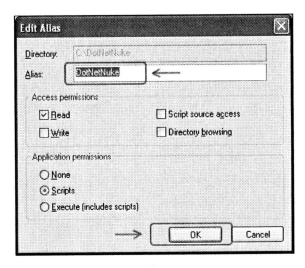

Using the Virtual Directory Creation Wizard

If you are not using Windows XP, you may need to set up your virtual directory using the **IIS Manager** and the **Virtual Directory Creation Wizard**. You will find the IIS Manager in the Control Panel | Administrative Tools section. Once you have IIS open, drill down until you see Default Web Site, right-click and select New | Virtual Directory.

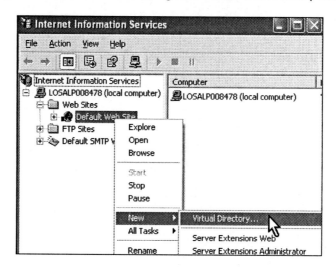

Click Next to begin the wizard. Then, enter an alias for your website. Type in DotNetNuke and then click Next.

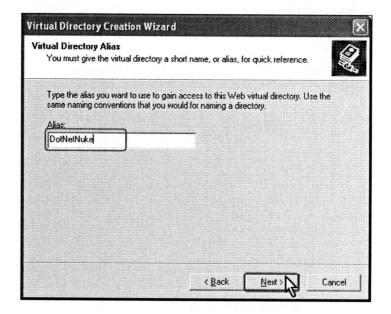

The next dialog box will ask you for the physical location of your DotNetNuke files. This is how IIS matches the virtual directory alias name to the web application files.

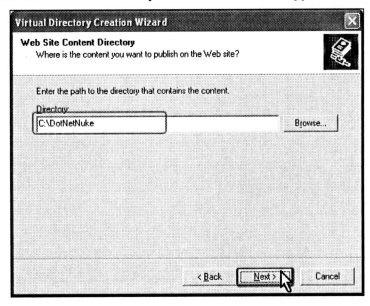

Type C:\DotNetNuke in the Directory: field and click Next. On the Access Permissions page, leave all the default permissions and click Next to save the settings.

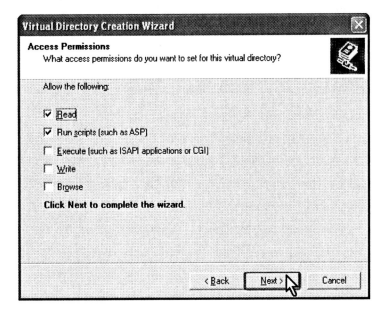

Click Finish to exit the wizard.

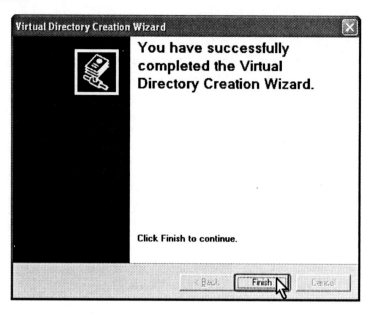

Verifying Default Documents

Default documents allow you to access a web page by typing in just the folder name. DotNetNuke uses default.aspx as its default page when running the portal. To ensure default.aspx is specified as a default document for your virtual directory, scroll down in IIS until you find the DotNetNuke Virtual Directory. Right-click and select Properties.

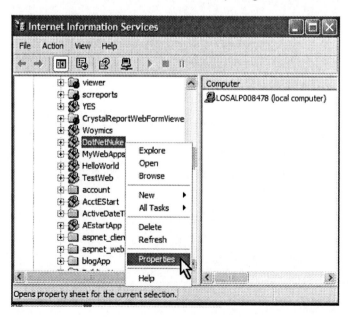

Select the Documents tab and confirm that you see default.aspx (in addition to default.asp) in the box. If you see it, click OK to close the properties box.

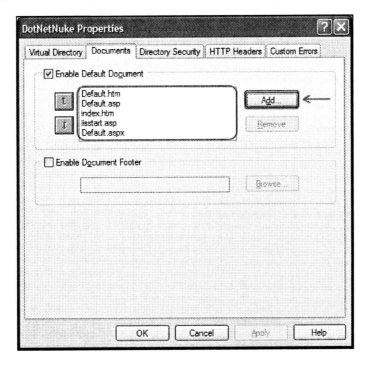

If default.aspx does not exist, click on the Add button to type it into the Default Document Name box and click OK. This will successfully complete the setup of the virtual directory for DotNetNuke.

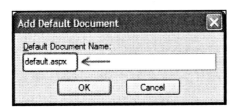

Setting up the Database

We will be covering using Microsoft SQL Server 2000. You can also use the **Microsoft Database Engine (MSDE)**, which is a free version of SQL Sever 2000, to handle the data for your portal (for more on how to use MSDE, you'll find a wonderful article at http://www.vb123.com/toolshed/99_accvb/installing_msde.htm). To use SQL Server, you will need to create your database. We will be using the **Enterprise Manager** to accomplish this task. For the Enterprise Manager, click on the Start button, and go to

Programs | Microsoft SQL Server | Enterprise Manager. Drill down the (local) server by clicking on the plus (+) signs, right-click on Databases, and select New Database.

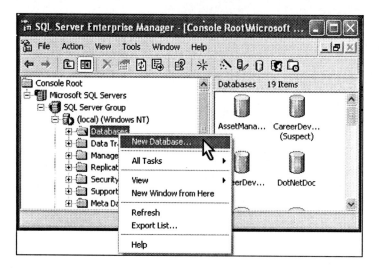

Type DotNetNuke into the name field and click OK.

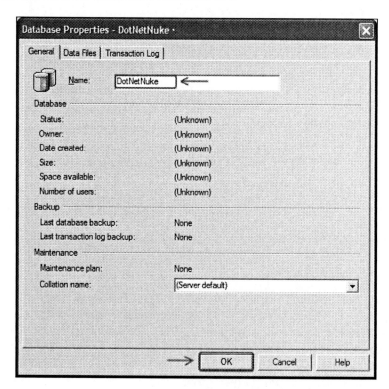

It will take a few moments for your database to be created. This will generate the system tables and stored procedures. The actual tables and procedures needed to run DotNetNuke will be created when you run the program for the first time.

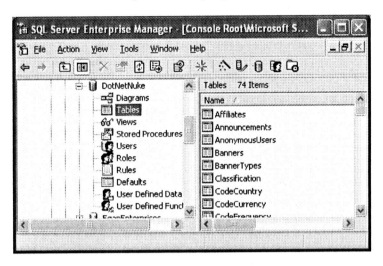

Once you create your database shell, you will need to modify some code in the web.config file to connect to SQL Server. Use Notepad to open up the C:\DotNetNuke\web.config file. We will explore the web.config file in detail while discussing the DotNetNuke architecture; for now we are only concerned with a few sections of the code. The web.config file is an XML-based file so be careful while working with this file.

You will find the line you need to modify in the <appSettings> section. In this section you will find a connection string for SQL Server. The connection string should already be set up to work on your local machine. If you did not name your database DotNetNuke in the last section, you will need to change the name of the database shown in this section. You will also need to supply it a user ID (uid) and password (pwd) according to how you have SQL Server set up on your machine.

```
<appSettings>
<add key="SiteSqlServer"
value="Server=(local);Database=DotNetNuke;uid=DNNID;pwd=DNNPwd;" />
</appSettings>
```

For additional help, please refer to the following websites:

http://www.connectionstrings.com/
http://www.sqlstrings.com/
http://aspnet101.com/aspnet101/tutorials.aspx?id=23

There are a few other optional sections of the web.config that we may be concerned about at this time. The first one has to do with debugging the application using Visual Studio. If you plan to work with DotNetNuke as a developer and will be using Visual Studio to manage your project you will want to turn on debugging for the DotNetNuke solution. To do this simply set the compilation debug section to true as shown below. (The case is important—default is false.)

```
<!-- set debugmode to false for running application -->
    <compilation debug="true" />
```

The second optional section you may want to modify has to do with how DotNetNuke sets up your database. You will find the items you need to modify in the <data defaultProvider="SqlDataProvider"> section near the end of the file. There are two attributes that you may consider modifying, objectQualifier and databaseOwner. The object qualifier will append your table names with whatever you place between the quotes. Since DotNetNuke uses some table names like Users, which may be in use in other programs, the object qualifier ensures that there will be no name collisions between tables. The database owner determines what SQL Server user will be the owner of the tables. An example of possible qualifiers is shown below.

```
objectQualifier="DNN"
databaseOwner="dbo"
```

Finally, you will also find another set of keys in the <appSettings> section that you can use during the installation process. The InstallProcedure and InstallTemplate keys work together to determine how your portal will be created. The first key, as shown below, determines the type of installation the DotNetNuke framework will perform.

```
<add key="InstallProcedure" value="3.0" />
```

The value of this key tells the framework whether to use scripts (value = 2.0), or to use the new template-based installation (value = 3.0), which allows you to customize how your portal is configured by reading an XML-based file for configuration. You use the InstallTemplate key to tell the framework where to find this file.

```
<add key="InstallTemplate" value="DotNetNuke.install" />
```

The framework comes loaded with a template that installs the base configuration of DotNetNuke. We will leave the default settings for our installation. Templates will be covered later in this book.

Once this is complete save the web.config file and you are ready to run DotNetNuke for the first time. To do this, navigate to http://localhost/DotNetNuke in your browser. The first time you access your portal it might take a few moments to come up. This is because it is running the database scripts required to set up your SQL Server database.

Once all the scripts have run, you will see the image below:

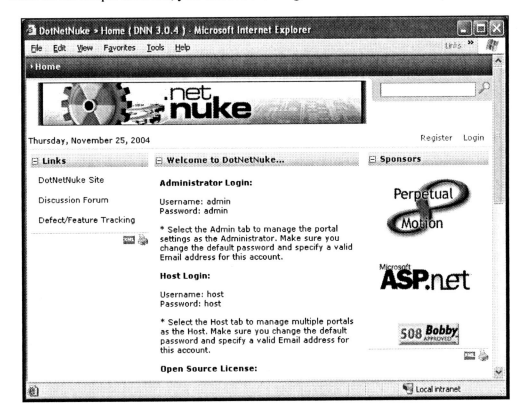

Upgrading

If you already have a DotNetNuke portal and would like to upgrade from version 2.x to version 3.x, a few steps are required. The amount of modification you have made to your installation will affect the amount of time required to complete your upgrade. If you read the readme.txt file that comes in the documentation folder you will see that it says only two things under the upgrade section:

1. Make sure you always back up your database before upgrading to a new version.
2. The application will automatically execute the necessary database scripts.

What it doesn't tell you is exactly how to upgrade.

Upgrade Checklist

If you are upgrading from a version before 3.0 there are a couple of things you will need to be aware of:

- **Do you have any custom modules, either built by you or purchased?** Since versions of DotNetNuke above version 3.0 employ a few changes to the module structure, some of these custom modules may no longer work. You will need to check to see if an updated version of the module is available and upgrade each module.

- **Have you made any modifications to the core architecture in the previous version?** Since we will be using the code from the new ZIP file, any changes you made to the old code will no longer be available. You will need to redo those changes in the updated framework after you update the files. For this reason, it is strongly recommended that you make no modifications to the core architecture itself.

So if you have not done much to your site except use the standard modules then the steps to upgrade are fairly straightforward.

Back Up Your Database

1. Open Enterprise Manager, drill down on the (local) server, and open up the database folder. Look for DotNetNuke and right-click on it to bring up the menu. Select All Tasks and Backup Database to begin the backup procedure.

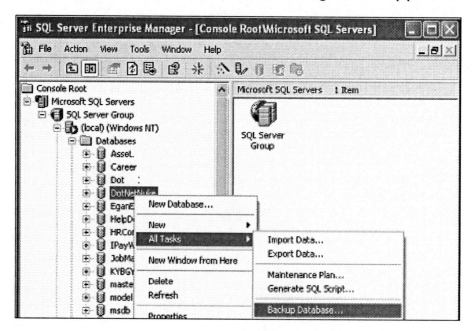

2. On the General tab, leave all the default settings and click on Add. In the File Name box, enter the location where you would like the backup saved and fill in a name for your backup.

3. It is common for you to put an extension of .bak at the end of the file name, but it is not necessary. Click the OK button on the Select Backup Destination dialog and then click OK again on the General tab. You will receive a message box when the backup completes successfully.

Back up Your DotNetNuke files

Whenever you are about to make changes to your site it is always a good idea to back up the physical files located at c:\DotNetNuke. Make a copy of this folder and store it in a safe place.

1. Unzip and copy new files in place of old files. Unzipping the files over the top of the existing files will allow you to keep any extra skinning or module files from the previous version. When you unzip the file, it will only replace the DNN files contained in the ZIP file.

2. Modify the new web.config file to point to your database. Even if you have made extensive additions to your web.config file, it is still a good idea to use the web.config file that comes with the new versions, since this may contain other changes that are needed for your portal to function properly.

3. Open up Internet Explorer and navigate to http://localhost/DotNetNuke.

When the site begins to open it will check to see what version of DotNetNuke you are running and compare it against the version held in the database. If it is different, it will run the necessary scripts to upgrade your portal.

Since the configuration of your site, how many tabs you have, where your modules are located, etc. are all contained in the database, upgrading the files and the database is all that is needed to upgrade.

Setting Security Permissions

ASP.NET web applications will usually run using the built-in ASPNET account. To allow the extensive file uploading and skinning features in DotNetNuke, you will have to set some security permissions before they start working correctly. To change these permissions, open up Windows Explorer and browse to your DotNetNuke folder (usually c:\DotNetNuke). Right-click the folder, select Sharing and Security from the menu, and click on the Security tab. Add the appropriate user account and set permissions.

If you are using Windows 2000 (IIS5) the account that needs permissions on the DotNetNuke folder is the {Server}\ASPNET user account, where {Server} is the name of your machine running the DotNetNuke installation.

It must have read and write permissions for the DotNetNuke folder. If you are using Windows 2003 (IIS6), then instead of the ASPNET account you will need to give permissions to the NT AUTHORITY\NETWORK SERVICE user account. Again, it must have read and write permissions for the folder.

On an XP machine formatted to NTFS that is not part of a domain, the security tab may not be visible by default. To reveal the Security tab, open Windows Explorer, and choose Folder Options from the Tools menu. On the View tab, scroll to the bottom of the Advanced Settings and clear (click) the check box next to Use Simple File Sharing. Click OK to apply the change. You should now have a Security tab when viewing the properties of a file on an NTFS volume.

Logging In as Admin and Changing Passwords

The admin and host accounts will have complete control over your web portal. This makes changing the default passwords for the admin and host accounts one of the most important steps to take once you have your site up and running. The first page you see when you start up DotNetNuke gives you all the information you need to sign on.

First, we will log in as admin. For this, click on the Login icon in the upper right portion of the site. This will give you the Account Login screen. Enter admin for both the username and the password. When you do this, you will notice a few changes to the site.

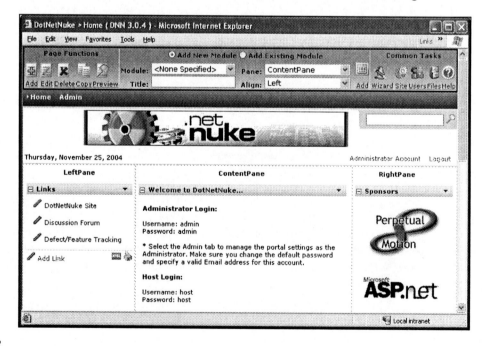

There is now an admin tool pane, and most text has a pencil icon next to it. You will now be able to edit the site. All the options available to you as an admin or host user will be covered in another chapter, for now we only want to change the default password. In the upper right corner, just below where you clicked the login icon, you will see a link for Administrator Account. Click on this to bring up the account screen for the admin account.

To change the password, fill out the Old Password, the New Password, the Confirm New Password, and all the other sections that are required (marked with an *). When finished filling out the information, click on the Update Password link to save your changes.

> You may remove some required items by unchecking the boxes next to the items. Note that this will remove the requirement for all users of your site.

When you are finished, log out of the admin account by clicking on the logout icon in the right-hand corner of the page. You can then change the host password by signing in as host, and navigating to Host | SuperUser Accounts. (We will discuss SuperUsers in upcoming chapters.)

Click on the pencil icon to modify the host account. Change the host password by filling in a new password in the Password box, retyping it in the Confirm box, and filling in a valid Email Address. Once this is complete, you can save the new password clicking on the Update link.

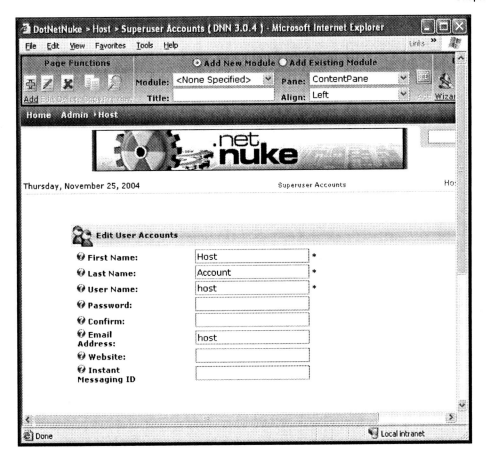

Summary

In this chapter, we have installed a local version of DotNetNuke using Microsoft SQL Server and covered how to set the correct permissions on our machine as well as how to upgrade from previous versions of DotNetNuke. We finished by changing the default passwords for the Host and Admin accounts. In the chapters that follow, we will explore all the features that are available to you as an admin or host user of the site. We will cover the modules and standard features that make DotNetNuke one of the fastest-growing web portals on the market today.

3

Users, Roles, and Pages

One of the most important and time-consuming aspects of running a DotNetNuke portal is trying to figure out how to administer the portal. From adding modules to working with users, it will take time before you start feeling comfortable with all the administration tasks associated with running a portal. The next few chapters are designed to give you a general understanding of how things work, and also to act as a reference for the tasks you have to perform only once or twice in a year. This chapter will familiarize you with managing users and pages within your portal. When you are done with this chapter you will possess a better understanding of the following areas:

- Creating and modifying user accounts
- How user accounts tie into the security of your site
- What DotNetNuke pages are and how to create and administer them
- How to structure your site using pages
- Discuss the new Membership Provider Model

User Accounts

If you are used to working within a network environment or have worked with different portals in the past then you are probably comfortable with the term "users" and how they interact with your portal. Everything that takes place on your portal revolves around users and user accounts. Whether users are required to register in order to use your services or you only need a few user accounts in order to manage the functionality and layout of your site, you will need to understand how to create and manage user accounts. We will start with a general description of a user, and then show you how to create and manage your users. In order to work through the examples, you will need to bring up your portal and sign in as admin.

What Is a User?

The simplest definition of a user is an individual who consumes the services that your portal provides. However, a user can take on many different roles; from a visitor just browsing (unregistered user) or the person who registers to gain access to your services (registered user), to the facilitator (Administrator or Host) who is responsible for the content and design of your portal. Just about everything in DotNetNuke revolves around the user, so before we can do anything else, we need to learn a little about user accounts.

Creating User Accounts

Before you create the user accounts you must set how users will be able to register on the site. You have the choice of four different types of registration: None, Private, Public (default), and Verified. To set the registration type for your portal go to the Site Settings link found on the Admin menu.

The User Registration section can be found under Advanced Settings | Security Settings:

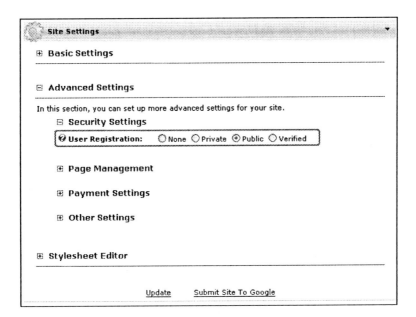

The type of registration you use depends on how you will be using your portal. What follows is a brief explanation of the different User Registration types.

Registration Setting	Description
None	Setting up user registration as None will remove the Register link from your portal. In this mode, users can only be added by the Admin or Host users. If you plan to have all sections of your site available to anyone then selecting none as your registration option is a good choice.
Private	If you select Private, the Register link will reappear. When users attempt to register, they will be informed that their request for registration will be reviewed by the administrator. The administrator will decide whom to give access to the site.
Public	Public is the default registration for a DotNetNuke portal. When this is selected, the users will be able to register for your site by entering the required information. Once the registration form is filled out, they will be given access to the site.

Registration Setting	Description
Verified	If you select Verified as your registration option, the users will be sent an e-mail with a verification code once they fill out the required information. This ensures that the e-mail address they enter in the registration process is valid. The first time they sign in, they will be prompted for the verification code. After they have been verified they will only need to type in their login name and password to gain access to the site.

Setting Required Registration Fields

The administrator has the ability to decide what information the user will be required to enter when registering. The place to accomplish this is not very straightforward.

When you log in as Admin, you will see the title Administrator Account in the upper right-hand corner of the current page (if you are using the default skin). Click this link to bring you to the Register page.

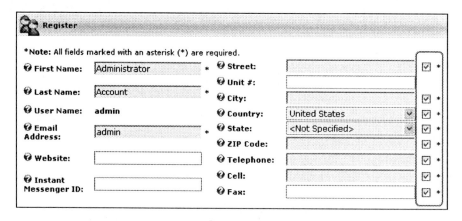

All users will be able to access this screen, for their own information, when they are signed on, but only the administrator will have additional checkboxes placed next to possible required fields. The unchangeable required fields are marked with an asterisk (*). If you would like to require a user to enter the additional information, place a checkmark next to all the relevant fields, and click on the Update link. Remember, the ability to mark required fields is only available from the administrators' Register page.

Registering a User Manually

As we discussed, you can set your portal registration to None. This will remove the Registration link from your site. So the only way to add users to your portal is to register them manually. To do this, go to Admin | User Accounts on the main menu. This will bring you to the **Manage Users** screen. There are actually two ways to add a new user from this screen. You can select Add New User from the drop-down menu on the right of the module or click on the Add New User link at the bottom of the module.

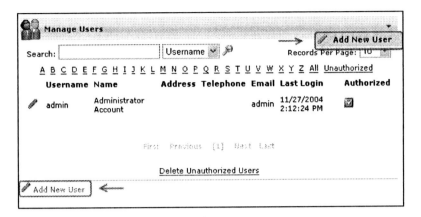

We will be setting up a user to help us administer the Coffee Connections site. We fill in the required information and click on the Update link.

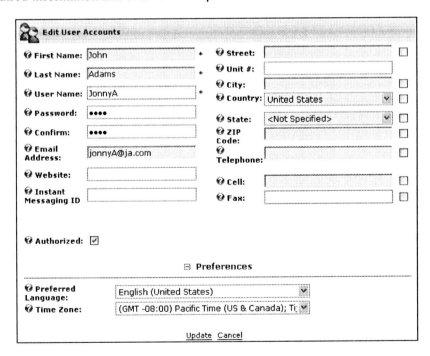

When we are done, we will test the account we just created. To do this we need to log off as admin by clicking on the Logout link in the upper right-hand corner of the current page. Then click on the Login link. Enter in the username and password of the user we just created. You will notice that while you are logged in as this user you lose access to all the updating functionality that the administrator account possesses.

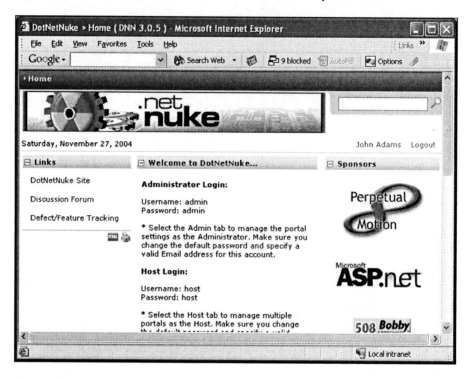

The ability to update the portal is not available to our new user because they do not have the authority to make the changes. Put another way, they do not belong to the right security role.

Understanding DotNetNuke Roles

We have just looked at how to add a user to your site, but are all users created equal? To understand how users are allowed to interact with the portal we will need to take a look at what a **Role** is and how it factors into the portal. There are plenty of real-world examples of roles we can look at. A Police station, for example, can have sergeants, patrol cops, and detectives and with each position comes different responsibilities and privileges. In a police station there are multiple people filling those positions (roles) with each sharing the same set of responsibilities and privileges.

Roles in our portal work the same way. Roles are set up to divide up responsibilities needed to run your portal. If we refer to the user stories we created in Chapter 1 we will see that one of them falls into the area of users and roles.

Site Updates

Administrators will have the ability to modify the site content easily using a web-based interface.

We want our portal to be easy for the administrators to manage. To do this we will need to settle on the different user roles needed for our site. To determine this we first need to decide on the different types of user that will access the portal. We will detail these user types below.

- **Administrator**: The Administrators will have very high security. They will be able to modify, delete, or move anything on the site. They will be able to add and delete users and control all security settings. (This role comes built into DotNetNuke.)

- **Home Page Admin**: The home page admins will have the ability to modify only the information on the home page. They will be responsible for changing what users see when they first access your site. (We will be adding this role.)

- **Forum Moderator**: The forum moderators will have the ability to monitor and modify posts in your forum. They will have the ability to approve or disapprove messages posted. (We will be adding this role.)

- **Registered User**: The registered users will be able to post messages in the forum and be able to access sections of the site set aside for registered users only. (This role comes built into DotNetNuke.)

- **Unauthenticated User**: The unauthenticated user is the most basic of the user types. Any person browsing your site will fall under this category. This user type will be able to browse certain sections of your portal but will be restricted from posting in the forum and will not be allowed in the Registered Users Only section. (This role comes built into DotNetNuke.)

Once you formulate the different user roles that will access the site, you will need to restrict users' access. For example; we only want the Home Page Admin to be able to edit items on the home page. To accomplish this DotNetNuke uses role-based security. Role-based security allows you to give access to portions of your website based on what role the user belongs to. The benefit of using a role-based security method is that you only have to define the access privileges for a role once. Then you just need to add users to that role and they will possess the privileges that the role defines. The diagram overleaf gives you an idea of how this works.

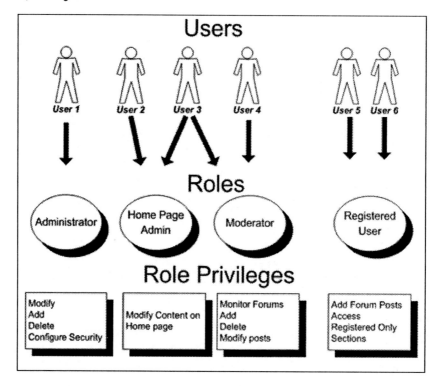

Looking at the diagram, we notice two things.

1. Users can be assigned to more than one role

2. More than one user can be assigned to a single role.

This gives us great flexibility when deciding on the authorization that users will possess in our portal.

To create the roles we have detailed, sign in as admin, and select Admin | Security Roles on the main menu.

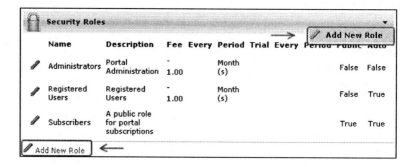

Notice that DotNetNuke comes with three roles already built into the system, the Administrators role (which we have been using), the Registered Users role, and the Subscribers role. We want to create an additional role for Home Page Admin. To do this you again have two choices. Either select Add New Role from the dropdown in the upper right or click on the Add New Role link near the bottom of the page. This will bring up the Edit Security Roles page. We will use this page to create the Home Page Admin role that we need.

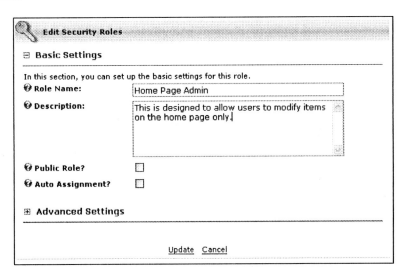

The basic settings shown in the screenshot are:

- Role Name: Make the name of your role short but descriptive. The name should attempt to convey its purpose.
- Description: Here you may detail the responsibilities of the role.
- Public Role?: Checking Public Role will give registered users of your site the ability to sign up for this role themselves. We will be creating a Newsletter Role and will demonstrate how this works when that is created.
- Auto Assignment?: If the Auto Assignment role is checked then users will automatically be assigned to this role as soon as they register for your portal.

Since we want to decide who will be able to modify our home page we will leave both of these unchecked. To save your settings click on the Update link.

The advanced settings section allows you to set up a fee for certain security roles. Depending on what you are offering on your portal, you can ask for a fee for a user to register for your portal or just to access particular sections.

Now to complete the roles that we will require for Coffee Connections, we will add two more security roles. (Admin, Registered Users, and Unauthenticated users come built into DotNetNuke.)

This role will be called Newsletter. We will be using this role to allow users to sign up for the newsletter we will be hosting at the Coffee Connections site. Set up the Security role with the following information

- Name: Newsletter
- Description: Allows users to register for the Coffee Connections Newsletter
- Public Role: Yes (checked)
- Auto Assignment: No (unchecked)

Click on the Update link to save this role.

This role will be called **Forum Admin**. We will be using this role to administer the forums at the Coffee Connections site. Set up the Security role with the following information:

- Name: Forum Admin
- Description: Allows user to administer Coffee Connections Forum
- Public Role: No (unchecked)
- Auto Assignment: No (unchecked)

Click on the Update link to save this role.

The security roles, by themselves, do not determine the security on your portal. As the diagram showed users and roles work together to form the basis of the security in your site.

Assigning Security Roles to Users

Security roles can be assigned to users by an administrator or, if Public Role is checked, can be assigned by the users themselves. To show you how users can sign up for security roles, log out as admin and log in as our sample user, JonnyA.

When signed on as JonnyA, in order to modify your user information, click on the user name in the upper right-hand corner of the portal. This will bring you to the Register screen shown opposite. This is the same screen we looked at when signed on as the administrator. Notice that the checkboxes to indicate the required fields have disappeared.

In the top section up the screen, you can change your password or personal information or Unregister from the site.

The bottom of the screen will show Preferences (Preferred Language and Time Zone), Change Password (which we looked at in Chapter 1), and the Membership Services (Public Security Roles) that are available to the user. These are the roles for which we checked the Public Role checkbox. To subscribe to the role, click on the Subscribe link.

After you have subscribed to a service, you can unsubscribe by clicking on the Cancel link. Since security roles such as Home Page Admin allow the user to modify the portal, they should not be assigned in this manner. As the administrator of the site, we want the ability to decide who is assigned to this role. To do this we will again need to sign off as JonnyA and sign back in as Admin.

Once logged in, select Admin | Security Roles on the main menu. Once there, click the pencil icon next to the Home Page Admin security role. Click on the Manage Users link that is located near the bottom of this screen. You will then be presented with the User Roles administration page.

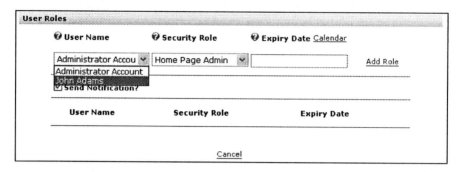

To add a user to a role, select them from the User Name dropdown. If you would like the role to expire after a specific date you may enter a date in the Expiry Date textbox or click on the Calendar link to select a date from a calendar. When you are done, click on the Add Role link to add the role to the user.

You can add as many users to the role as you wish. To remove a role from a user, click on the delete icon (☒) next to the user's name. If the Send Notification checkbox is checked, the portal will send an e-mail notification to the users when they are added or removed from the role.

Up to this point, we have added security roles, and added users to roles both as an admin and by allowing users to add themselves through membership services. However, the security role authorizations still need to be set. To do this we will introduce you to the page architecture of DotNetNuke and in the process show you how to add security roles to sections of our portal.

Understanding DotNetNuke Pages and tabIDs

As we have been navigating through to different pages you may have noticed that the page name shown in your browser's address bar has not changed. Although the **tabID** portion of the address changes, every time you click on another item on the menu, it keeps showing default.aspx. This is because DotNetNuke uses dynamic page generation to render the correct information for each page (e.g. http://localhost/ DotNetNuke/tabid/39/Default.aspx).

> You will see that some of the screenshots in this book as well as others you will find on your DotNetNuke portal refer to something called a **tab**. In previous versions of DotNetNuke the word tab' was used instead of the word Page.
>
> I am sure in time, that all of these references will be changed inside the portal. Until then be aware that the words tab and page are interchangeable.

In traditional web applications, pages are created in an application like Front Page, Dreamweaver, or Visual Studio .NET. The designer decides where to place the text, inserts images, saves the page, and then posts it to the website. Navigating the traditional web application takes you from one "physical" page to another "physical" page.

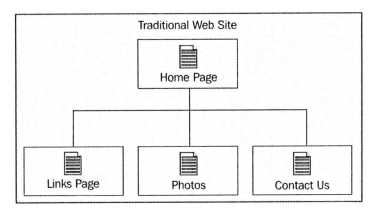

In DotNetNuke web portal, there is only one "physical" page used in the application. Instead of placing the information directly on the page, DotNetNuke holds the information for each page in the database. When a page is then requested on a DNN portal, the application looks in the database to determine what information should be on the page and displays it on Default.aspx. The database knows what information to pull from the database by looking at the tabID in the URL (e.g. http://localhost/ DotNetNuke/tabid/39/Default.aspx).

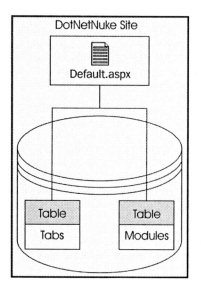

When users navigate to different items on the menu, they will see different information and will be presented with the illusion of multiple physical pages.

When you create new pages in DotNetNuke, you are not only creating the page information for the database but this same step will also build the navigation menu for your site.

To better understand the pages and menu structure we will create some new pages. To create a new page, we first need to log in as an admin. When you do you will see the Page Functions pane at the top of your portal.

To add a page, click on the Add link on the left side of the pane. We will be adding a page that will hold our Coffee House Search engine as well as a page that will eventually hold our forums. This admin screen is broken up into three different sections, Basic Settings, Copy Page, and Advanced Settings.

We will start with the Basic Settings:

This is where we enter the following information to set up our page:

- Page Name: This is the name that will show up on the menu. You want to keep this name short in order to save space on the menu.

- Title: This is used to display the name of the page on the Internet Explorer title bar. This can be more descriptive than the page name.

- Description: Enter a short description of what the page will be used for.

- Parent Page: As we discussed earlier, this information not only creates a page dynamically but is also used to create your site menu. If you would like this page to be positioned under another page in the menu select the parent page from the dropdown.

- Link Url: If you would like a menu item to link to information that already exists on your site you can fill in the Link Url information. You can link to an external resource (a page or file on another site), a page on your site (an existing "physical" page on your website), or a file on your site. This can be used to incorporate existing ASP or HTML files you may already have.

Under the Copy Page section you can select whether you would like to copy information from an existing page to create a new page.

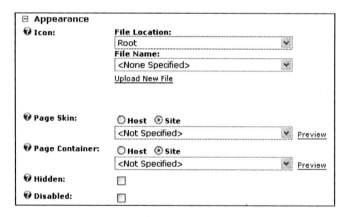

Select the page you would like to copy from the dropdown and check the Copy Content box if you would like the content of the modules copies as well.

The Advanced Settings section is broken up into three subsections, Appearance, Security Settings, and Other Settings.

The Icon drop-down box allows you to add an icon next to the page name on the menu. You can see an example of this on the Admin menu.

In the Admin menu the Admin page is the parent for Security Roles, as well as the others in the list. As you can see, if you use an icon it will be placed on the left of the page name.

The next portion of the Page Management panel deals with skinning. For now we will leave <Not Specified> selected. We will cover how these items work when we discuss skinning in Chapter 8.

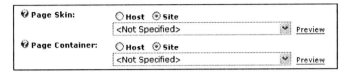

If you don't want the page to be displayed on the menu, check the Hidden checkbox. You can still access this page by creating a link to it in your portal. Administrators will be able to see and modify hidden pages using the page management section.

ⓦ Hidden:	☐
ⓦ Disabled:	☐

Checking the Disabled checkbox will allow a page to show up on the menu but will not allow the page to be shown. This is used to help with navigation for your site. The Admin page again is an example of this. It is used only as a parent page to allow you to navigate to the other pages beneath it. If you click on the admin menu item, no page will appear. If you check both hidden and disabled, you will only be able to access the page from Admin | Pages on the main menu. This can be useful if you would like to navigate to a page in a non-traditional way. For example; you can add a link to specific page using the links module that we will discuss in Chapter 4.

In the Security Settings we will start to tie the pages into the roles we created earlier. This will assign privileges to access the page.

⊟ Security Settings		View Tab	Edit Tab
ⓦ Permissions:	Administrators	☑	☑
	All Users	☐	☐
	Forums Admin	☐	☐
	Home Page Admin	☐	☐
	Newsletter	☐	☐
	Registered Users	☐	☐
	Subscribers	☐	☐
	Unauthenticated Users	☐	☐

- View Tab: Roles that are selected in this row will have the ability to view the page. This means that only those roles checked will be able to see this page. If you are not in one of these roles you will not see the page. This can be used to restrict portions of your portal to certain groups of people.

- Edit Tab: Roles that are selected in this role will have the ability to administer this page. This means that a user who belongs to any of the roles checked will have the ability to edit, modify, and delete information on this page. Remember these privileges apply to this page only.

We want to restrict this page to Registered Users and Administrators only. Select the checkbox next to Registered Users in the View Tab column.

In the Other Settings section you have the ability to add key words that are used by search engines to index your site. You may also show the page between certain dates by entering start and end dates. We will be leaving these sections blank.

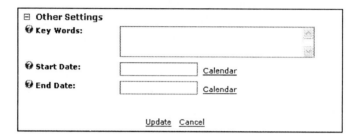

To save our settings for this page, click on the Update link. When it is complete, you will see your new page on the menu bar. Therefore, when you build a page you are creating both a page to add content to and an item for your menu.

Administering Pages

You have now seen how you can create a page using the Page Functions Pane. Next you will see how to work with all of your pages to build your menus in a straightforward manner. To get to the Page Administration section select Admin | Pages on the main menu.

By using the icons on the page admin pane you will be able to create a new page, edit or view an existing page, or modify where the link to the page appear on your menu. You will notice that neither the Host nor Admin menus items appear on this page. You are not able to modify those menus in this context. To test this, highlight the Coffee House Search menu item and click on the View Selected Page icon (magnifying glass). This will bring us right back to the page that we just created. Notice that the page is separated into three distinct panes. The LeftPane, ContentPane, and RightPane (You may need to click on the Preview icon in the Page Functions pane if the panes are not visible).

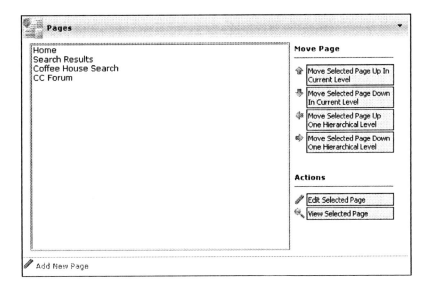

Take time to try out the functionality on this page and get comfortable with how you can edit, move, and modify your pages. Once we have created our page we will want to add information to it. To do this we need to add modules to our new page.

Membership Provider Model

In the upcoming version of Visual Studio 2005 and .NET Framework 2.0 (code named Whidbey), Microsoft has added controls to help with the tedious task of setting up a membership system on your website. Along with the new controls comes a membership provider model that gives developers the ability to choose what data store they will use to store their user information. In preparation for this advancement, DotNetNuke 3.0 has back-ported this model to work with the DotNetNuke framework. This allows you to decide whether you want to use the default tables in DotNetNuke to hold your user or use another data store for this purpose. We will cover providers in greater detail in Chapter 12, which discusses the Provider model.

Summary

In this chapter we covered the concepts of users, roles, and pages. This should lay a foundation for the rest of the information we will be covering in this book. Most of the concepts we will cover will deal with one or all of these items. In the next chapter we will introduce you to the concept of modules and discuss the sample modules that come prepackaged with DotNetNuke.

4
Standard DotNetNuke Modules

As we discovered in the last chapter, DotNetNuke dynamically builds its pages using the tabID to retrieve the information for each page from the database. This includes the modules that are located on each page as well as the content in those modules. In this chapter we will cover the following:

- The basic concepts of the module
- How to add modules to a page and how to remove them
- The standard modules that come pre-packaged with DNN

DotNetNuke Modules

Adding content to DotNetNuke is done using modules. Modules are used as building blocks for your portal. Each module is designed to perform a given task. From providing links, to storing contacts, to adding a simple welcome message for your users, modules are what make your portal buzz. We will first discuss modules in general, discussing the features that all modules have in common. Then, we will discuss how to add, delete, and set properties on modules. Finally, we will cover all the standard modules that come prepackaged with DotNetNuke. We will discuss their practical purposes and any administration or modification needed to work with the module.

Adding a Module

To begin, make sure you are logged in as admin and then navigate to the Coffee Connections Search tab we created earlier. We will then turn our attention to the Module Admin pane at the top of the page. We will be using this pane to work with the modules on our page.

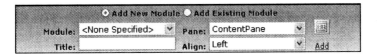

To demonstrate the common module features we will be using the Text/Html module. Select Text/Html in the module dropdown.

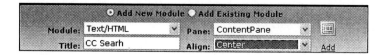

The Pane dropdown allows you to decide in which pane (or section) of the page you would like to place the module. Our choices for a default skin are Left, Right, or Content (center). These choices will vary depending on the skin you are using on your portal. We will be placing the Text/HTML module in the ContentPane. The Align dropdown allows you to left-, center-, or right-justify the module within the pane you select and the Title box allows you to create a title for the module.

To add the module to the tab, just click on the Add link located to the right of the Align dropdown. This will place the Text/HTML module into the content pane.

Module Settings

To access a module's settings you need to access the settings menu. To do this, use the drop-down icon in the right-hand corner of the module. From this menu you will be able to do the following:

- Access the Edit page for the module
- Import or Export content
- Syndicate the information in the module using RSS
- Access online Help and documentation
- Change module Settings
- Print contents of the module
- Delete the module
- Move the module

Editing a Module

The first item on the menu allows you to modify the content of the module. The Edit page as well as the name of the link may be different for each module depending on its functionality. The module developer can decide what shows up on the menu. We will cover how to use this option on each of the standard modules.

Importing and Exporting Content

DotNetNuke 3.0 allows you to export the content from one module and import it into another module. You can test this by going to the home page and using the export function on the Welcome to DotNetNuke Text\Html box. If you then go to the Text/Html box we placed on our Coffee House Search page, you can use the import function to import the information into this page.

Syndicate Information

You can also syndicate the information contained in your module allowing others to pull your information using RSS Readers. (We will discuss this further when we look at the News Feeds module.)

Online Help and Documentation

This item allows the developer of the module to have online help available to help users of the module.

Editing Module Functionality

The Settings menu item allows you to edit the basic functionality of each module. This will be the same for all modules. Let's take a look at this section. On the Text/HTML module, select Settings from the Edit menu.

This will bring up the Module Settings page. This section is divided up into three sections: general settings, security settings, and page Settings.

> When creating a module, you have the choice of adding custom settings to the Settings section. We will cover this when we learn how to develop custom modules later in this book.

Basic Settings

The first item on this page allows you to set a title to show at the top of your module. The title will default to the name of the module (in this case, Text.html). This is followed by the permissions for the module, which work in the same way as the role privileges on the page. Note that these permissions override the ones set on the page. So, you can, for example, keep a tab available to the All Users role but only allow users in the "registered users" role to see the modules on that tab. Keep in mind that the overriding only works one way. If you restrict the page to registered users and then try to give All Users access to the modules on the tab, they won't see the module because they will never see the page. The default permissions will be inherited from the page.

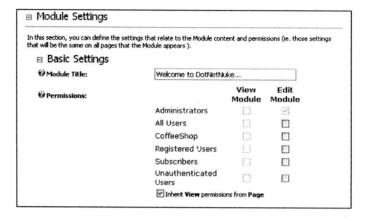

Advanced Settings

The Header and Footer sections allow you to enter information that will appear at the top and bottom of your module. Just as you did with the page, you can also decide on showing this module during a specific date range. In addition, you can also make a module show up on all the tabs (pages) that you create. You might want to do this if you have a set of links that you want on every tab.

Page Settings

This final section deals mostly with the appearance of the module.

If you would like an icon to appear before the title, select one from the File Name dropdown or upload a new icon by clicking on the Upload New File link.

The next section allows you to modify the look and feel of your module. You can change the alignment of the text by selecting Left, Right, or Center from the list. Change the background color by entering a color code into the Color box, or add a border by entering a thickness in the Border box.

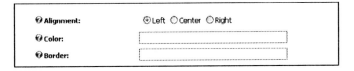

When you looked at the Text/HTML module, you may have noticed a small minus (-) sign in the upper left-hand corner next to the title. This gives the users of your site the ability to show or hide the content of each module.

You can set the default setting to Minimized, Maximized, or None, which will allow users to hide the content.

The next section allows you to determine whether you would like the title displayed on your module, whether you will allow users to print the contents and if RSS syndication is allowed. Just check the boxes to enable these features.

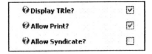

In addition, you may select a module container to skin your individual modules. Module containers are discussed in Chapter 8.

The Cache Timeout is used to speed up the rendering of your page. Caching stores a representation of the data contained in your module for the number of seconds that you place in this box. That means that subsequent attempts to access this page (even by other users) will show the same data. If the text in this module does not change very often then set this to a high number like 360. If this data is dynamic, or changes frequently, then set it to a low number or leave it at zero.

You can make the settings for this module the default settings and/or apply the settings to all modules in your site. The final option is to move your module to another page by selecting the page name from the dropdown. When you are finished with your modifications click the Update link to save your settings.

Standard Modules

DotNetNuke comes prepackaged with nineteen standard modules for you to use on your portal. As we cover each module we will first give you the official description for the module as stated on the DotNetNuke main website. We will then discuss the modules in the following context:

- Practical purposes
- Administration and Modifications
- Special features

Account Login Module

The Account Login module permits users to log in to your portal. It features a Register button that a user can use to become a registered user of your portal, and a Password Reminder button.

Practical Purposes

The Account Login module is a unique standard module. It is used to allow user login for your site. The site will come pre-loaded with this module already working on the site.

The default login will appear on a page all by itself. You may find that you want to add other modules or images when a user is logging into the portal. To accomplish this you will need to use the Account Login module.

Administration and Modification

To show you how this works we will need to add a new page to the site. Create a page with the following attributes:

- Name: Login
- Title: Login Tab
- Hidden: Checked
- View Tab Roles: Administrators; Unauthenticated Users

We do not want users to be able to navigate here so we make it a hidden page. We also want to make it available to unauthenticated and administrator roles.

Since we are not able to navigate to this page, we will need to access it from the Admin | Pages menu.

Highlight the Login tab we just created and click on the viewing icon (magnifying glass). Once on the Login tab, select Account Login in the Module drop-down section of the Module pane and add it to the ContentPane by clicking on the Add icon. Your tab should look like the following screenshot.

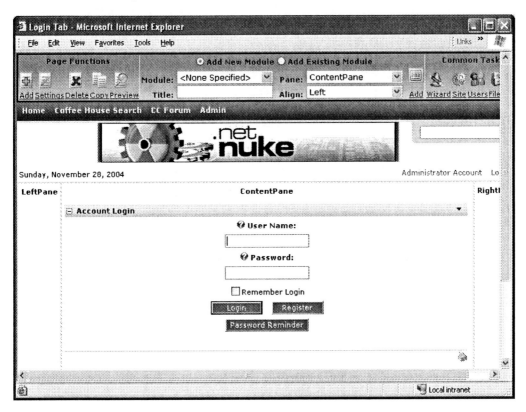

Next, we want to modify some settings on the Login module. Hover your mouse cursor over the Edit icon and select Settings. Modify the following properties:

- Visibility: None

- Permissions (View): Administrators; Unauthenticated Users

We change the Visibility to None to avoid users inadvertently minimizing the module and not seeing it when they attempt to login.

To use this tab for logging in instead of the default login we will need to go to the Admin | Site Settings tab. We will need to change two properties:

- Login page (Under Advanced Settings | Page Management): Login
  Setting this property to our login tab will tell DotNetNuke to use our new tab instead of the default tab. Just select our tab from the dropdown.

- Home page (Under Advanced Settings | Page Management): Home
  The default behavior of the login control is to stay on the current page as soon as a user is authenticated. Since we have made this page only available to administrators and unauthenticated users, after users log in successfully, they will see an error on the page. To change this behavior we will set the Home Tab Property to our Home tab. This will direct users to the home page once they have been authenticated.

Once you have set these properties click on the Update link to save your settings. We now have the ability to add further content to the Admin tab. We will show you how this is done as we talk about other standard modules.

Special Features

Registration is built into the login control. Clicking on the Register button will bring the user to a registration page to create an account.

The login control gives users the ability to have the portal remember their login name and password. If the Remember Login checkbox is selected it will save the users' information in a cookie on their machine. The next time they navigate to the site they will automatically be authenticated.

If the users forget their password, they will be able to enter their username and click on the Password Reminder button. This will e-mail their login information to the e-mail account they used when they registered.

Announcements Module

The Announcements module produces a list of simple text announcements consisting of a title and brief description. Options include a "read more" link to a file, tab or other site, announcement publish date, and expiration date.

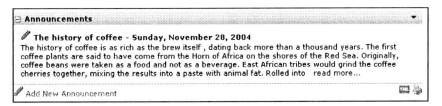

Practical Purposes

- **What's New Section**: This is a great use for the Announcements module. It is usually put on the home page of your site. It gives a headline with a short description of the content. It allows you to show a lot of information in a short amount of space by giving the users a Read More link for the items they want to read about more.

- **Article Listing**: The Announcements module allows you to link to pages internally and externally. This allows you to link to either articles you write or those that you have found on the Internet.

Administration and Modification

To create an announcement, click on the Add New Announcement link.

This will bring up the Edit Announcements page. The properties of an announcement are as follows:

- Title: Type in a short title for the announcement, this will be displayed in bold at the top of the announcement.

- Add Date: If this checkbox is checked, the date will be added to the title of the announcement.

- Description: The description is what allows you to give a short teaser of the full announcement. You can also use this to give a short announcement without giving a link to a larger article.

- Link: You have three choices as to where to link your announcement; you can link to any Internet URL, as we have done above, link to a tab on your site, or link to a file located in your folders. The last option allows you to link to any PDF, HTML, or Word document file located on your portal.

- Track: If this is checked, the module will track the number of times the link has been clicked.

- Log: If this is checked, the module will track who clicks on the read more link and when.

- Open Link in a New Window: As the title explains, this will cause a new browser window to open when a user clicks on the read more link.

- Expires: You may elect to have the announcement expire if you chose. Either type in or select from a calendar (by clicking on the Calendar link) a date when the announcement will be deleted.

- View Order: By default, announcements are ordered by the date that they are added or updated to the module. You can override this by placing a number in the view order box. The announcements will then be ordered numerically by the view order. If no number is entered, the order will be zero.

Special Features

Once you save your announcement, you will have the ability to track which announcements have the greatest interest to your users. To see this information, click on the pencil icon next to a particular announcement. (This option will be available only if the Preview option is unchecked.) At the bottom of the Edit Announcement page you can see how many times this announcement has been clicked and a log of who has clicked on it (if the Log option is checked).

Banner Module

For a discussion on how to use the Banner module in conjunction with vendor advertising, see the *Vendors* sub-section under the *Host Tools* section in Chapter 5.

Contacts Module

This module renders contact information for a particular group of people. You could, for example, use it for a project team or a certain department. A contact includes an Edit page, which allows authorized users to edit the contacts data stored in the SQL database.

Practical Purposes

- Storing a list of contacts on your portal for all users
- Storing internal company phonebook information protected by security roles

Administration and Modification

To add a new contact, sign on as admin, hover the mouse cursor over the pencil icon by the Contacts title, and click on the Add New Contact link.

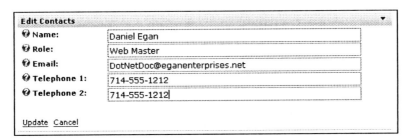

- Name: Enter a name for the contact
- Role: Enter the role for this contact; this is not a security role, this should be the title of the contact (Manager, Owner, Partner, etc.)
- Email: Enter the e-mail address for this contact
- Telephone 1: Enter a primary phone number for this contact
- Telephone 2: Enter a secondary phone number for this contact

Click Update to save your settings.

Special Features

- Mailto hyperlink created by contacts' e-mail address is cloaked by creating a JavaScript function utilizing `String.fromCharCode` to keep spambots from harvesting e-mail addresses
- Call link available if page is browsed by a wireless telephone

Discussions Module

The Discussions module produces a simple threaded newsgroup-style text discussion. Each discussion includes a Read/Reply Message page, which allows authorized users to reply to existing messages or add a new discussion topic.

Practical Purposes

- The Discussions module can be used to facilitate a forum-like atmosphere where visitors to your portal are allowed to read questions and post answers to individual threads in the discussion.
- Depending on the security settings you apply to the module, you could also use the Discussions module as Frequently Asked Question section. In module settings you determine who can edit the content.

Administration and Modification

To add a new discussion question, sign on as admin and click on Add New Thread.

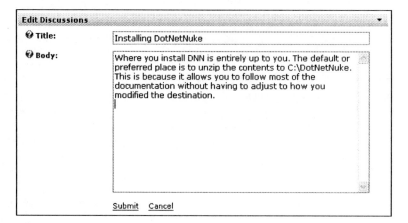

- Title: Enter a title for the discussion. This should be a short descriptive title that will grab a user's attention. When saved, it will be followed by the time it was added and the user who added it.
- Body: Enter the body of the discussion. This will be what the users will read when they click on the discussion link.

Clicking on the link brings you to the body of the discussion.

Special Features

When editing a discussion thread, the system will tell you when and by whom the thread was last modified. This will allow you to track changes made by the administrators of this module. The administrator account has the rights to reply, edit, or delete a discussion thread. You can give others the ability to add or reply to a thread by modifying the roles that can edit content in module settings.

Documents Module

The Documents module produces a list of documents with links to view (depending on users' file associations) or download the document.

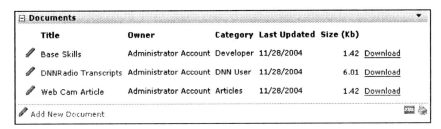

Practical Purposes

- Can be used as a document repository for Word, Excel, PDF, and so on
- Can be used to give access to programs, modules, presentations, and so on contained inside a ZIP file
- Can be used as a resource section by adding links to downloads on other sites

Administration and Modification

To add a new document, sign on as admin and click on the Add New Document link.

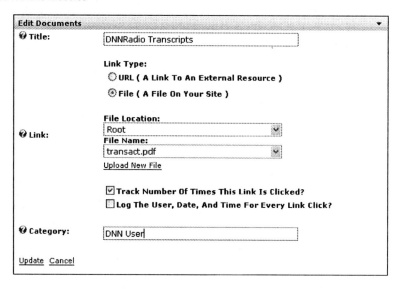

- Title: Fill in the title of the document.

- Link: Select a URL or file. Use a URL for content located on another site. Specify the file location for content located on this site. Either select the file from the dropdown or enter the URL for the download. You can use the upload link to upload new content to the portal.

- Track and Log: Check the Track and Log checkboxes if you would like this module to track downloads for this content. It will give you a detailed list at the bottom of the Edit screen showing you the date and time each user downloads this item.

- Category: Enter in a category for this download. The category is used to help organize the downloads.

Click on Update to save your settings.

Special Features and Additional Information

The owner of the download, as listed in the module, will be the user who adds the download to the module. Also, items will sort by *when* you added them to the module. There is no way to re-sort this information other than by removing and re-adding the items in the order that you would like them.

Events Module

The Events list/calendar module produces a display of upcoming events as a list in chronological order or in calendar format. Each event can be set to automatically expire on a particular date or to re-occur after a specified number of days, weeks, months, or years.

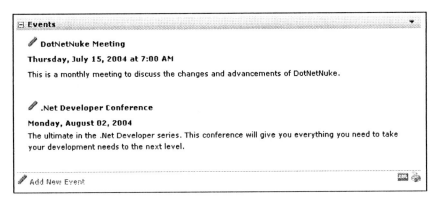

Practical Purposes

- Listing upcoming events for an organization
- Keeping track of upcoming deadlines in a calendar format
- Listing recurring appointments or reminders

Administration and Modification

The Events module is the first standard module that we have discussed that utilizes the module-settings page for additional options. To see the custom options for this module, hover the cursor over the Edit menu and click on the Settings menu item.

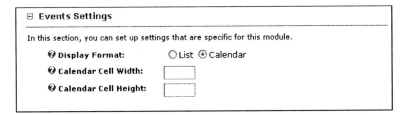

You have the option to have the events displayed as a list or inside a calendar. The Calendar display is the default but List is a better-looking display format for the data. If you choose to use Calendar, you can modify the size of each date cell. To do this, enter the cell height and cell width in pixels. To save your settings click on the Update link.

To add a new event, sign on as admin, and click on the Add New Event link.

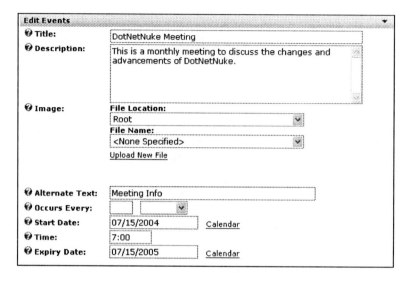

- Title: Enter a title for the event. This will be displayed in bold on the first line of the event for the list view or inside the cell for the calendar view.

- Description: Enter a description for the event. This will be displayed in regular text under the title in list view and inside the cell for the calendar view. If you are using calendar view you will want to keep the description short. This will give you a better presentation of the data.

- Image: If you would like an icon to show up on the left of the event title select one from the dropdown or click on the Upload New File link to upload a new one.

- Alternate Text: Enter in alternative text for the image if using an icon. The alternate text will be displayed when you hover the cursor over the icon associated with this event.

- Occurs Every: Enter a recurring pattern for this event. If this is a meeting or event that happens on a regular basis you can choose to have the event automatically appear on a daily, weekly, monthly, or yearly basis.

- Start Date: This is the date when the pattern will start if this is a recurring event. For a one-time event, this is the date of the event.

- Time: Enter the time for the event either using military time or with and AM or PM at the end of the time.

- Expiry Date: This is the date that the event will stop showing up on the calendar if this is a recurring event.

Special Features and Additional Information

The alternate text will not show when not using an icon. It will also not show when logged in as an admin. To view the alternate text select an icon for the event, save the event, log out as admin, and hover over the icon.

FAQs Module

The FAQs module produces a list of linked frequently asked questions. The corresponding answer is displayed when a question is clicked.

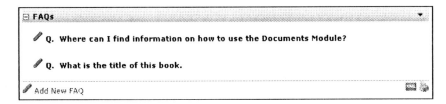

Practical Purposes

- List product FAQs
- Display special contact information

Administration and Modification

To add a new FAQ, sign on as admin and click on the Add New FAQ link.

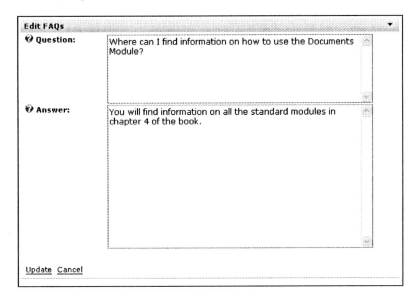

- Question: Enter the FAQ Question.
- Answer: Enter the FAQ Answer.

Click on Update to save your changes.

Special Features and Additional Information

The question is presented as a hyperlink. When the question is clicked, the answer will be shown. This helps to save space on your page by only showing the answers to the questions when they are requested.

Feedback Module

The Feedback module produces a form for visitors to send messages to a specific e-mail address. If users are already logged in, their name and e-mail address will be automatically placed into the form.

Practical Purposes

- Have users request content or changes on your portal
- Use as a Contact Us section
- Allow users to give general feedback about your portal

Administration and Modification

The Feedback module is a simple but extensively used standard module.

By default, all Feedback modules send the e-mail to the administrator of the site. If you would like to send the feedback to a specific e-mail address, log on as admin, go to Module Settings on the Module Edit menu, and add the e-mail address into the Send To box found in the Feedback Settings section. Click on the Update link when finished.

⊟ **Feedback Settings**

In this section, you can set up settings that are specific for this module.

🕲 **Send To:**

Special Features and Additional Information

When we discussed the general features of modules earlier in this chapter we looked at an option that would put a module on every tab. The Feedback module would be a good candidate for this action. It fits nicely on either the left or the right pane and allows your users to contact you with questions without having to go to any particular tab to use the module.

IFrame Module

IFrame is an Internet Explorer browser feature, which allows you to display content from another website within a frame on your portal.

IFrame did not work on Netscape browsers prior to version 6.0.

Practical Purposes

- Display dynamic content from another website
- Keep users up to date on information on other sites

Administration and Modification

To modify the IFrame module, sign on as admin and click on Edit IFrame Options.

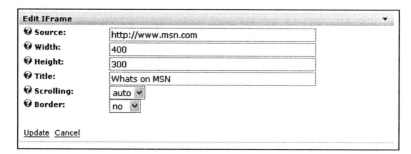

- Source: Enter a source for the IFrame (the source is the webpage you would like to be displayed in the IFrame). The IFrame captures a web page from another site like a mini browser.

- Width: Enter the width for the IFrame in pixels. This is how much of the page will show in your module.

- Height: Enter the height of the IFrame in pixels. This is how much of the page will show in your module.

- Title: Enter the title for your IFrame. This title will not change the title of your module. To change the title of the module you will need to go to Module Settings.

- Scrolling: Select a scrolling option. Since you are only showing a portion of the web page as determined in the Width and Height options, you will determine whether you would like to allow users to scroll the page for more information. Your options are Auto (Scrollbars will appear when needed), Yes (Scrollbars will be shown at all times), and No (Scrollbars will not be available).

- Border: Select whether you would like a border. Yes will display a border around your IFrame, No will not.

Click Update to save your settings.

Special Features/Additional Information

Since the IFrame allows you to show content from other websites, you must make sure that you have permission to do this before setting up the IFrame. Contact the webmaster of the site to find out if this is allowed.

Image Module

The Image module produces an image from a relative or absolute URL—the image file does not need to reside on the host system. Height and width attributes for the image can be entered, which will provide adjustment of the image dimensions.

Practical Purposes

- Display image links to other websites
- Display pictures or images for logos associated with our portal

Administration and Modification

To modify the Image module sign on as admin and click on the Edit Image Options link.

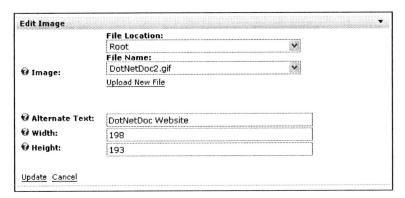

- Image: Enter the image to show for this module. You can select an image from your site by using the File Location and File Name options and selecting it from the dropdown. You can also upload a new image using the Upload New File link. Your third option is to link to an image on another site. To do this, select the URL options and enter the address of the image.

- Alternate text: The alternate text is shown when a user hovers the cursor over the image.

- Width: Enter the width for the image in pixels.

- Height: Enter the height for the image in pixels.

Click on Update to save your settings.

Special Features and Additional Information

If you leave the width and height of the image blank, it will automatically be set to the size of the image you are selecting.

Links Module

The Links module produces a list of hyperlinks to any tab, image, or file on the portal or to a web page, image, or file on the Web. The links can be set to display as a vertical or horizontal list or as a drop-down box. The links appear alphabetically by default. An indexing field facilitates custom sorting. A supplemental description can be set to appear either on mouse rollover or on the click of a dynamically generated link.

Practical Purposes

- Link to resources connected to your portal
- Link to pages on your site
- Link to internal site documents

Administration and Modification

To add a new link to the Links module, sign on as admin and click the Add Link link.

Edit Links

Title: DotNetNuke Site

Link Type:
- URL (A Link To An External Resource)
- Page (A Page On Your Site)
- File (A File On Your Site)

Link:
Location: (Enter The Address Of The Link)
http://www.dotnetnuke.com
Select An Existing URL

☑ Track Number Of Times This Link Is Clicked?
☐ Log The User, Date, And Time For Every Link Click?
☐ Open Link In New Browser Window?

Description: The Official DotNetNuke Website

View Order: 1

Update Cancel Delete

- Title: Enter the title for the link. The title is what the users see in the module and it is what they click on to open the link.

- Link Type: The Links module allows you to link in three different ways:
  - URL: Allows you to link to an external web page (like Yahoo or MSN).
  - Page: Allows you to link to a page on your site. With this option you can create a Quick Links menu that allows users to quickly navigate to particular pages without having to navigate the main menu.
  - File: Acts as an option to the Documents module and allows you to give your users access to documents on your site.

- Link: Enter the destination of the link. Your options here will depend on what type of link you are using. If you are using URL, you can enter the address into the textbox. If using Page, you will be presented with a dropdown of all your pages. If you are using File, you will be show a dropdown displaying the files on you portal.

- Log and Track boxes: Check these options. This will allow you to see how many users have used the links you provided.

- Open Link in New Browser Window: Check this box if you want your link to open in a new window (for example, when you link to another website or file).

- Description: The description section describes what the link is used for. You will be able to see this depending on the options you select.

- View Order: This will be used to sort your links numerically. If nothing is entered, this will default to zero and the links will be sorted by when they were added.

Special Features and Additional Features

The Links module gives you a choice of how you would like to view the content. To edit these options, sign on as admin and go to Settings on the Module Edit menu. You will find the settings under Link Settings.

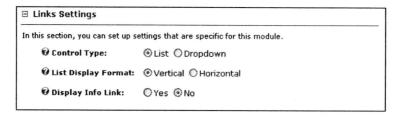

- Control Type: Select the control type you would like to use for your links. The default view for the Links module is to display them in a List but you can choose to have them displayed in a Dropdown.

- List Display Format: Select the format in which you want to display your links—vertically or horizontally.

- Display Info Link: If Yes is selected, an ellipsis will be placed next to the link. When it is clicked it will show the description of the link you entered when you created the link.

News Feed (RSS) Module

The News Feed module provides visitors with up-to-date, topical, information on a wide range of topics (see http://w.moreover.com/categories/category_list_rss.html for one of the more comprehensive selections). Information includes a title linked to the source document, source, and publication date.

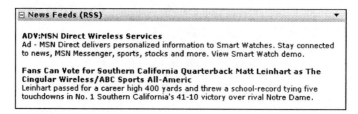

Practical Purposes

- Supply users with information updates on other sites
- View favorite blogs directly on your portal

Administration and Modification

RSS (Rich Site Summary or **Really Simple Syndication)** is an XML-based format for syndicated content. It is designed to allow individuals to distribute news or articles in a format that is easy for programs to read (XML). This allows you to gather relevant content from other sites without needing to rewrite the content or update articles on your site. There are many places to get RSS-syndicated content. One of the better known is `http://www.moreover.com`.

To add an RSS feed to your site, sign in as admin and click on Edit Newsfeed link.

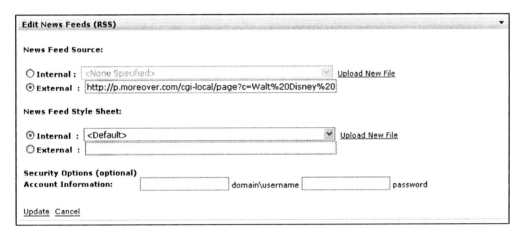

- News Feed Source: You can select a news feed generated from your portal *or* from an external source. Type in the URL location for the news feed.
- News Feed Style Sheet: XSL style sheets allow you to determine how the data appears in your module. If none is selected it will use the default XSL `RSS91.xsl`, which is located in the `DesktopModules/News` folder. You can leave the default, or link to an XSL style sheet on the Internet or on your site.
- Security Options (optional): Some news feeds are not free and will require you to give a username and password to use them.

Click Update to save your changes.

Special Features

RSS feeds are a great way for you to add important and relevant information to your site with very little effort.

Text/HTML Module

The Text/HTML module provides for the input of simple or HTML-formatted text. Simple text is input in a standard textbox and a filter converts carriage returns (paragraph breaks) to HTML breaks. HTML-formatted text can be input directly or generated by an alternative rich text input utility that provides a number of advanced WYSIWYG features as well as a gallery of all uploaded images.

Practical Purposes

- Adding welcome information to your home page
- Creating short tutorials with bolding, highlighting, and images
- Building professional looking ads to place on your site

Administration and Modification

To edit the Text/HTML module, sign in as admin and select the module's Edit menu.

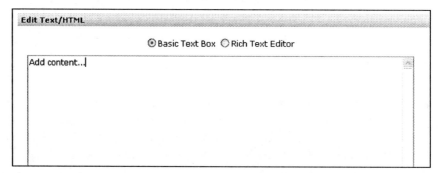

When adding content, you have two options: you can add text to the module using the basic textbox, or you can use the Rich Text Editor.

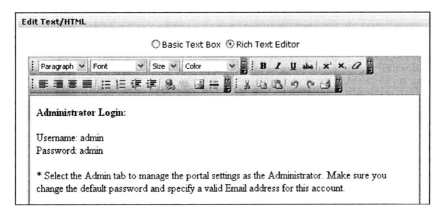

You are able to edit the text in many different ways. You can use tables to organize data, insert images, and modify the color, type, and size of the font. To accomplish this DotNetNuke uses the FreeTextBox version 3.0. FreeTextBox is a freely available control that can be used with ASP.NET. To save your data click on the Update link.

Special Features and Additional Information

Because of its versatility, the Text/HTML module is probably the most widely used module on a DotNetNuke site. Most tabs are filled with static data and this module fits the bill.

User Accounts Module

The User Account module permits registered users to add, edit, and update their user account details. Membership services are also managed here.

Practical Purpose

This module can be used to create a page that has many different user modules on it.

Administration and Modification

By default, the user account module is found when a users click on their name in the header. You are not allowed to modify this page. So if you want to combine the User Accounts module with other modules you can add it to any tab you would like.

Special Features and Additional Information

There are two sections to the User Account module. The first section is used to edit and update the users' information.

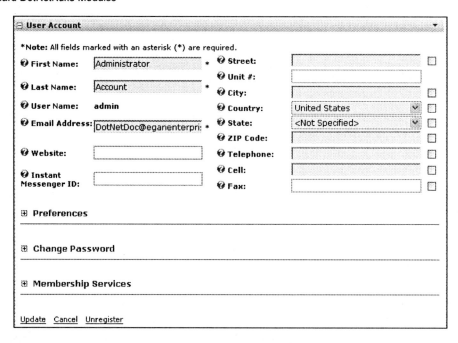

Here you are able to change your password and personal information, or unregister from the portal completely. The bottom section holds all the available member services. These services are set up by the admin when creating user roles. If the role is set up as a public role it will show up in this section.

User Defined Table Module

User Defined Table allows you to create a custom data table for managing tabular information.

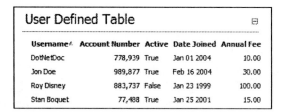

Practical Purpose

This module can be used to display relevant user information.

Administration and Modification

When using the User Defined Table module, the first thing you must do is to decide what columns you would like in your table. To do this, sign on as admin, hover over the pencil icon next to the User Defined Table title, and click on Manage User Defined Table.

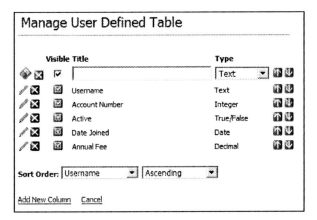

Click on Add New Column. This will present you with the dialog boxes necessary to create a new column for your table.

- Visible: If you don't want the column to be visible to non-admin roles, uncheck the Visible checkbox.

- Title: Enter a title for the column.

- Type: Enter a type for the data. You can choose from Text, Integer, True/False, Date, and Decimal. Select the appropriate type from the dropdown. Data will be validated according to the type you select.

- Sort Order: You may choose to sort any of the columns as Ascending or Descending.

Click on the save icon to save the current column to the database.

Repeat the previous steps for each of the columns you require. Use the arrows to determine the order of the columns.

When you are finished adding columns, click Cancel.

After you have created your columns, you can add rows of data. To do this, make sure you are signed on as admin, hover the cursor over the pencil icon next to the User Defined Table title, and click on Add New Row.

Edit User Defined Table

Username: DotNetDoc

Account Number: 778939

Active: True

Date Joined: 01/01/2004

Annual Fee: 10.00

Update   Cancel

- Enter the data for the row. The data you enter will be validated from the type you selected when setting up the columns. If the data you enter is not valid, you will be shown an error message at the top of the page.
- Click on Update to save your row.
- Repeat these steps for additional rows.

Special Features and Additional Information

Since it is impossible to predict the different types of data that portal administrators may want on their site, the User Defined Table module gives you the ability to customize your site with data that is pertinent to you and your users.

XML/XSL Module

The XML/XSL module renders the result of an XML/XSL transform. The XML and XSL files are identified by their UNC paths in the xmlsrc and xslsrc properties of the module. The XML/XSL module includes an Edit page, which persists these settings to the SQL database.

Practical Purpose

You can use this module for presenting XML data in a readable format.

Administration and Modification

News feeds are not the only application to use XML to deliver data. Whether you have a program on your local intranet or you are trying to access a web service, the XML/XSL module allows you to translate the XML data to a readable format fit for your web page.

Special Features and Additional Information

Like the User Defined module, the XML/XLS module gives you tremendous flexibility on the type of information you can present to your users. Using standard XML data, you can create different XLS style sheets to present the data differently for different users.

Summary

In this chapter we covered the standard modules that come prepackaged with DotNetNuke. We covered their basic uses as well as situations they may be used in. You will use these modules to build the content of your portal. In the next chapter we will cover the administration options you have available to you as well as the differences between the admin and host logins.

5
Host and Admin Tools

Running a DotNetNuke site requires someone to administer the site. There are two built-in roles for accomplishing the tasks associated with this. The host and admin roles are very similar in nature and ability, but possess some important differences. In this chapter, we will learn the following:

- The difference between host and admin
- How to access and use the admin tools
- How to access and use the host tools

The Difference Between Host and Admin

There has always been a bit of confusion about what differentiates the admin and host roles. To understand the difference, you first have to look into how DotNetNuke works. An implementation of DotNetNuke is not restricted to one portal. DotNetNuke has the ability to run multiple portals from one database. This is where the difference between the roles comes in.

The host has the responsibility of, for lack of a better word, hosting the portals. The host will have access to any parent and/or child portals that are created, as well as all the administrative functions. This user is sometimes called a **superuser**. In previous versions of DotNetNuke, you were only allowed *one* superuser per installation. Starting with DotNetNuke 3.0, you can add additional users with superuser abilities. This really helps to divide the tasks needed to run a portal.

The admin role on the other hand is responsible for only one portal. There can be more than one admin for every portal, but unlike the superusers, they only have the ability to access one portal. While the superuser has access to both host tools and the admin tools, the admin will only see the admin tools.

Admin Tools

When you sign on to your DotNetNuke portal using an admin login, you will see an admin menu item appear on the menu bar. In this section we will cover these menu items in detail.

The first admin menu item is Site Settings. The Site Settings cover a wide range of services for a site. Because of this, we cannot cover this in one section of the book. We will walk through each item on the Site Settings page and either describe its functionality or point you to where you can find the information in this book.

Site Settings

Like the other admin screens we have seen, the Site Settings page lays out several options that allow the administrator to customize the portal experience. These settings are divided into three sections: Basic Settings, Advanced Settings, and StyleSheet Editor. We will begin with the Basic Settings section.

Basic Settings

The Site Details are used to tailor your portal with the information that describes what your site is used for:

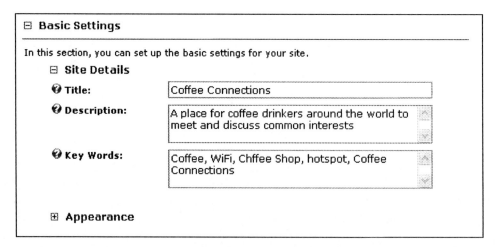

- Title: The title or name for your website. This will be displayed in the top bar of your browser along with the current tab information.

- Description and Key Words: Used by search engines when describing your site. The key words should be entered in a comma-separated format.

The Appearance section controls the basic look and feel of your site.

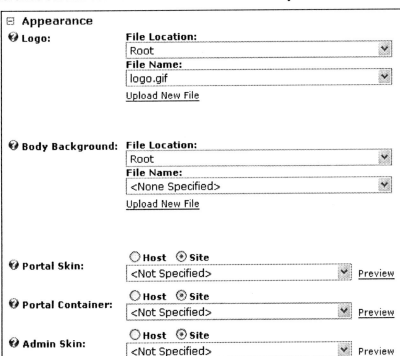

- Logo: If you are using the default look of DotNetNuke, you can change the logo from the DotNetNuke logo.gif to one of your choice.

- Body Background: As an alternative to skinning your site, you can choose to change the background of your site to any image you would like. To do this, select the image from the dropdown. You will need to upload the image to your site first. The ease of using skins makes this option almost obsolete.

- Portal Skin, Portal Container, Admin Skin, and Admin Container: This section allows you to select a skin for your portal. There are different sections for Admin and Portal skins because Admin sections of the site usually use only one frame and portal sections utilize three or more. You can find our more about skinning your portal in Chapter 8.

Advanced Settings

The advanced settings are divided into three different sections: Page Management, Payment Settings, and Other Settings. We will first look at Page Management.

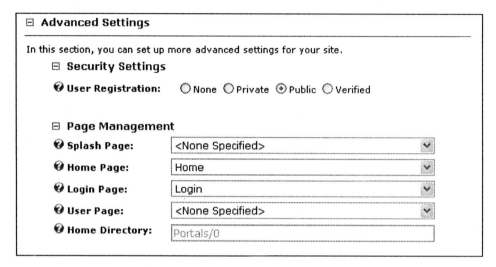

- **Splash Page:** Lets you choose from a dropdown a splash page that will load before your site is shown (if you want your site to begin with a splash page).

- **Home Page:** Determines where users are redirected to when they first navigate to your portal. The default is the Home page. You may select any page on your portal from the dropdown.

- **Login Page:** Determines where the users are redirected to once they log in to your portal. Select a page from the dropdown.

- **User Page:** By default, administrators can't edit the user account information page, but can place the User Accounts Module on a separate page along with other modules of their choosing. To change the default user accounts page to a different tab, you can select the page from the dropdown box.

- **Home Directory:** The physical path of your portal's location.

The Payment Settings section, as the name implies, allows you to add payment processing to your portal:

- **Currency, Payment Processor, Processor UserId, and Processor Password:** DotNetNuke gives you the ability to charge users for subscribing to a service on your site (see *Understanding DotNetNuke Roles* in Chapter 3). The only payment processor fully integrated into DotNetNuke at this time is PayPal.

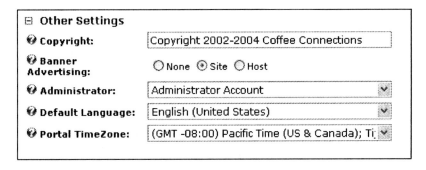

The Other Settings section helps you customize your portal to fit the company's identity.

- Copyright: The copyright notice that appears on the footer of each page on the portal. Change this to reflect your portal name.
- Banner Advertising: Allows you to decide whether you want banner advertising to be on a single site or on all the sites under the host.
- Administrator: The default administrator for this site. You can to select anyone who has been added to the administrator role.
- Default Language: Beginning with DotNetNuke 3.0, localization has been integrated into the DotNetNuke portal. At the time of writing, only English and German were available, but many more are on the way. You can set the default language of your portal by selecting it from the dropdown.
- Portal Time Zone: Allows you to localize your portal's time zone.

Stylesheet Editor

The Stylesheet Editor section is the final portion of the Site Settings.

- Edit Style Sheet: This will allow you to edit the CSS stylesheet for the DotNetNuke site. You can change the look and feel of the site by modifying the styles located in the stylesheet. This section has been made somewhat obsolete because of the new skinning solution for DotNetNuke.

```
⊟ Stylesheet Editor
/* ===============================
   CSS STYLES FOR DotNetNuke
   ===============================
*/


/* PAGE BACKGROUND */
/* background color for the header at the top of the page  */
.HeadBg {
}

/* background color for the content part of the pages */
Body
{
}

/* background/border colors for the selected tab */
.TabBg {
}
```

Pages Menu

You will find a discussion on pages under the *Understanding DotNetNuke Pages and tabIDs* section in Chapter 3.

Security Roles

You will find a discussion on Security roles under *Understanding DotNetNuke Roles* in Chapter 3.

User Accounts

You will find a discussion of user accounts under *User Accounts* in Chapter 3.

Vendors

You will find a discussion of vendors under the *Host Tools* section in this chapter.

Site Log

The site log gives you access to log files that keep track of most things that happen on your portal.

```
┌──────────────────────────────────────────────────────────────────────┐
│  ▮▮  Site Log                                                      ▼   │
│                                                                        │
│   ⚠   Your Hosting Provider Has Limited Your Portal To 60 Days Of Site Log History. │
│  ──────────────────────────────────────────────────────────────────── │
│     ❷ Report Type:      │ Affiliate Referrals            ▼│            │
│     ❷ Start Date:       │ 11/23/2004        │  Calendar               │
│     ❷ End Date:         │ 11/30/2004        │  Calendar               │
│                              Display   Cancel                          │
└──────────────────────────────────────────────────────────────────────┘
```

To use the site report, select one of the following options from the dropdown, select a Start Date and End Date, and click on the Display link.

- **Affiliate Referrals:** You can track when users enter your site from sites that are affiliated with you. To make this work, the link coming from the affiliate site must add a querystring to the URL. For example, instead of pointing the link to `http://www.CoffeeConnections.net`, you would point it to `http://www.CoffeeConnections.net?AffiliateID=108`. You would need to give different IDs to different affiliates. When someone logs in using one of those links, it is recorded into the database and you then have the ability to view reports of this data.

- **Detailed Site Log:** This report gives you the name of the user, the date and time they entered your site, the website they came from (referrer), the type of browser they are using (user agent), their IP address (UserHostAddress), and the name of the tab they entered on.

- **Page Popularity:** This report gives you the Page Name, number of times the page has been visited, and when the tab was last visited.

- **Page Views By Day, Week, Month, Hour:** The report gives you summarized views of how many visitors have been on your site.

- **Site Referrals:** This report gives you the website that referred users to the site (referrer), the number of times users came from the site, and the last time a user was referred by the site. Unlike the Affiliate Referral, this tracks users from *any* website, and not just those with which you have a relationship.

- **User Agents:** This report gives the types of browsers (user agents) used to browse your site as well as the number of times each browser was used.

- **User Frequency:** This report gives you the number of times each user has logged onto your site. It also displays the last time users logged on.

- User Registration by Country: This report details what country your users come from. The report depends entirely on the country the users select when registering on your portal.

- User Registrations by Date: This report sorts the registrations on your site by the date the users registered. It provides you with the date and the number that registered on each date.

Newsletter

As an administrator, you can send out bulk e-mails to your users. The Newsletter section contains all that you need to send newsletters to your users.

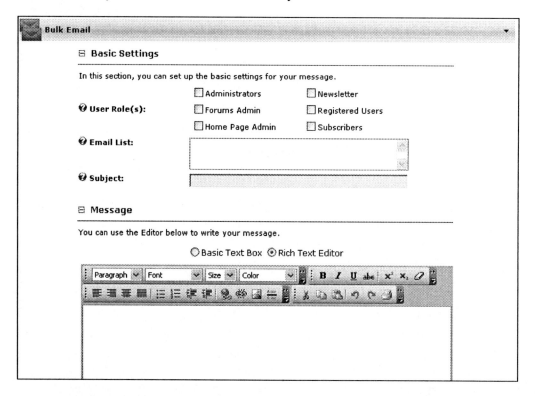

- User Roles: You can send an e-mail to a select group of users based on the user roles you set up for your portal. (For more information on user roles, see *Understanding DotNetNuke Role* in Chapter 3.)

- Email List: Optionally, you can send e-mails to e-mail addresses in this e-mail list. You will need to make sure that you separate each e-mail address with a semi-colon.

- Subject: This will appear on the subject line when the e-mail is received.
- Message: The body of the message that you want to send. You may use either a Basic Text Box or the Rich Text Editor (FreeTextBox). For more information on the FreeTextBox and other rich text editors in DotNetNuke please see Chapter 12, which discusses the Provider model.

- Attachment: You can add an attachment to be sent out in the e-mail. Select the attachment from the drop-down box or upload a new file. For more information on uploading files, see the *File Manager* section in this chapter.
- Priority: You can set the priority of your e-mail to Low, Normal, or High.
- Send Method: You have two choices on how to send your message. The first method will send a separate e-mail to each user that will be personalized with their user name. The second method will send one e-mail with all the users entered into the BCC (Blind Carbon Copy) section of the e-mail. The e-mail will not be personalized, and all users will see the same message.
- Send Action: Selecting Synchronous will have your web page wait while the e-mails are sent. Selecting Asynchronous will send the e-mails on a new thread behind the scenes. Use this option when sending a personalized e-mail.
- Click Send Email when your message is complete.

File Manager

The file manager allows the administrator to upload files to the portal. This control has been upgraded from previous versions. It gives the user much more flexibility for working with files.

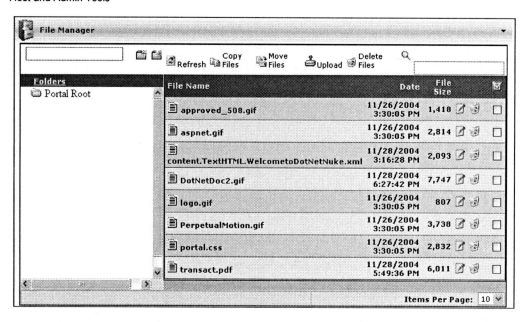

One of the nicer new features is the ability to upload files to folders other than the default Portal Root folder.

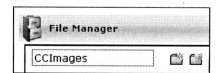

To create a new folder, type a name into the folder box and click on the New Folder icon (the folder icon with an asterisk in the corner). This will then allow you to upload files to this folder. To upload a new file to the portal, from within the file manager, click on the Upload icon.

- Click on the Browse button to select the file to upload. This will open the Choose File dialog box. Navigate to the location of the file you would like to upload and select it. This will place the location of the file in the browse textbox.

- Select the folder where you would like to upload the file. Notice that the folder we created in the last exercise is now available to us.

- Click on the Add button to add the file to the list of files to be uploaded. The file must first be added to the list before it can be uploaded to the portal.

- Decompress Zip Files?: If you have selected a ZIP file to be uploaded to your portal, you can either have the files inside the ZIP file extracted (box is checked) or upload the ZIP file in its entirety (box is unchecked).
- Repeat these steps for all files to be uploaded.
- Click on Upload New File to finish the procedure.

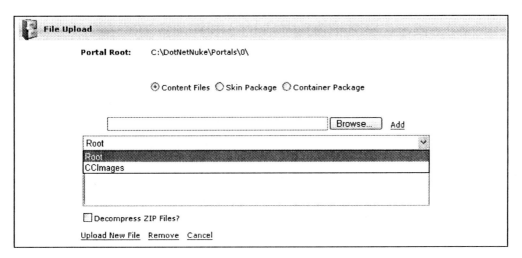

On the bottom of the admin File Upload page are some options you can set to allow other users to upload files.

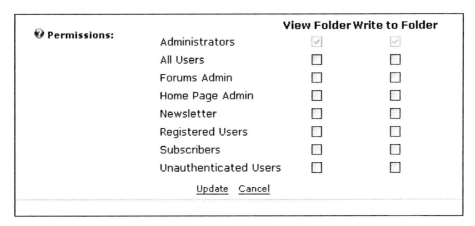

- Check the boxes next to the roles allowed to upload files.
- Click on Update to save your settings.

Recycle Bin

The Recycle Bin allows you to recover modules or tabs that you deleted.

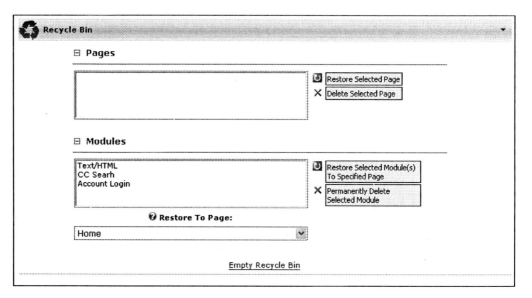

- To restore a page or module to its original location highlight it and click on the restore icon (🔄). Note, a module cannot be restored if the page it was on has also been deleted. Restore the page before restoring the module.
- To delete a page or module permanently, highlight it and click on the delete icon (❌).

Log Viewer

The log viewer gives the administrator of the portal the ability monitor all transactions that occur on the portal.

General Exception Errors will only show up in the log viewer when you are signed on as a superuser (host).

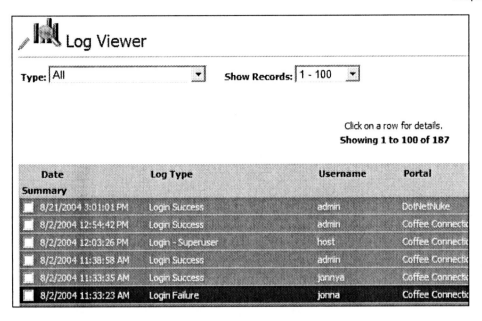

The log will track many different pieces of information; among the most useful is the Exception. To view the details for any log entry just click on the row. This will give you a detailed explanation of the log entry.

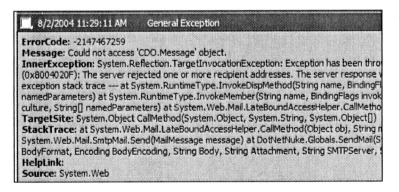

This information is very helpful when attempting to track down errors generated by your portal. To alert you to errors happening to other users, DotNetNuke gives you the ability to send error notices to any e-mail address. To set this up, expand the Send Exceptions section at the bottom of the log viewer.

It is important to note that the e-mails will not be encrypted when sent. So be careful if sensitive data is involved.

To Specified Email Address

Email Address:

Message (optional):

Send Selected Exceptions

- Email Address: The e-mail address of the person you would like the error notification to be sent to. This will send the addressee the detailed error message, including the stack trace. To send to more than one address, separate them with a semi-colon (;).
- Message: A message to accompany the exception.
- Click on Send Selected Exceptions link to save your settings.

Skins

This section allows you to browse through all of the skins and containers that have been uploaded to your portal. You can find a discussion on skins in Chapter 8.

Languages

Starting with DotNetNuke version 3.x you have the ability to localize your portal to the language of you choice.

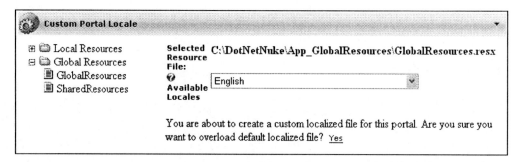

Currently only English and German are supported but many more languages are on the way. If you would like to learn more about localization please refer to the DotNetNuke localization white paper found in the C:\DotNetNuke\Documentation\Public folder.

Host Tools

To access the host tools, you will first need to log on as the host for your portal. Once you have done this you will see the host menu. We will cover each of the tools that are available to you as a superuser.

Host Settings

The first menu item on the host menu is Host Settings. They are separated into Basic Settings and Advanced Settings. The host settings cover a very wide range of services for your portal. Because of this, we will walk through each item on the host settings page and either describe its functionality or point you to where you can find the information in this book.

Basic Settings

As we have seen when we looked at the admin Site Settings, the Basic Settings on the Host Settings page gives you the ability to customize your hosting environment.

The Host Details cover the contact information for your portal.

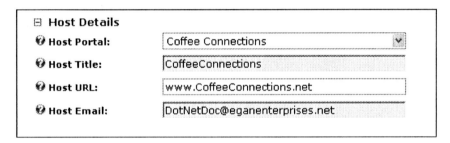

- Host Portal: The portal that serves as the host for all other parent or child portals that you create.

- Host Title: The text for the hyperlink that is displayed. The Host Title is located on the footer of every tab in your portal.

- Host URL: The location to which the user will be taken to when the Host Title hyperlink is clicked.

- Host Email: The e-mail address used when sending out certain administration e-mails.

The Appearance section controls the basic look and feel of the site:

- Host Skin, Host Container, Admin Skin, and Admin Container: This section allows you to select a skin for your portal. There are different sections for admin and portal skins, because admin sections of the site usually use only one frame and portal sections utilize three or more. You can find out more about skinning your portal in the Chapter 8.

- Show Copyright Credits: Unchecking this box will remove the DotNetNuke copyright from the footer and the (DNN 3.X) from the IE header.

- Use Custom Error Message: DotNetNuke uses a custom provider for its error handling. If you would like to turn this feature off and use the default ASP.Net error handling, uncheck this box.

- Payment Settings: This section allows you to set up a payment processor for your site and gives you the ability to charge for hosting multiple DotNetNuke sites.

Advanced Settings

The Advanced Settings section is used to make configuration changes to your portal to enable it to work in certain restricted environments.

Some intranet or Internet configurations need to use a proxy server to allow modules to make web requests to the Internet. An example of this is the RSS NewsFeed module, which requests data from a news feed source on the Internet. This next section allows you to configure DotNetNuke to use a proxy server:

⊟ **Proxy Settings**	
🌏 **Proxy Server:**	
🌏 **Proxy Port:**	
🌏 **Proxy Username:**	
🌏 **Proxy Password:**	
🌏 **Web Request Timeout:**	

- Proxy Server: The IP address of the proxy server
- Proxy Port: The port that the proxy server uses to fulfill web requests
- Proxy Username: The username needed to connect through the proxy server
- Proxy Password: The password needed to connect through the proxy server
- Web Request Timeout: The time, in seconds, for which DotNetNuke will attempt to fulfill a web request

For the e-mail functionality to work on your portal, you will need to configure your SMTP (Simple Mail Transfer Protocol) server. Once the correct information has been entered, you can click on the Test link to determine whether it is working. If the test succeeds, you will receive a message that says Email Sent Successfully. If there is an error, it will say Could not access 'CDO.Message' object. This is a generic error message; look in the log viewer for specific details.

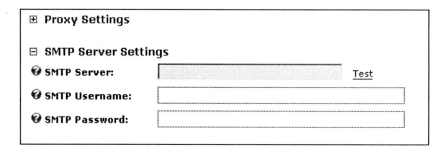

- SMTP Server: The address of your mail server. This can be obtained from your ISP. It is usually your domain name with mail replacing the www.
- SMTP Username: The username for your SMTP server, if required.
- SMTP Password: The password for you SMTP server if required.

The Other Settings section is set up to hold all the information that does not fit into any particular group.

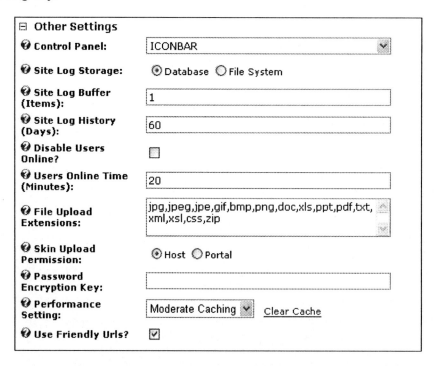

- Control Panel: When signed on as host or admin, you will see a control panel at the top of the screen. If you prefer the version of the control panel that existed in 2.x, you can choose the Classic option.

- Site Log Storage: You can select whether you would like the site logs to be stored in your database or in the file system.

- Site Log Buffer (Items): The site log buffer is a setting for the number of Sitelog records that have to be reached before DotNetNuke writes them to the database. They are held in memory before they are written to the database. This can help to speed things up on a busy site. Be careful when increasing this number, because if the application is reset you will loose the records in the buffer. Setting the number to 1 before you reset the application will prevent this from happening.

- Site Log History (Days): This tells the system how many days of history to keep for your site log. The default is 60 days.

- Disable Users Online and Users Online Time (Minutes): For more information on users online, please refer to Chapter 9.

- File Upload Extensions: This setting restricts the files users are able to upload to your site. This is done for security purposes so that users are not able to upload malicious script files to the server. Separate file extensions (without a period) by using a comma.

- Skin Upload Permissions: This setting determines who has the authority to upload new skins to the site. Setting it to Portal allows portal administrators to upload skins.

- Password Encryption Key: By default, user passwords are stored in the database using plain text. To encrypt the passwords enter a password encryption key in this box. The key can use any keyboard character. When a key is entered and the settings are updated, all passwords currently in the database will be encrypted.

- Performance Settings: The performance settings are used to speed up the rendering of your portal. Caching stores a representation of the data contained in your page. This means that subsequent attempts to access this page (even by other users) will show the same data. Setting this to Heavy Caching will keep the cached data the longest. To clear the cache click on the Clear link.

- Use friendly URLs?: Checking this box (default) will create URLs that are search-engine friendly. Search engines, for the most part, prefer URLs without querystrings. This option will create the URL in a friendlier version, allowing your site to perform better on search sites.

| Upgrade Log For Version: | 01.00.10 ▼ | Go |

The last item on the Host Settings tab is the Upgrade Log For Version section. When you upgrade DotNetNuke from one version to the next, it keeps a log file. To view the log files for a particular version, select the version from the dropdown and click on Go.

Portals

For a discussion on running multiple portals, please refer to Chapter 11 on *Creating Multiple Portals*.

Module Definitions

For a discussion of modules and module definitions, please see Chapter 7 *Creating Custom Modules*.

File Manager

The file manager under the host settings functions just as the file manager under the Admin menu (see the *Admin Tools* section in this chapter). The only difference is that the host, by default, is able to upload not only content files, skin packages, and container packages, but also custom modules.

Vendors

DotNetNuke comes equipped with vendor and banner advertising integration. To set up a new vendor for your site, click on the Add New Vendor link at the bottom of the page:

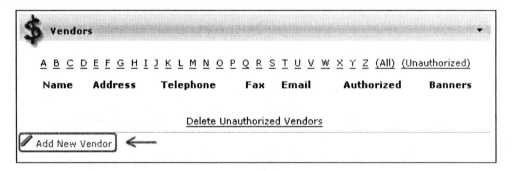

Fill out the vendor information and click on Update to save the vendor. Once you have saved the vendor information, you can add banners to this vendor by editing the vendor record.

To add a banner to a vendor, edit a vendor, open the Banner Advertising section, and click on Add New Banner:

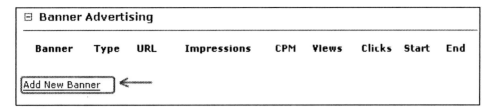

This allows you to add the specifications necessary to associate banner ads with your vendors.

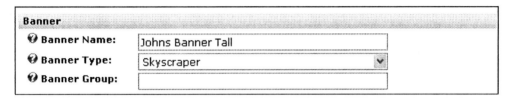

- Banner Name: Enter the name of the banner. This can be anything you want. Make it descriptive to help organize your banners.
- Banner Type: This refers to the size of the banner. Banners can be anything from large skyscraper banners to tiny micro banners.
- Banner Group: To better organize your banners, type in a banner group.

The next section determines where the banner ad is located. You can chose between a file on your site and a URL to a file located on another site.

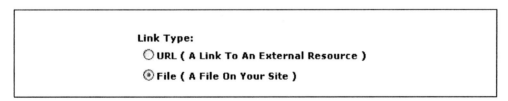

Once you make your selection, you will be able to point to the correct file. Select the location and the name of the banner ad file:

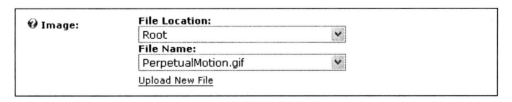

If you selected URL, you would need to enter the URL of the file.

Text/Script:	Please come and visit Johns Shop
URL:	http://www.JohnsShop.com

Next you will want to determine what happens when the user clicks on a banner.

- Text/Script: The alternative text to be displayed with the banner.
- URL: The URL that users will be redirected to when they click on a banner ad. If no URL is listed here, the URL in the vendor setup will be used.

CPM/Cost:	0.10
Impressions:	100
Start Date:	01/15/2004 Calendar
End Date:	01/15/2006 Calendar
Criteria:	⦿ OR ◯ AND

- CPM/Cost: The amount you will charge for every 1000 impressions. An impression is how many times the banner is displayed on the site.
- Impressions: The number of impressions the vendor has paid for.
- Start Date and End Date: Start and end dates for the ad campaign.
- Criteria: Used to determine whether to stop the ads after the date has expired or the number of impressions has been reached.

When you are done adding the banner details, click on the Update link to save your data.

To view your banners on the portal, you will need to add a banner module to one of your pages. Once you have added a banner module, select Edit from the module drop-down menu.

To edit the banner, enter the Banner Source and Banner Type to display your banner. Since the vendor was created from the Host tools, you will need to select Host for the source. By using the information you used to set up your banner in the vendor section, you can decide the types or groups of banners you would like displayed. When you are finished adding the information, click on the Update link to save your settings.

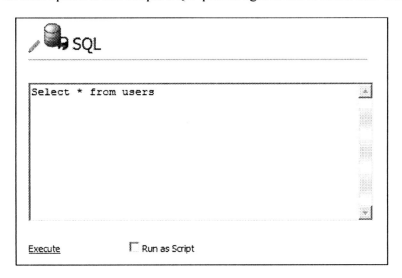

SQL

Use the SQL host option to run simple SQL queries against the DotNetNuke database.

Simply type in your SQL statement and click on the Execute link. You will then be presented with a simple tabular representation of your data. Since this is part of the DotNetNuke framework, you can also run scripts that use the <objectQualifier> and <databaseOwner> tags.

Schedule

With the addition of users online and site log in DotNetNuke 2.0, there arose a need to schedule recurring tasks. To address this, the core team developed the **scheduler**. The scheduler allows you to perform recurring actions on the portal. For more information on how to use the scheduler, please see the DotNetNuke Scheduler.doc located in the C:\DotNetNuke\Documentation\Public folder.

Languages

Starting with DotNetNuke version 3.x, you can localize your portal to the language of you choice. Currently only English and German are supported, but many more are on the way. If you would like to learn more about localization, refer to DotNetNuke Localization.doc in the C:\DotNetNuke\Documentation\Public folder. We will look into localization further when we discuss designing custom modules in Chapter 7.

Search Admin

You may have noticed in the upper right-hand corner of your screen, a box with a small magnifying glass.

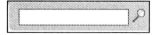

DotNetNuke gives the portal visitors the ability to search the portal for relevant information. The administration for the functionality is found on the host menu.

Search Admin	
Maximum Word Length:	
Minimum Word Length:	
Include Common Words:	☐
Include Numbers:	☐

Update   Cancel   Re-Index Content

In this section, you can set parameters for the search engine to follow. You can set the maximum and minimum word length to follow as well as decide if you want to ignore common words (and, or, the, etc.) and/or numbers. We will look further into the search functionality when we discuss custom modules in Chapter 7.

Lists

Many of the controls in DotNetNuke use lists to populate the information need to fulfill a task. A good example of this is the user account registration control.

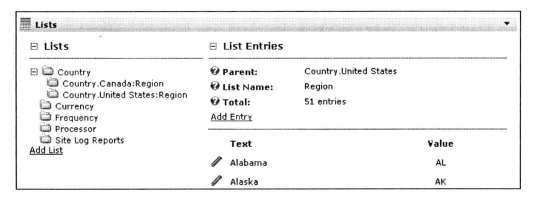

When users register for your site, they are presented with drop-down lists that allow them to select their country and region/state. This section allows the host to add items or remove items from the list. This allows you to customize the items show in the list.

Superuser Accounts

In previous versions of DotNetNuke, only one host (superuser) account was available. This restriction has been fixed in version 3.0 with the addition of the SuperUser section. From here, you can create additional users who will have the same abilities as the host.

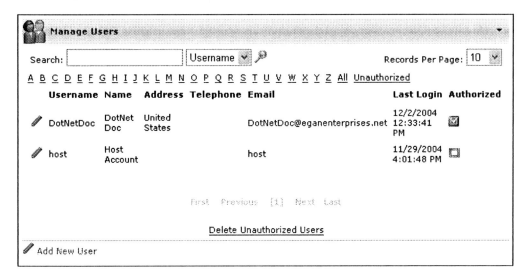

Remember that these users will have the freedom to control access to every part of your portal, from creating portals to deleting users, so be careful when issuing these sign-ons.

Extra Options on the Admin Menu

When you are signed on as a superuser, you may notice a few extra items on the Admin menu. If you look at the Site Settings, you will see an extra section called Host Settings that allows a superuser to control certain aspects of the portal. In addition, if you view the Log Viewer on the Admin menu when signed on as a superuser, you will see exceptions generated by the portal. These exceptions are logged here by the framework, but are only available to the superuser. Finally, at the bottom of the Site Settings pane, you will see an extra section for Portal Aliases.

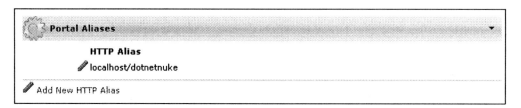

The portal alias of the site must be located in this section. When you first set up your site on a local machine, it will be added for you, but when you upload your site to a remote server, you will need to add the URL of your site to this section. We will cover deploying to a remote server in Chapter 10.

Common Tasks

So far we have used the icon bar at the top of the portal to work with pages and to install modules. The last section of the icon bar is used to perform common administrative tasks.

These are shortcuts to common tasks that you can find on the administrative menus and are meant to help you be more productive. The only item on the Common Tasks bar that we have not yet talked about is the Wizard. We will discuss this in more detail in Chapter 11 on running multiple portals.

Summary

This chapter has covered a variety of information. It should have given you, as the administrator of a DotNetNuke portal, the skills needed to maintain your website. In the next chapter, we will delve deep into the core of the DotNetNuke architecture and find out what really makes our portal run.

Understanding the DotNetNuke Core Architecture

In this chapter, we will be exploring the core functionality of the DotNetNuke architecture. We will start with an overview of the architecture, touching on key concepts employed by DotNetNuke. After this, we will examine some of the major sections that make up the framework. Finally, after we learn about the objects that make up the core, we will follow a request for a page through this process to find out how each page is dynamically created.

Architecture Overview

As we discussed in the previous chapter, as opposed to traditional web applications that may rely on a multitude of web pages to deliver content, DotNetNuke uses a single main page called Default.aspx. The content for this page is presented dynamically by using a tabID value to retrieve from the DotNetNuke database the skins and modules needed to build the page requested. Before we move on, we should discuss what is meant by a **tab** and a **page**. As you read this chapter, you will notice the word tab is sometimes used when referring to pages in your DotNetNuke portal. In the original IBuySpy application, pages were referred to as tabs because they resembled tabs when added to the page.

This continued in the original versions of the DotNetNuke project. With the release of version 3.0, an effort has begun to rename most of these instances to reflect what they really are: pages. Most references to "tabs" have been changed to "pages", but the conversion is not complete. For this reason, you will see both—tabs and pages—in the database, in the project files, and in this text. We will use these terms interchangeably throughout this text as we look into the core architecture of DNN.

> You may notice a file called `DefaultDesktop.aspx` in the DotNetNuke application. In previous versions of DNN, this served the same purpose as `Default.aspx`. It is kept around for backwards compatibility.

We will begin with a general overview of what happens when a user requests a page on your DotNetNuke portal. The process for rendering a page in DotNetNuke works like this: a user selects a menu item; this calls the `Default.aspx` page, passing the `tabid` parameter in the querystring to let the application identify the page being requested. The example `http://www.dotnetnuke.com/Default.aspx?tabid=476` demonstrates this.

> DotNetNuke 3.0 has introduced something called **URLRewriting**. This takes the querystring shown above and rewrites it so that it is in a format that helps increase search-engine hits. We will cover the HTTP Module that is responsible for this later in this chapter. The rewritten URL would resemble `http://localhost/DotNetNuke/tabid/476/Default.aspx`.
>
> While referring to URLs in this chapter we will be using the non-rewritten version of the URL. This can be turned off at the Host Settings page.

The querystring value (`?tabid=476`) is sent to the database, where the information required for the page is retrieved.

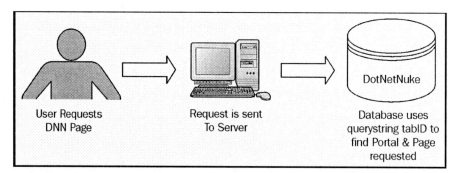

User Requests DNN Page	Request is sent To Server	Database uses querystring tabID to find Portal & Page requested

The portal that the user is accessing can be determined in a number of ways, but as you can see from the `DNN_Tabs` table, each page/tab contains a reference to the portal it belongs to in the `PortalID` field. Once the server has a reference to the page that the user requested (using the tabID), it can determine what modules belong on that page.

	DNN_Tabs
PK	**TabID**
	TabOrder
I1	PortalID
	TabName
	IsVisible
I2	ParentId
	Level
	IconFile
	DisableLink
	Title
	Description
	KeyWords
	IsDeleted
	Url
	SkinSrc
	ContainerSrc
	TabPath
	StartDate
	EndDate

	DNN_TabModules
PK	**TabModuleID**
U1	**TabID**
U1	**ModuleID**
	PaneName
	ModuleOrder
	CacheTime
	Alignment
	Color
	Border
	IconFile
	Visibility
	ContainerSrc

	DNN_Modules
PK	**ModuleID**
I1	**ModuleDefID**
	ModuleTitle
	AllTabs
	IsDeleted
	InheritViewPermissions
	Header
	Footer
	StartDate
	EndDate
	PortalID

Although there are many more tables involved in this process, you can see that *these* tables hold not only the page and modules needed to generate the page, but also what pane to place them on (PaneName) and what skin and containers to apply (SkinSrc or ContainerSrc).

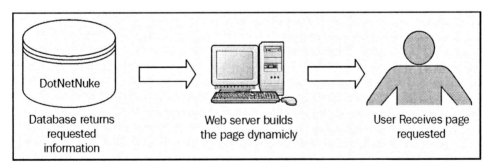

Database returns requested information	Web server builds the page dynamicly	User Receives page requested

All of this information is returned to the web server, and the Default.aspx page is constructed with and returned to the user who requested it along with the required modules and skins.

Now, this is of course a very general overview of the process, but as we work through this chapter, we will delve deeper into the code that makes this process work, and in the end show a request work its way through the framework to deliver a page to a user.

Diving into the Core

There are over 80,000 lines of code in the DotNetNuke application. There is no possible (or even practical) way to cover the entire code base. In addition to this, version 3.0 has gone through a major namespace restructuring to better categorize the classes contained in the application. To help you transverse the many namespaces present in the application, Subzero-Solutions (http:www.subzero-solutions.net) has created a class browser for DotNetNuke. This can be found at http://dnn3.subzero-solutions.net/.

In this section, we will go in depth into what I believe are the main portions of the code base: The PortalSettings as well as the companion classes found in the portals folder; the web.config file including the HTTP Modules and Providers; and the Global.aspx and Globals.vb files.

We will start our discussion of the core with two objects that play an integral part in the construction of the architecture. The Context object and the PortalSettings class will both be referred to quite often in the code, and so it is important that you have a good understanding of what they do.

Using the Context Object in Your Application

ASP.NET has taken intrinsic objects like the Request and the Application objects and wrapped them together with other relevant items into an intrinsic object called Context.

The Context object (HttpContext) can be found in the System.Web namespace. Below you will find some of the objects that make up the HttpContext object.

Title	Description
Application	Gets the HttpApplicationState object for the current HTTP request.
Cache	Gets the Cache object for the current HTTP request.
Current	Gets the HttpContext object for the current HTTP request.
Items	Gets a key-value collection that can be used to organize and share data between an IHttpModule and an IHttpHandler during an HTTP request.
Request	Gets the HttpRequest object for the current HTTP request.
Response	Gets the HttpResponse object for the current HTTP response.

Title	Description
Server	Gets the `HttpServerUtility` object that provides methods used in processing Web requests.
Session	Gets the `HttpSessionState` instance for the current HTTP request.
User	Gets or sets security information for the current HTTP request.

Notice that most of the descriptions talk about the "current" request object, or the "current" response object. The Global.aspx file, which we will look at soon, reacts on every single request made to your application, and so it is only concerned with whoever is "currently" accessing a resource.

The HttpContext object contains all HTTP-specific information about an individual HTTP request. The HttpContext.Current property in particular can give you the context for the current request from *anywhere* in the application domain. The DotNetNuke core relies on the HTTPContext.Current property to hold everything from the Application Name to the Portal Settings and through this makes it available to you.

The PortalSettings Class

The portal settings play a major role in the dynamic generation of your pages and as such will be referred to quite often in the other portions of the code. The portal settings are represented by the PortalSettings class, which you will find in the Components\ Portal\PortalSettings.vb file. As you can see from the private variables in this class, most of what goes on in your portal will at some point need to access this object. This object will hold everything from the ID of the portal to the default language, and as we will see later, is responsible for determining the skins and modules needed for each page.

```
Private _PortalId As Integer
        Private _PortalName As String
        Private _HomeDirectory As String
        Private _LogoFile As String
        Private _FooterText As String
        Private _ExpiryDate As Date
        Private _UserRegistration As Integer
        Private _BannerAdvertising As Integer
        Private _Currency As String
        Private _AdministratorId As Integer
        Private _Email As String
        Private _HostFee As Single
        Private _HostSpace As Integer
        Private _AdministratorRoleId As Integer
        Private _AdministratorRoleName As String
        Private _RegisteredRoleId As Integer
        Private _RegisteredRoleName As String
        Private _Description As String
```

```
Private _KeyWords As String
Private _BackgroundFile As String
Private _SiteLogHistory As Integer
Private _AdminTabId As Integer
Private _SuperTabId As Integer
Private _SplashTabId As Integer
Private _HomeTabId As Integer
Private _LoginTabId As Integer
Private _UserTabId As Integer
Private _DefaultLanguage As String
Private _TimeZoneOffset As Integer
Private _Version As String
Private _DesktopTabs As ArrayList
Private _ActiveTab As TabInfo
Private _PortalAlias As PortalAliasInfo
```

The Portal class itself is simple. It is filled by using the only instance method of the
class, the GetPortalSettings method. The method is passed a tabID and a
PortalAliasInfo object. You already know that the tabID represents the ID of the page
being requested, but the PortalAliasInfo is something new. This class can be found in
the same folder as the PortalSettings class and contains the following information:

- PortalID: This is the ID the portal is assigned in the database.

- PortalAliasID: Since each portal can have more that one alias, this ID
  references the specific alias used for the portal.

- HTTPAlias: This is the actual alias used to access the portal
  (www.MyPortal.com, localhost/dotnetnuke, etc.).

From this object, we can retrieve all the information associated with the portal. If you
look past the initial declarations, you can see that the portal settings are saved in cache
for the time that is specified in on the Host Settings page.

```
Public Sub GetPortalSettings(ByVal TabId As Integer, _
                    ByVal objPortalAliasInfo As PortalAliasInfo)
        Dim objPortals As New PortalController
        Dim objPortal As PortalInfo
        Dim objTabs As New TabController
        Dim arrTabs As ArrayList
        Dim objTab As TabInfo
        Dim objModules As New ModuleController
        Dim arrModules As ArrayList
        Dim objModule As ModuleInfo
        Dim objSkins As New UI.Skins.SkinController
        Dim objSkin As UI.Skins.SkinInfo

' data caching settings
    Dim intCacheTimeout As Integer
' calculate the cache settings based on the performance setting
    intCacheTimeout = 20 * _
    Convert.ToInt32(Common.Globals.PerformanceSetting)
```

A drop-down box on the Host Settings page (admin\host\hostsettings.ascx) is used to set the cache.

- No Caching: 0
- Light Caching: 1
- Moderate Caching: 3
- Heavy Caching: 6

The value in this dropdown ranges from 0 to 6; the code above takes the value set in the dropdown and multiplies it by 20 to determine the cache duration. Once the cache time is set, the method checks if the portal settings object already resides there. Retrieving these settings from the database for every request would cause your site to run slow, so placing them in a cache for the duration you select helps increase the speed of your site.

```
PortalId = objPortalAliasInfo.PortalID
' get portal settings
objPortal = CType(DataCache.GetCache("GetPortalSettings" & _
            PortalId.ToString), PortalInfo)
```

If the object is not already cached, it will use the PortalId passed to the GetPortal method to retrieve the portal settings from the database. This method is located in the PortalController class (components\Portal\PortalController.vb) and is responsible for retrieving the portal information from the database.

```
If objPortal Is Nothing Then
        ' get portal settings
        objPortal = objPortals.GetPortal(PortalId)
```

This will fill a PortalInfo object (components\Portal\PortalInfo.vb), which, as the name suggests, holds the portal information. This object in turn is used to create the PortalSettings object. Once this is complete, the PortalSettings object is added to the HTTPContext to make it available to the rest of the core code.

```
' Add the PortalAlias to Context, as this is needed before
' PortalSettings have been set

If Not (HttpContext.Current Is Nothing) Then
    HttpContext.Current.Items.Add _
    ("UrlRewrite:PortalAlias", Me.PortalAlias)
End If
```

After the portal settings are saved, the tabs are retrieved. Like the portal settings themselves, the tabs are saved in cache to save resources. In the get portal tabs section, the code will loop through all of the non-host tabs on the site. Although I don't suggest changing the core code very much (because of upgrading problems you may face in the future), you can capture the admin tabs here and decide whether you want to show them.

```
' get portal tabs
    arrTabs = CType(DataCache.GetCache("GetTabs" & _
                    Me.PortalId.ToString), ArrayList)
        If arrTabs Is Nothing Then
            arrTabs = objTabs.GetTabs(Me.PortalId)
            If Not arrTabs Is Nothing Then
```

After all the portal tabs are iterated through and added to an ArrayList, the host tabs are collected. Again, you can change the default behavior of the host tabs in this section.

```
' host tab
    objTab = objTabs.GetTab(Me.SuperTabId)
        If Not objTab Is Nothing Then
            ' set custom properties
            objTab.StartDate = Date.MinValue
            objTab.EndDate = Date.MaxValue
            objTab.Url = NavigateURL(objTab.TabID, Null.NullString, _
                            "portalid=" & objTab.PortalID.ToString)
        arrTabs.Add(objTab)
        End If

' host child tabs
    Dim arrHostTabs As ArrayList = _
                objTabs.GetTabsByParentId(Me.SuperTabId)

    If Not arrHostTabs Is Nothing Then
            For Each objTab In arrHostTabs
            ' set custom properties
            objTab.StartDate = Date.MinValue
            objTab.EndDate = Date.MaxValue
            objTab.Url = NavigateURL _
                (objTab.TabID, Null.NullString, "portalid=" & _
                    objTab.PortalID.ToString)
                        arrTabs.Add(objTab)
        Next
    End If
```

The method ends by taking the lists of tabs that were just created and uses them to call the GetSkin and GetPortalTabModules, which will apply both the skins and modules that are associated with each tab. You will see the PortalSettings class referenced many times as we work through the rest of the code, so gaining a good understanding of how this class works will help you as you move along.

Working with the Configuration Files

Next, we will continue our exploration of the DotNetNuke architecture by looking at a couple of files in the main DotNetNuke folder. The DotNetNuke download is broken up into many different solutions. This has been done so that you can open up only the files that you are concerned with. In this section, we will work with the core DotNetNuke project along with the Providers used by the core. To get started, we will want to open up the solution file located at C:\DotNetNuke\Solutions\DotNetNuke.Providers\ DotNetNuke.Providers.sln.

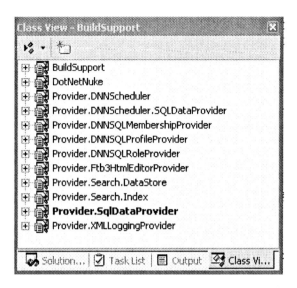

We want to start by looking at the DotNetNuke project. Expand the DotNetNuke project to expose two very important files, the web.config file, and the Global.aspx file.

The web.config File

The web.config file is an XML-based file that contains configuration information specific to your web application. At run time, ASP.Net stores this configuration information in cache so that it can be easily retrieved by your application. If changes are made to this file, ASP.NET will detect the changes and automatically apply the new configuration. The web.config file is very extensible: it allows you to define new configurations and write handlers to process them. DotNetNuke takes full advantage of this ability, as we will discover as we move through this file.

We will only touch on the areas of the web.config file that are specifically used in DotNetNuke. In the DotNetNuke project, open up the web.config file. The first section in the file is the local configuration settings. Here we find the settings for our provider models. For our providers to work, we need a configuration section and configuration section handler.

Configuring the Providers Used in DotNetNuke

<configSections> is broken into two separate groups. The first group, <dotnetnuke>, describes the providers that are available to the application.

```
<sectionGroup name="dotnetnuke">
    <section name="data" type="DotNetNuke.Framework.
        Providers.ProviderConfigurationHandler, DotNetNuke" />
    <section name="logging" type="DotNetNuke.Framework.
        Providers.ProviderConfigurationHandler, DotNetNuke" />
```

```
        <section name="scheduling" type="DotNetNuke.Framework.
            Providers.ProviderConfigurationHandler, DotNetNuke" />
        <section name="htmlEditor" type="DotNetNuke.Framework.
            Providers.ProviderConfigurationHandler, DotNetNuke" />
        <section name="searchIndex" type="DotNetNuke.Framework.
            Providers.ProviderConfigurationHandler, DotNetNuke" />
        <section name="searchDataStore" type="DotNetNuke.Framework.
            Providers.ProviderConfigurationHandler, DotNetNuke" />
        <section name="friendlyUrl" type="DotNetNuke.Framework.
            Providers.ProviderConfigurationHandler, DotNetNuke" />
    </sectionGroup>
```

This custom configuration section handles the different providers integrated into the framework. Providers give the developer the ability to have a pluggable architecture. The data provider, for example, lets us decide which data store to use (Access or SQL Server), while the logging provider allows us to decide what logger we would like to use for our web application. The framework separates the act of logging from the type of logger being used. To change the logging, or any of the other providers, you would need to write your own provider to handle the functions as you see fit.

> For more information on the Provider model and creating custom providers, refer to Chapter 12 on implementing the Provider model.

The first declaration states the name that you will use when you refer to this section in your configuration file. In other words, this is the tag you need to look for in your web.config file in order to see the providers that will handle this functionality:

```
name="data"
```

It also includes the type, which is the configuration section handler. This should include the Global Assembly Cache location information for the class.

```
type="DotNetNuke.Framework.Providers.ProviderConfigurationHandler,
DotNetNuke"
```

The type declaration follows the following configuration.

```
type="configuration section handler class, assembly"
```

The providers serve the following functions:

- The data Provider: Gives the ability to decide which datastore type you would like to use. The DotNetNuke framework is prepackaged with SQL Server and Access (default), but there are others, such as MySQL and Oracle, which are in development by third-party providers.

- The logging Provider: Used for all logging associated with the core framework. This handles, among other things, exception handling.

- The scheduling Provider: One of the newer features, along with the logging, this provider helps to facilitate reoccurring functionality.

- The `htmlEditor` Provider: The default HTML WYSIWYG editor is the FreeTextBox. This configuration setting allows you to substitute other rich textbox components for the FreeTextBox.

- The `searchIndex` Provider: The default provides, if implemented, the ability to search the content of the modules located on your portal.

- The `searchDataStore` Provider: The default provides the ability to search for information inside the datastore you have selected as your data provider.

- The `friendlyUrl` Provider: The default provides the ability to rewrite the URL in a manner that is friendly to search engines.

There is a second group in the configuration section that can be found in the `<system.web>` section group. Again, the group's name signifies where the configuration for the providers will be handled. If you look closely, you will notice a few differences in this section. First, you will notice that the `type` holds a fully qualified name that includes the `Version`, `Culture`, and `PublicKeyToken` associated with the assembly:

```
type="Microsoft.ScalableHosting.Configuration.MembershipConfigHandler
, MemberRole, Version=1.0.0.0, Culture=neutral,
PublicKeyToken=b7c773fb104e7562"
```

The second thing you will notice is that the namespace for these assemblies starts with `Microsoft` instead of `DotNetNuke`. That is because DotNetNuke version 3.0 uses a "backported" version of the `Membership` Provider, which will become available in the next version of ASP.NET (version 2.0, code-named Whidbey). As opposed to the DataProvider model, which is also based on the Whidbey provider model, the `Membership` Provider does not use a custom version of the model. DotNetNuke uses the provider as designed by Microsoft.

> There's more information on the Membership provider in the `Membership.doc` under the `C:\DotNetNuke\Documentation\Public` folder.

The providers in this section cover:

- `Membership`: This is used to address the linking of users to specific portals.

- `rolesManager`: This is used to determine that authorizations each user has once signed on to the portal.

- `profiles`: This is used to address the personal information associated with each user.

- `anonymousIdentification`: This allows the portal to support anonymous users. As we saw in our discussion of roles, anonymous user is a default role given to all users before they are authenticated.

Handling the Providers

The configuration section only tells the application where each provider will be handled. The configuration section has a companion section in the web.config file. This defines the configuration section handlers. You will find two handler sections in the web.config file, one for each group we described above. The first handler section we will look at is the <dotnetnuke> section. This corresponds to the sectionGroup name in the configuration section.

The <dotnetnuke> Group

Within the <dotnetnuke> section, we see the handlers for our individual providers, beginning with the HTML provider. The first node in this section defines the default provider. The defaultProvider attribute is advised, but is optional. If it's left out, the first provider in the list will serve as the default. The default as well as the *only* provider for the htmlEditor is the Ftb3HtmlEditorProvider.

> For a complete description of how to create an additional htmlEditor provider, please see Chapter 12 on implementing the provider model.

The next node starts the provider section; it is followed by a <clear/> node. This node is used to clear out the providers from the configuration settings that may have been added in the machine.config file. The final node is the <add/> node. This node is used to add our provider to the list of available providers. This list is used by the DotNetNuke core to tell it what is handling each section that uses a provider. Inside this node, we need to define a few attributes:

- name: This is the friendly name of our provider. This will be the name of the class you create to handle this functionality.
- Type: This again follows the [namespace.class],[assembly name] format.
- providerPath: This attribute points to where the provider class can be found within the application structure.

After the end of the <add/> node, the structure is completed with the closing tags for add, providers, and htmlEditor.

```
<dotnetnuke>
  <htmlEditor defaultProvider="FtbHtmlEditorProvider" >
    <providers>
      <clear/>
      <add name = "FtbHtmlEditorProvider"
          type = "DotNetNuke.HtmlEditor.FtbHtmlEditorProvider
                ,DotNetNuke.FtbHtmlEditorProvider"
          providerPath = "~\Providers\HtmlEditorProviders\
                FtbHtmlEditorProvider\"/>
    </providers>
  </htmlEditor>
```

The next two configuration handlers are for the search facility built into the DotNetNuke framework. The searchIndex and searchDataStore follow the same configuration as the htmlEditor. We will look further into these providers when we create a custom module in Chapter 7.

This is followed by the data provider. In previous versions, there were two providers supplied by default with DotNetNuke: the AccessDataProvider (the default) and SqlDataProvider. In version 3.0, you will find only the SqlDataProvider is available. The task of creating an Access provider has been given to a third party (BlackJacket Software, http://www.blackjacketsoftware.com/).

```
<data defaultProvider="SqlDataProvider">
  <providers>
    <clear />
    <add name="SqlDataProvider" _
         type="DotNetNuke.Data.SqlDataProvider, _
                    DotNetNuke.SqlDataProvider"
         connectionStringName="SiteSqlServer"
         upgradeConnectionString=""
         providerPath="~\Providers\DataProviders\SqlDataProvider\"
         objectQualifier=""
         databaseOwner="dbo"/>
  </providers>
</data>
```

The data provider has some additional attributes we did not see in the HTML provider.

- connectionStringName: This provides the name of the connection string you will use for your portal. This string can be found in the <appSettings> section of the web.config file.

- upgradeConnectionString: This connection string is used for installation and updates. It is only used to run the upgrade scripts. This can be used to run the updates using a database user with more privileges.

- objectQualifier: The objectQualifier is used to allow multiple installations to run inside the same database. If for example you added CC1 in the object qualifier before you installed DotNetNuke, all the tables and stored procedures would be prefixed with CC1. This would allow you to run another DotNetNuke implementation inside the same database by setting the object qualifier in the second one to CC2. Inside the database, you would have two of every stored procedure and table. Each pair would be named according to the pattern CC1_users, CC2_users, which would keep them separate.

- databaseOwner: The databaseOwner is set to dbo. This is the default database owner in SQL Server. Some hosting companies will require you to change this to reflect your user.

The next configuration handler is for the logging provider. The logging provider handles all logging, including errors, associated with the portal.

```
<logging defaultProvider="XMLLoggingProvider" >
  <providers>
    <clear/>
    <add name = "XMLLoggingProvider"
       type = "DotNetNuke.Logging.XMLLoggingProvider,
                 DotNetNuke.XMLLoggingProvider"
       configfilename="LogConfig.xml.resources"
       providerPath =
          "~\Providers\LoggingProviders\XMLLoggingProvider\" />
  </providers>
</logging>
```

This is followed by the handler for the DNNScheduler:

```
<scheduling defaultProvider="DNNScheduler" >
  <providers>
    <clear/>
    <add name = "DNNScheduler"
       type = "DotNetNuke.Scheduling.DNNScheduler,
                 DotNetNuke.DNNScheduler"
       providerPath = "~\Providers\SchedulingProviders\
                         DNNScheduler\"
       debug="false"
       maxThreads="-1"
       enabled="true"/>
  </providers>
</scheduling>
</dotnetnuke>
```

The scheduler has a few additional attributes we have not seen so far.

- debug: When this is set to true, it will add additional log entries to aid in debugging scheduler problems.

- maxThreads: This sets the maximum number of thread-pool threads to be used by the scheduler (1-10). Setting it to -1 tells the scheduler to determine this on its own.

- enabled: Setting this to false will turn off the scheduler entirely. It can be used to aid the debugging process to alleviate having to debug in a multi-threaded environment.

The final handler for this section is for handling friendly URLs. We will be looking further into this functionality when we discover the HTTP Modules that DotNetNuke employs later in this chapter.

```
<friendlyUrl defaultProvider="DNNFriendlyUrl">
  <providers>
    <clear />
    <add name="DNNFriendlyUrl"
         type= _
         "DotNetNuke.Services.Url.FriendlyUrl.DNNFriendlyUrlProvider,
          DotNetNuke.HttpModules.UrlRewrite" />
  </providers>
</friendlyUrl>
```

The <system.web> Group

The <system.web> section of the web.config file is where most of the configuration of your ASP.NET web application is placed. We will be discussing most of the information contained in this section (including the HTTP Modules) but for now, we'll concentrate on the providers that are defined in this section. As we saw in the <dotnetnuke> section earlier, here we see the information needed to handle our provider. The first provider we find in the <system.web> section is the membership provider. The setup is similar to those we have already seen with the exception of the additional attributes.

```
<membership userIsOnlineTimeWindow="15">
    <providers>
        <add name="DNNSQLMembershipProvider"
type="DotNetNuke.Security.Membership.DNNSQLMembershipProvider, _
DNNSQLMembershipProvider"
                connectionStringName="SiteSqlServer"
                enablePasswordRetrieval="true"
                enablePasswordReset="true"
                requiresQuestionAndAnswer="false"
                requiresUniqueEmail="false"
                passwordFormat="Encrypted"
                applicationName="/"
                description="Stores and retrieves membership data _
                from the local Microsoft SQL Server database" />
    </providers>
</membership>
```

One thing that might catch your eye here is the type. In the config section associated with these providers, the type was Microsoft.ScalableHosting.Security. SqlMembershipProvider, and here you can see that it is DotNetNuke.Security. Membership.DNNSQLMembershipProvider. This might throw you off until you look at the provider class. You can find it in the Provider.DNNSQLMembershipProvider project. If you have the DotNetNuke.Providers solution open, you will find this in the Solution Explorer.

```
Public Class DNNSQLMembershipProvider
    Inherits Microsoft.ScalableHosting.Security.SqlMembershipProvider

        Public Overrides Property ApplicationName() As String
            Get
                If Convert.ToString( _
                HttpContext.Current.Items _
                ("ApplicationName")) = "" Then
                    Return "/"
                Else
                    Return Convert.ToString _
                    (HttpContext.Current.Items("ApplicationName"))
                End If
            End Get
            Set(ByVal Value As String)
                HttpContext.Current.Items("ApplicationName") = Value
            End Set
        End Property
    End Class
```

As you can see, this class inherits from Microsoft's `SqlMembershipProvider` and overrides the `ApplicationName` property. In the original version of the `Membership` provider, the `ApplicationName` was declared in the `web.config` file and only allowed *one* datastore per IIS account. This would of course cause problems with running multiple portals within DotNetNuke. As a result, Microsoft will be modifying this property to allow dynamic specification and has already added this feature to the backported version in use with DotNetNuke. As far as DotNetNuke is concerned, `ApplicaitonName` can be thought of as the same thing as `Portal`. We will explore this further when we look at the `Global` class later in this chapter.

You will also find the `roleManager`, `profile`, and `anonymousIdentification` providers in the `<system.web>` section of the `web.config`. With the exception of the `anonymousId entification` provider, they all follow the same pattern as the `Membership` provider, inheriting the `Microsoft` provider and overriding the `ApplicationName` property.

> More information on the attributes associated with each provider can be found as comments directly above each provider in the `web.config` file.

HTTP Modules

Located at the beginning of the `<system.web>` section is the `HTTPModule` section. HTTP Modules allow you to intercept a request for a page and modify it. To explore this code, you will need to open up a second solution. The solution that holds the HTTP Modules is at `C:\DotNetNuke\Solutions\DotNetNuke.HTTPModules\DotNetNuke.HTTPModules.sln`.

HTTP Modules give you the ability to intercept the request for a page and modify the request in some way. In DotNetNuke, they have been added to abstract some of the code that used to reside inside the Global.asax.vb file. This gives a greater degree of modularity and allows developers to change behavior without affecting the core architecture. An HTTP Module is a class that implements the IHTTPModule interface. This interface has two methods you need to implement.

- Init: This method allows an HTTP Module to register its event handlers to the events in the HttpApplication object.

- Dispose: This method gives the HTTP Module an opportunity to perform any clean up before the object gets garbage-collected.

These methods are called when they are hooked into the **HTTP Pipeline**. The HTTP Pipeline refers to the path followed by each request made to your application. The following diagram shows the path a typical request takes through the pipeline.

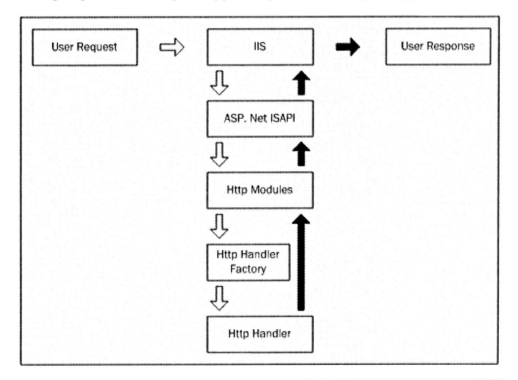

For more information on how HTTPModules work within the HTTP Pipeline, check out this great MSDN article by George Sheperd at http://msdn.microsoft.com/msdnmag/issues/02/05/asp/.

HTTP Modules plug themselves into the ASP.NET request process by adding entries into the web.config file. This allows them to intercept the request before it is returned in order to modify the request to perform certain actions. DotNetNuke uses this process for a number of things.

To see an example of this we will look at the Exception module. It is first declared in the web.config file.

```
<add name="Exception" type="DotNetNuke.HttpModules.ExceptionModule, _
                DotNetN XE "HTTPModules, system.web section
group:Exception module"uke.HttpModules.Exception" />
```

This will place the ExceptionModule in the HTTP Pipeline, allowing it to intercept each request. Let's take a look at the ExeptionModule class found in the HttpModule.Exception project. As we learned earlier, the Init method is called when the module is hooked into the pipeline with a declaration in the web.config file. In this method, we add an event handler to the application.Error event that is thrown whenever an error happens in your application:

```
Public Class ExceptionModule

    Implements IHttpModule
    Public ReadOnly Property ModuleName() As String
        Get
            Return "ExceptionModule"
        End Get
    End Property

    Public Sub Init(ByVal application As HttpApplication) _
                        Implements IHttpModule.Init
        AddHandler application.Error, AddressOf Me.OnErrorRequest
    End Sub
```

The OnErrorRequest method is then called and the error is passed to the Error provider designated in the web.config file. The actual logging of the error is done by the logging provider. The default implementation of DotNetNuke comes with a single logging provider, XMLLoggingProvider, but you may write your own provider to fit your needs.

```
    Public Sub OnErrorRequest(ByVal s As Object, ByVal e As EventArgs)

        Dim Context As HttpContext = _
            CType(s, HttpApplication).Context.Current
        Dim Server As HttpServerUtility = Context.Server
        Dim lex As New Exception("Unhandled Error: ", _
            Server.GetLastError)
        Dim objExceptionLog As New _
                Services.Log.EventLog.ExceptionLogController
        objExceptionLog.AddLog(lex)
    End Sub

    Public Sub Dispose() Implements IHttpModule.Dispose
    End Sub

End Class
```

As opposed to the first two HTTP Modules you have seen, the UrlRewrite module is quite extensive. Just like the others, the first thing that is needed is a designation in the HTTPModules section of the web.config file.

```
<add name="UrlRewrite" _
     type="DotNetNuke.HttpModules.UrlRewriteModule, _
     DotNetNuke.HttpModules.UrlRewrite" />
```

You can view the UrlRewrite HTTPModule by looking in the HTTPModule.UrlRewrite project. This class is responsible for taking a querystring that looks like this:

```
http://www.dotnetnuke.com/Default.aspx?tabid=476
```

and converting it to look like this:

```
http://localhost/DotNetNuke/tabid/476/Default.aspx
```

There are a few reasons why you would want to rewrite your URLs; among them are a cleaner appearance or hiding the physical page names, but probably the most important reason for DotNetNuke is to increase traffic to your site. Search engines crawl your site with bots that look to catalog your pages. Search bots prefer non-dynamic web pages. By using URL rewriting, you can increase the popularity of your links on the major search engines.

As you look at this module, you can see that although the code that does the URL rewriting is extensive, it is hooked into the pipeline in the same fashion as the other modules. The Init method is used to add an event handler to Application .BeginRequest, which fires every time a user requests a page on your site, so that on every request to your site the OnBeginRequest method is called and the URL is rewritten before it is sent on its way.

```
Public Sub Init(ByVal application As HttpApplication) _
               Implements IHttpModule.Init

        AddHandler application.BeginRequest, _
        AddressOf Me.OnBeginRequest

End Sub
```

The rest of the HTTP Modules follow this same pattern, and although they differ in complexity, they all accomplish their task by intercepting the request. We will visit a few of these again when we develop a custom module in the next chapter.

Application Settings

Let's look at one of the remaining sections of web.config. Below <configSettings> you will find a section called <appSettings>. This section holds three items that are of interest to us: SiteSqlServer, InstallProcedure, and InstallTemplate:

```
<appSettings>
    <add key="SiteSqlServer"
         value="Server=(local);Database=DotNetNuke;uid=;pwd=;" />
```

```
<add key="InstallProcedure" value="3.0" />
<add key="InstallTemplate" value="DotNetNuke.install" />

</appSettings>
```

The SiteSqlServer is used to hold the connection string for your datastore. As we saw earlier, this is referenced in the data provider. The next two keys deal with how DotNetNuke will be installed. Previous versions of DotNetNuke used install scripts to set up your portal. Version 3.0 introduced templates, which allows you to create a template that will set up your portal the way you like it. The template install is the default (value="3.0") with a companion key used to tell the framework which template to use.

The Global Files

The Global.aspx.vb and Globals.vb files share similar names but the parts they play in DotNetNuke are vastly different. The Global.aspx.vb is used by DotNetNuke to handle application-level events raised by the ASP.NET runtime. The Globals.vb file, on the other hand, is a public module that contains global utility functions. Before we take a look at these files, we first want to look at what object is being passed around in these transactions.

Global.aspx.vb

Much of the logic that used to reside in the Global.aspx.vb file has now been abstracted to the HTTP Modules. We will look into the code that remains.

Application Start

When the first request is made to your application (when the first user accesses the portal), a pool of HttpApplication instances are created and the Application_Start event is fired. If you have a very busy site, this will (theoretically) fire just once and on the first HttpApplication object in the pool. When there is inactivity on your portal for a certain amount of time the application (or worker process aspnet_wp.exe) will be recycled. When this happens, your application will restart (and this event will fire again) when the next request is made for your application.

In the Application_Start, we are using the Context object and the System .Reflection namespace to initialize some global variables. As we will see shortly, the global variables reside in the Globals.vb file. In addition to this, we use the AutoUpgrade method to determine if an upgrade is needed for the site as well as to start the scheduler. These are performed in the Application_Start because we want them to only be called once.

```
Sub Application_Start(ByVal Sender As Object, _
        ByVal E As EventArgs)
        ' global variable initialization
        ServerName = Server.MachineName
```

```
        If HttpContext.Current.Request.ApplicationPath = "/" Then
            ApplicationPath = ""
        Else
            ApplicationPath = _
            HttpContext.Current.Request.ApplicationPath
        End If
        ApplicationMapPath = _
        HttpContext.Current.Server.MapPath(ApplicationPath)

        HostPath = ApplicationPath & "/Portals/_default/"
        HostMapPath = HttpContext.Current.Server.MapPath(HostPath)

        AssemblyPath = _
        System.Reflection.Assembly.GetExecutingAssembly.Location

        'Perform automatic upgrade
        Services.Upgrade.Upgrade.AutoUpgrade(HttpContext.Current)

         'Cache Mapped Directory(s)
        CacheMappedDirectory()

        ' log APPLICATION_START event
        LogStart()

        'Start Scheduler
        StartScheduler()
    End Sub
```

Examining Application_BeginRequest

The Application_BeginRequest is called for each request made to your application. In other words, this will fire every time a page (tab) is accessed in your portal. This section is used to implement the scheduler built into DotNetNuke. Starting in version 2.0, two items, "users online" and "site log", required recurring operations. You can find out more about the scheduler by looking at the DotNetNuke Scheduler.doc document found in the C:\DotNetNuke\Documentation\Public folder.

```
Sub Application_BeginRequest(ByVal sender As Object, _
                             ByVal e As EventArgs)
    Try
        If Services.Scheduling. _
        SchedulingProvider.SchedulerMode = _
        Scheduling.SchedulerMode.REQUEST_METHOD _
        AndAlso _
        Services.Scheduling. _
        SchedulingProvider.ReadyForPoll Then
            Dim RequestScheduleThread As Threading.Thread
            RequestScheduleThread = _
            New Threading.Thread _
            (AddressOf          Scheduling. _
            SchedulingProvider. _
            Instance.ExecuteTasks)
            RequestScheduleThread.IsBackground = True
            RequestScheduleThread.Start()
            Services.Scheduling. _
            SchedulingProvider.ScheduleLastPolled = Now
        End If
```

```
        Catch exc As Exception
            LogException(exc)
        End Try
    End Sub
```

Application Authenticate Request

Previous versions of DotNetNuke did the authentication for each request in the `Application_AuthenticateRequest` section of the `global.asax` file. In version 3.0, this has been moved to the `HttpModule.DNNMembership` module. This can be found in the `DNNMembershipModule.vb` file in the `HTTPModule.DNNMembership` project.

Forms authentication is the default authentication model currently used in DotNetNuke, so we will keep our discussion centered on this authentication type. Forms authentication works by determining the identity of the user by using a login page. If users try to access an area of your application that they are not authorized to view, they are directed to a login page. DotNetNuke uses forms authentication in a different manner. If you look back at the `web.config` file where we configured the authentication type, you will notice that we do not have a login redirection path.

```
<!-- Forms or Windows authentication -->
    <authentication mode="Forms">
    <forms name=".DOTNETNUKE" protection="All" timeout="60" />
    </authentication>
```

In DotNetNuke, all users are allowed to access the `Default.aspx` page, but within the page we check to see what they are authorized to see.

In the `OnAuthenticateRequest` method, which is sinked in the `Init` method to the `Application.AuthenticateRequest` event, we first declare a few variables we will need for authentication.

```
Dim Context As HttpContext = CType(s,
HttpApplication).Context.Current
Dim Request As HttpRequest = Context.Request
Dim Response As HttpResponse = Context.Response
```

Before we proceed, we check to see if we are upgrading, and if so, we skip authentication all together.

```
'First check if we are upgrading
If Request.RawUrl.EndsWith("Upgrade.aspx") Then
    Exit Sub
End If
```

Next, we set the `OriginalApplicationName` and get an instance of the `PortalSettings` class by calling the `PortalControler.GetCurrentPortalSettings` method. This simple method returns the `PortalSettings` that are being held in the context object.

```
' Obtain PortalSettings from Current Context
Dim _portalSettings As PortalSettings = _
CType(HttpContext.Current.Items("PortalSettings"), _
```

138

```
                     PortalSettings)
                     Dim OriginalApplicationName As String = _
                     Globals.GetApplicationName
```

After we determine that the user is authenticated and that we have a PortalSettings object, we use the GetUser method of the Membership object to retrieve the user.

```
If Request.IsAuthenticated = True And _
                    Not _portalSettings Is Nothing Then
    Dim objMembershipUser As MembershipUser = _
                    Membership.GetUser(True)
```

If this request turns up nothing, we check if the user is signed on as a SuperUser:

```
    If objMembershipUser Is Nothing Then

        'could be a SuperUser, try super user application name

        Globals.SetApplicationName(Common.Globals.glbSuperUserAppName)
            objMembershipUser = Membership.GetUser
        Globals.SetApplicationName(OriginalApplicationName)

    End If
```

We then go on to set cookies for the current user.

```
If Not Request.Cookies("portalaliasid") Is Nothing Then
    Dim PortalCookie As FormsAuthenticationTicket = _
    FormsAuthentication.Decrypt _
    (Context.Request.Cookies("portalaliasid").Value)
```

The user base for DotNetNuke is on a per-portal basis; if they switch portals, their cookies should expire. This will force them to sign in to authenticate to the new portal.

```
        ' check If user has switched portals
        If _portalSettings.PortalId <> _
            Int32.Parse(PortalCookie.UserData) Then

            ' expire cookies if portal has changed
            Response.Cookies("portalid").Value = Nothing
            Response.Cookies("portalid").Path = "/"
            Response.Cookies("portalid").Expires = _
            DateTime.Now.AddYears(-30)

            Response.Cookies("portalroles").Value = _
            Nothing
            Response.Cookies("portalroles").Path = "/"
            Response.Cookies("portalroles").Expires = _
            DateTime.Now.AddYears(-30)

            ' check if user is valid for new portal
            Dim objUsers As New UserController
            Dim objUser As UserInfo = _
            objUsers.GetUserByUserName _
            (_portalSettings.PortalId, _
            Int32.Parse(Context.User.Identity.Name))
            If objUser Is Nothing Then
                ' log user out
                Dim objPortalSecurity _
                As New PortalSecurity
```

```
                                objPortalSecurity.Signout()
                                ' Redirect browser back to home page
                                Response.Redirect(Request.RawUrl, True)
                                Exit Sub
                        End If
                End If
        End If
End If
```

If the user is authenticated, a variable called `objRoleController` is instantiated to hold the roles that the user belongs to and an `objUserController` object is instantiated so that the `GetUsersByUserName` function can be called. This function will return to us all the relevant information for this user. The `arrPortalRoles` variable, as the name suggests, will be an array used to hold the portal roles for this user.

```
Dim arrPortalRoles() As String
Dim objRoleController As New RoleController
Dim objUserController As New UserController
```

The current-user information is retrieved from cache or is hydrated from the database.

```
Dim Username As String
Dim intUserId As Integer = -1
Dim objUserInfo As UserInfo
Dim UserInfoCacheKey As String = _
        objUserController.GetCacheKey(_portalSettings.PortalId, _
        Context.User.Identity.Name)
If Globals.PerformanceSetting = _
   Globals.PerformanceSettings.HeavyCaching _
   AndAlso Not DataCache.GetCache(UserInfoCacheKey) Is Nothing Then

    objUserInfo = _
      CType(DataCache.GetCache(UserInfoCacheKey), UserInfo)
Else
    objUserInfo = _
      objUserController.GetUserByUsername(_portalSettings.PortalId, _
      Context.User.Identity.Name)

    If Common.Globals.PerformanceSetting = _
      Common.Globals.PerformanceSettings.HeavyCaching Then

        UserInfoCacheKey = _
        objUserController.GetCacheKey(_portalSettings.PortalId, _
        objUserInfo.Username)

        Dim intExpire As Integer = _
        Globals.PerformanceSetting.HeavyCaching
        DataCache.SetCache(UserInfoCacheKey, objUserInfo, _
        TimeSpan.FromMinutes(intExpire))
    End If
End If
```

The `intUserID` and `UserName` variables are set using the `UserInfo` object.

```
If Not objUserInfo Is Nothing Then
                intUserId = objUserInfo.UserID
                Username = objUserInfo.Username
Else
```

```
                    'The user is authenticated because they have
                    'an auth cookie, but it is possible that
                    'their cookie contains the userid instead
                    'of the username.
                    Dim objPortalSecurity As New PortalSecurity
                    objPortalSecurity.SignOut()
                    Exit Sub
          End If
```

Since users are allowed to set permanent cookies by selecting the Remember Login checkbox when signing in, we need to call the UpdateUserLogin function so that the database is updated to show that they have accessed the portal.

```
    ' authenticate user and set last login ( this is
    ' necessary for users who have a permanent Auth cookie set )

  If objMembershipUser Is Nothing Then

        Dim objPortalSecurity As New PortalSecurity
        objPortalSecurity.SignOut()
```

If this is the first request after the user is authenticated, an authentication ticket is created for the user and stored in a cookie.

```
  Else ' valid Auth cookie

  ' create cookies if they do not exist yet for this session.
    If Request.Cookies("portalroles") Is Nothing Then

      ' keep cookies in sync
        Dim CurrentDateTime As Date = DateTime.Now

      ' create a cookie authentication ticket
        Dim PortalTicket As New FormsAuthenticationTicket _
        (1, Username, CurrentDateTime, CurrentDateTime.AddHours(1), _
        False, _portalSettings.PortalAlias.PortalAliasID.ToString)

  ' encrypt the ticket
    Dim strPortalAliasID As String = _
    FormsAuthentication.Encrypt(PortalTicket)

  ' send portal cookie to client
    Response.Cookies("portalaliasid").Value = strPortalAliasID
    Response.Cookies("portalaliasid").Path = "/"
    Response.Cookies("portalaliasid").Expires = _
    CurrentDateTime.AddMinutes(1)
```

The user ID is then passed to the GetRolesByUser procedure and used to fill the arrPortalRoles with the roles the user belongs to. This is then turned into a comma-delimited string to represent this user's roles and is placed in a cookie called portalroles.

```
  ' get roles from UserRoles table
    arrPortalRoles = objRoleController.GetPortalRolesByUser _
        (intUserId, _portalSettings.PortalId)
```

```
' create a string to persist the roles
  Dim strPortalRoles As String = Join(arrPortalRoles, New Char() _
{";"c})

' create a cookie authentication ticket
  Dim RolesTicket As New FormsAuthenticationTicket _
    (1, objUserInfo.Username, CurrentDateTime, _
    CurrentDateTime.AddHours(1), False, strPortalRoles)

' encrypt the ticket
  Dim strRoles As String = FormsAuthentication.Encrypt(RolesTicket)


' send roles cookie to client
  Response.Cookies("portalroles").Value = strRoles
  Response.Cookies("portalroles").Path = "/"
  Response.Cookies("portalroles").Expires =
CurrentDateTime.AddMinutes(1)
```

The portalroles cookie is then read to see what authorizations it possesses.

```
If Not Request.Cookies("portalroles") Is Nothing Then

    ' get roles from roles cookie
    If Request.Cookies("portalroles").Value <> "" Then
        Dim RoleTicket As FormsAuthenticationTicket = _
        FormsAuthentication.Decrypt _
        (Context.Request.Cookies("portalroles").Value)

        ' convert the string representation of the
        ' role data into a string array
    Context.Items.Add("UserRoles", ";" + RoleTicket.UserData + ";")
    Else
        Context.Items.Add("UserRoles", "")
    End If

        Context.Items.Add("UserInfo", objUserInfo)
End If
```

Finally, the UserInfo object is stored in the current context object for later retrieval.

```
If CType(HttpContext.Current.Items("UserInfo"), UserInfo) Is Nothing Then
        Context.Items.Add("UserInfo", New UserInfo)
End If
```

Compared to other versions of DotNetNuke, the Global.aspx.vb file is almost empty. As we just observed, HTTP Modules have taken over most of the duties of this file, and this minimal code is all that is needed.

The Globals.vb File

As part of the namespace-reorganization effort associated with DotNetNuke version 3, general utility functions, constants, and enumerations have all been placed in a public module named Globals. Since items in a .NET module are inherently shared, you do not need to instantiate an object in order to use the functions found here. In this module, you will find not only global constants:

```
Public Const glbAppVersion As String = "03.00.07"
Public Const glbAppTitle As String = "DotNetNuke"

Public Const glbTrademark As String = "DotNetNuke"

Public Const glbRoleAllUsers As String = "-1"
Public Const glbRoleSuperUser As String = "-2"
Public Const glbRoleUnauthUser As String = "-3"
```

and application-wide constants:

```
Private _ApplicationPath As String
Private _ApplicationMapPath As String
Private _AssemblyPath As String
Private _HostMapPath As String
Private _HostPath As String
Private _ServerName As String
Private _HostSettings As Hashtable
Private _PerformanceSetting As PerformanceSettings
```

but also a tremendous number of public functions to help you do everything, from retrieving the domain name:

```
Public Function GetDomainName(ByVal Request As HttpRequest) As String
```

to setting the focus on a page:

```
Public Sub SetFormFocus(ByVal control As Control)
```

This one file contains a wealth of information for the developer. Since there are more than 1600 lines in this file and the methods are fairly straightforward, we will not be stepping through this code.

Putting It All Together

We have spent some time looking at some of the major pieces that make up the core architecture. You might be asking yourself how all this works together. In this section, we will walk you through an overview version of what happens when a user requests a page on your portal.

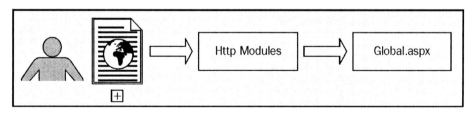

When a user requests any page on your portal, the HTTP Modules that have been declared in the web.config file are hooked into the pipeline. Some of the modules, like the LoggingModule, run their code when the Init method is called. Others such as the UrlRewriteModule use the Init method to attach event handlers to application events.

The request then goes through the Global.aspx page. As just mentioned, some of the events fired here will be intercepted and processed by the HTTP Modules, but the authentication of the user will be done in this file.

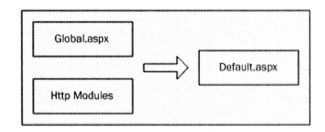

Next, the page that was requested, Default.aspx, will be processed. As we stated at the beginning of this chapter, all requests are sent to the Default.aspx page and all the controls and skins needed for the page are created dynamically by reading the tabID from the querysting. So let's begin by looking at the HTML for this page.

The HTML of the page is pretty simple and straightforward. The attributes at the top of the page tell us that the HTML page inherits from the DotNetNuke.Framework.CDefault class, which is found in the Default.aspx.vb code-behind page. We will be examining this class soon.

```
<%@ Page CodeBehind="Default.aspx.vb" language="vb"
AutoEventWireup="false" Explicit="True"
Inherits="DotNetNuke.Framework.CDefault" %>
<%@ Register TagPrefix="dnn" Namespace="DotNetNuke.Common.Controls"
Assembly="DotNetNuke" %>
<!DOCTYPE HTML PUBLIC "-//W3C//DTD HTML 4.0 Transitional//EN">
```

The title and meta-tags are populated with variables we will find in the code-behind file:

```
<HTML>
    <HEAD id="Head">
        <TITLE>
            <%= Title %>
        </TITLE>
        <%= Comment %>
        <META NAME="DESCRIPTION" CONTENT="<%= Description %>">
        <META NAME="KEYWORDS" CONTENT="<%= Keywords %>">
        <META NAME="COPYRIGHT" CONTENT="<%= Copyright %>">
        <META NAME="GENERATOR" CONTENT="<%= Generator %>">
        <META NAME="AUTHOR" CONTENT="<%= Author %>">
        <META NAME="RESOURCE-TYPE" CONTENT="DOCUMENT">
        <META NAME="DISTRIBUTION" CONTENT="GLOBAL">
        <META NAME="ROBOTS" CONTENT="INDEX, FOLLOW">
        <META NAME="REVISIT-AFTER" CONTENT="1 DAYS">
        <META NAME="RATING" CONTENT="GENERAL">
```

After the meta-tags, placeholders are set to hold CSS and Favicons. These are declared in this manner so that the actual files can be determined by the skin being used on the site.

This is followed by a script declaration for the file; this declaration is responsible for the module drag-and-drop capability of DotNetNuke 3.

```
<style id="StylePlaceholder" runat="server"></style>
<asp:placeholder id="CSS" runat="server"></asp:placeholder>
<asp:placeholder id="FAVICON" runat="server"></asp:placeholder>
<script src="<%= Page.ResolveUrl("js/dnncore.js") %>"></script>
</HEAD>
```

The body of the HTML is relatively bare. The important code in this section is the `SkinPlaceholder`, used to inject the selected skin into the body of the page.

```
<BODY ID="Body" runat="server" ONSCROLL="__dnn_bodyscroll()"
BOTTOMMARGIN="0" LEFTMARGIN="0"
    TOPMARGIN="0" RIGHTMARGIN="0" MARGINWIDTH="0" MARGINHEIGHT="0">
    <noscript></noscript>
    <dnn:Form id="Form" runat="server" ENCTYPE="multipart/form-
data" style="height:100%;>
        <asp:Label ID="SkinError" Runat="server"
CssClass="NormalRed" Visible="False"></asp:Label>
        <asp:placeholder id="SkinPlaceHolder" runat="server" />
        <INPUT ID="ScrollTop" runat="server" NAME="ScrollTop"
TYPE="hidden">
        <INPUT ID="__dnnVariable" runat="server"
NAME="__dnnVariable" TYPE="hidden">
    </dnn:Form>
</BODY>
</HTML>
```

Now we will venture into the code-behind class for this file. If you look past the `Imports` statements, you will see that this class is declared `MustInherit` and itself inherits from the `DotNetNuke.Framework.PageBase` class.

```
Public MustInherit Class CDefault
    Inherits DotNetNuke.Framework.PageBase
```

The class is declared `MustInherit` since we only want this class to be used as a code-behind file. Its base class handles the localization for the page and of course, since this is a web page, inherits from `System.Web.UI.Page`. All we are going to peek at in the file is the `ReadOnly PortalSettings` property.

```
Public ReadOnly Property PortalSettings() As PortalSettings

    Get
        PortalSettings = PortalController.GetCurrentPortalSettings
    End Get

End Property
```

This allows the page to have easy access to the portal settings by calling the `GetCurrentPortalSettings` method. Next, we can see the variable declarations we were introduced to in the HTML file.

```
Public Comment As String = ""
Public Title As String = ""
```

```
Public Description As String = ""
Public Keywords As String = ""
Public Copyright As String = ""
Public Generator As String = ""
Public Author As String = ""

Protected ScrollTop As System.Web.UI.HtmlControls.HtmlInputHidden
Protected SkinError As System.Web.UI.WebControls.Label
Protected SkinPlaceHolder As System.Web.UI.WebControls.PlaceHolder

Protected CSS As System.Web.UI.WebControls.PlaceHolder
Protected FAVICON As System.Web.UI.WebControls.PlaceHolder
```

As we move through this file, you will see how these variables are filled.

The first procedure that is run in the page is the `Page_Init` method. Most of the action required to generate our request resides in this section. The first few lines of the method call the `InitializeComponent` method, which is a default web-form designer procedure, the `InializePage`, which generates the information to fill the meta-tags, and the `ManageRequest`, which collects the affiliate information and updates the site log.

If you look at a couple of pieces of code in, we can see some of the files we looked at earlier in use. In the `InitializePage` method, we make use of both the `PortalSettings` class and the `Current` property of the `HTTPContext` object to retrieve the `TabName`:

```
objTab = objTabs.GetTabByName(Request.QueryString("TabName"),
CType(HttpContext.Current.Items("PortalSettings"),
PortalSettings).PortalId)
```

The `ManageRequest` method on the other hand makes use of the `Globals` class to find the `SiteLogStorate` setting:

```
If Convert.ToString(Common.Globals.HostSettings("SiteLogStorage")) _
    <> "" Then
    strSiteLogStorage = _
    Convert.ToString(Common.Globals.HostSettings("SiteLogStorage"))
End If
```

When these two methods complete, the process of loading the skin begins. The process starts by creating a user control to hold the skin and a `SkinControler` that will do the work of loading the skin.

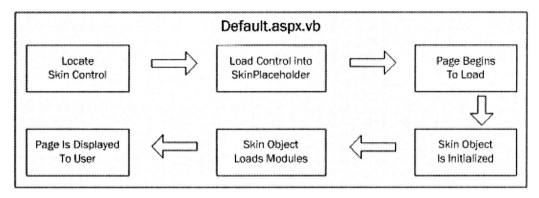

After determining whether the request is a skin preview, the code moves on to load the skin. There are three possible outcomes when loading the skin: it is for an admin page, it is for a regular page, or there was an error and it loads the default skin. Regardless of which section is invoked, the skin is loaded using the LoadSkin method.

```
ctlSkin = LoadSkin(PortalSettings.ActiveTab.SkinSrc)
```

This method reads the physical path of the skin control and loads it into our ctlSkin variable. And finally after calls to ManageStyleSheets and ManageFavicon, the control is added to the page by using the SkinPlaceholder that we looked at earlier in the HTML page:

```
' add skin to page
SkinPlaceHolder.Controls.Add(ctlSkin)
```

At this point, you may be thinking to yourself, "I understand how the skin is dynamically added to the page for a user's request, but how are the modules dynamically added?" Well, to get the answer to that question, we will need to look at the skin control itself. You can find the skin control (skin.vb) in the admin\Skins folder. We will not look at this entire class, but if you look closely at the Page_Init method, which is called when the control is instantiated, you will see how the modules are created. The method first determines the number of panes available on the skin and then dynamically populates the modules assigned to each pane.

```
' dynamically populate the panes with modules
If PortalSettings.ActiveTab.Modules.Count > 0 Then

    ' loop through each entry in the configuration system for this tab
    For Each objModule In PortalSettings.ActiveTab.Modules
```

It will check for the authorization of the user as it goes.

```
' if user is allowed to view module and module is not deleted
If PortalSecurity.IsInRoles(objModule.AuthorizedViewRoles) = True _
    And objModule.IsDeleted = False Then
```

and then finally inject the module into the skin.

```
' inject the module into the skin
InjectModule(parent, objModule, PortalSettings)
```

This procedure will be repeated for all of the modules associated with that page, and the request is finally completed and presented to the user. We did not, of course, cover every piece of code that is called in the process, but hopefully have given you a path to follow to continue researching the core architecture on your own.

Summary

In this chapter we have taken a look at how the core of DotNetNuke works. We looked at a general overview, examined important pieces of the framework, and finally followed a request through its paces. We will be expanding on this knowledge as we venture into the world of custom-module creation in Chapter 7.

7

Creating Custom Modules

In this chapter, we are going to walk you through creating a custom module for the CoffeeConnections portal. A custom module can consist of one or more custom web controls. The areas we will cover are:

- Creating a private assembly project to build and debug your module

- Creating View and Edit controls

- Adding additional options to the module settings page

- Implementing the `IActionable`, `ISearchable`, and `IPortable` interfaces

- Using the Dual List Control

- Creating a SQLDataProvider

- Packaging your module

- Uploading your module

Coffee Shop Listing Module Overview

One of the main attractions for the CoffeeConnections portal is that users will be able to search, by zip code, for coffee shops in their area. After searching, the users will be presented with the shops in their area. To allow the focus of this chapter to be on module development, we will present a simplified version of this control. We will not spend time on the ASP.NET controls used or validation of these controls, instead we will focus only on what is necessary to create your own custom modules.

Setting Up Your Project (Private Assembly)

The design environment we will be using is Visual Studio .NET 2003. The files used in DotNetNuke come pre-packaged as a VS.NET solution and it is the best way to create custom modules for DotNetNuke. Visual Studio will allow us to create **private assemblies (PA)** which will keep our custom module code separate from the DotNetNuke framework code.

A private assembly is an assembly (`.dll` or `.exe`) that will be deployed along with an application to be used in conjunction with that application. In our case, the main application is the DotNetNuke core framework. The private assembly will be a project that is added to the DotNetNuke solution (`.sln`). This will keep our module architecture separate from the DotNetNuke core architecture but will allow us to use Visual Studio to debug the module within the framework. Since building our modules in a PA allows us to have separation from the DotNetNuke core framework, upgrading to newer versions of DotNetNuke is a simple process.

> Even though the DotNetNuke framework is built using VB.NET, you can create your module private assemblies using any .NET language. Since your module logic will be compiled to a `.dll`, you can code in the language you like.

The DotNetNuke project is divided into many different solutions enabling you to work on different parts of the project. We have already seen the HTTP Module solution and the Providers solutions. Since we want to look at the default modules that have been packaged with DotNetNuke we will be using the `DotNetNuke.DesktopModules` solution.

> You can even create a new solution and add the DotNetNuke project to the new solution. You would then need to create a build support project to support your modules. We are using the `DotNetNuke.DesktopModules` solution so that you are able to look at the default modules for help in design process.

To set up your private assembly as part of the `DotNetNuke.DesktopModules` solution, take the following steps:

1. Open up the DotNetNuke Visual Studio.NET solution file (`C:\DotNetNuke\Solutions\DotNetNuke.DesktopModules\DotNetNuke.DesktopModules.sln`).

2. In the Solution Explorer, right-click on the DotNetNuke solution (not the project) and select Add | New Project:

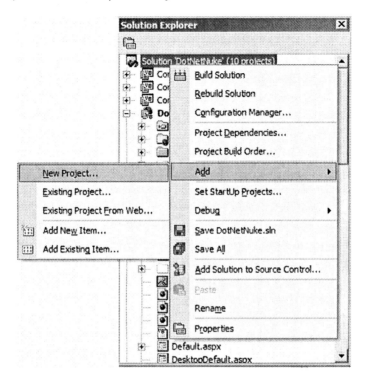

3. In Project Types, make sure that Visual Basic Projects is highlighted and select Class Library as your project type. Our controls are going to run in the DotNetNuke virtual directory, so we do not want to create a web project. This would create an additional virtual directory that we do not need.

4. Your project should reside under the C:\DotNetNuke\DesktopModules folder. Make sure to change the location to this folder.

5. The name of your project should follow the following convention. CompanyName.ModuleName. This will help avoid name conflicts with other module developers. Ours is named EganEnterprises.CoffeeShopListing. You should end up with a new project added to the DotNetNuke solution.

If you have installed URLScan, which is part of Microsoft's IIS Lockdown Tool, you will have problems with folders that contain a period (.). If this is the case, you can create your project using an underscore instead of a period. Refer to http://www.microsoft.com/technet/security/tools/locktool.mspx for more information on the IIS Lockdown Tool.

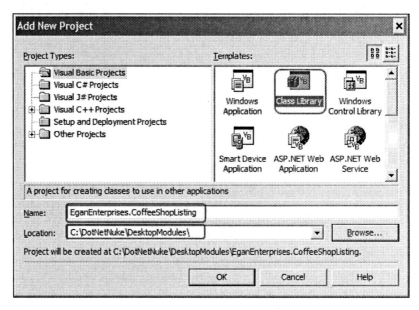

6. You need to modify a few properties to allow you to debug our project within the DotNetNuke solution:

- In the Common Properties folder, under the General section remove the Root namespace. Our module will be running under the DotNetNuke namespace, so we do not want this to default to the name of our assembly.

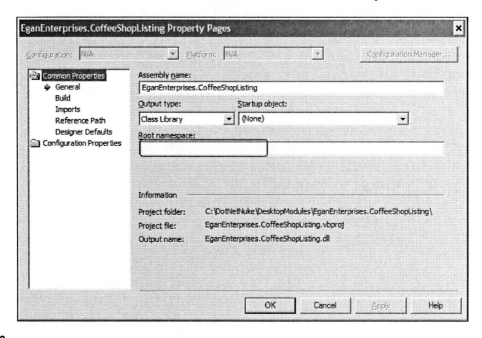

- Delete the `Class1.vb` file that was created with the project.
- Right-click on our private assembly project and select Properties.

7. In the `Common Properties` folder, under the Imports subsection, we want to add imports that will help us as we create our custom module. Enter each of the namespaces below into the namespace box and click on Add Import.

- DotNetNuke
- DotNetNuke.Common
- DotNetNuke.Common.Utilities
- DotNetNuke.Data
- DotNetNuke.Entities.Users
- DotNetNuke.Framework
- DotNetNuke.Services.Exceptions
- DotNetNuke.Services.Localization
- DotNetNuke.UI

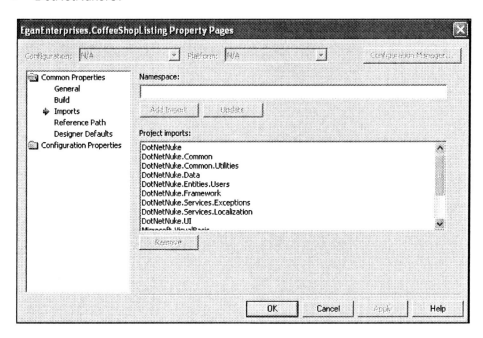

8. Click OK to save your settings

When we run a project as a private assembly in DotNetNuke, the DLL for the module will build into the DotNetNuke `bin` directory. This is where DotNetNuke will look for the assembly when it tries to load your module. To accomplish this, there is a project called BuildSupport inside each of the solutions. The BuildSupport project is responsible for taking the DLL that is created by your project and adding it to the DotNetNuke solution's bin folder.

To allow the BuildSupport project to add our DLL, we need to add a reference to our custom module project.

1. Right-click on the reference folder located below the BuildSupport project and select Add Reference.

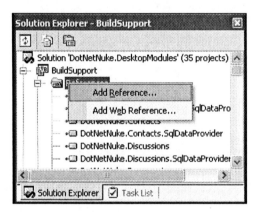

2. Select the Projects tab.
3. Double-click on the EganEnterprises.CoffeeShopListing project to place it in the Selected Components box.
4. Click OK to add the reference.

Finally, we want to be able to use all of the objects available to us in DotNetNuke within our private assembly, so we need to add a reference to DotNetNuke in our project.

1. Right-click on the reference folder located below the EganEnterprises .CoffeeShopListing private assembly project we just created and select Add Reference.
2. Select the Projects tab.
3. Double-click on the DotNetNuke project to place it in the Selected Components box.
4. Click OK to add the reference.

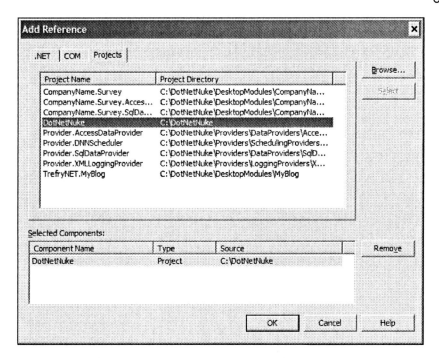

Before moving on, we want to make sure that we can build the solution without any errors. We will be doing this at different stages in development to help us pinpoint any mistakes we make along the way.

After building the solution, you should see something similar to the following in your output window.

```
--------------------- Done ---------------------
     Build: 35 succeeded, 0 failed, 0 skipped
```

The number you have in `succeeded` may be different but make sure that there is a zero in `failed`. If there are any errors fix them before moving on.

Creating Controls Manually in Visual Studio

When using a Class Library project as a starting point for your private assembly, you cannot add a Web User Control to your project by selecting Add | New Item from the project menu. Because of this we will have to add our controls manually.

> An optional way to create the user controls needed is to create a Web User Control inside the DotNetNuke project and then drag the control to your PA project to make modifications.

Creating the View Control

The View control is what a non-administrator sees when you add the module to your portal. In other words, this is the public interface for your module.

Let's walk through the steps needed to create this control.

1. Making sure that your private assembly project is highlighted, select Add New Item from the Project menu.

2. Select Text File from the list of available templates and change the name to `ShopList.ascx`.

3. Click Open to create the file.

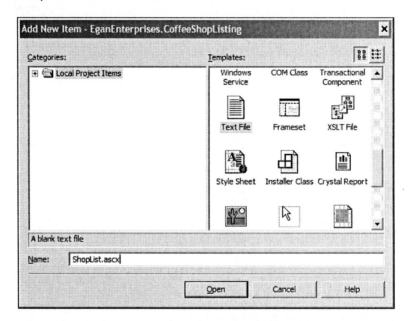

4. Click on the HTML tab and add the following directive to the top of the page:

```
<%@ Control language="vb" AutoEventWireup="false"
        Inherits="EganEnterprises.CoffeeShopListing.ShopList"
        CodeBehind="ShopList.ascx.vb"%>
```

Directives can be located anywhere within the file, but it is standard practice to place them at the beginning of the file. This directive sets the language to VB.NET and specifies the class and code-behind file that we will inherit from.

5. Click the save icon on the toolbar to save the page.

6. In the Solution Explorer right-click on the `ShopList.ascx` file and select View Code.

This will create a code-behind file for the Web User Control that we just created. The code-behind file follows the format of a normal Web User Control that inherits from `System.Web.UserControl`. This control, though based on `web.UserControl`, will instead inherit from a class in DotNetNuke. Change the code-behind file to look like the code that follows. Here is the code-behind page in its entirety minus the Web Form Designer Generated Code:

```
Imports DotNetNuke
Imports DotNetNuke.Security.Roles

Namespace EganEnterprises.CoffeeShopListing

    Public MustInherit Class ShopList
        Inherits Entities.Modules.PortalModuleBase
        Implements Entities.Modules.IActionable
        Implements Entities.Modules.IPortable
        Implements Entities.Modules.ISearchable

        Private Sub Page_Load(ByVal sender As System.Object, _
        ByVal e As System.EventArgs) Handles MyBase.Load
            'Put user code to initialize the page here
        End Sub

Public ReadOnly Property ModuleActions() As _
DotNetNuke.Entities.Modules.Actions.ModuleActionCollection _
Implements DotNetNuke.Entities.Modules.IActionable.ModuleActions

    Get
        Dim Actions As New _
        Entities.Modules.Actions.ModuleActionCollection
        Actions.Add(GetNextActionID, _
        Localization.GetString( _
        Entities.Modules.Actions.ModuleActionType.AddContent, _
        LocalResourceFile), _
        Entities.Modules.Actions.ModuleActionType.AddContent, _
        "", _
        "", _
        EditUrl(), _
        False, _
        Security.SecurityAccessLevel.Edit, _
        True, _
        False)
        Return Actions
    End Get
End Property

Public Function ExportModule(ByVal ModuleID As Integer) _
As String Implements _
DotNetNuke.Entities.Modules.IPortable.ExportModule
    ' included as a stub only so that the core
    'knows this module Implements Entities.Modules.IPortable
End Function

Public Sub ImportModule(ByVal ModuleID As Integer, _
ByVal Content As String, _
```

```
            ByVal Version As String, _
            ByVal UserID As Integer) _
            Implements DotNetNuke.Entities.Modules.IPortable.ImportModule
                ' included as a stub only so that the core
                'knows this module Implements Entities.Modules.IPortable
            End Sub

            Public Function GetSearchItems( _
            ByVal ModInfo As DotNetNuke.Entities.Modules.ModuleInfo) _
            As DotNetNuke.Services.Search.SearchItemInfoCollection _
            Implements DotNetNuke.Entities.Modules.ISearchable.GetSearchItems
                ' included as a stub only so that the core
                'knows this module Implements Entities.Modules.IPortable
            End Function

        End Class
End Namespace
```

Let's break up the code listing above so that we can better understand what is happening in this section. The first thing that we do is add an `Imports` statement for `DotNetNuke` and `DotNetNuke.Security.Roles` so that we may access their methods without using the fully qualified names.

```
Imports DotNetNuke
Imports DotNetNuke.Security.Roles
Namespace EganEnterprises.CoffeeShopListing
```

Next, we add the namespace to the class and set it to inherit from `Entities.Modules` `.PortalModuleBase`. This is the base class for all module controls in DotNetNuke. Using the base class is what gives our controls consistency and implements the basic module behavior like the module menu and header. This class also gives us access to useful items such as User ID, Portal ID, and Module ID among others.

This section then finishes up by implementing three different interfaces. These interfaces allow us to add enhanced functionality to our module. We will only be implementing the `IActionable` interface in this file. The others will only be placed in this file to allow the framework to see, using reflection, whether the module implements the interfaces. The actual implementation for the other interfaces occurs in the controller class that we will create later.

```
        Public MustInherit Class ShopList
            Inherits Entities.Modules.PortalModuleBase
            Implements Entities.Modules.IActionable
            Implements Entities.Modules.IPortable
            Implements Entities.Modules.ISearchable
```

Since we will be implementing the `IActionable` interface in this file, we will now look at the `IActionable ModuleActions` properties that need to be implemented.

The core framework creates certain menu items automatically. These include the movement, module settings, and so on. You can manually add functionality to the menu by implementing this interface.

To add an action menu item to the module actions menu, we need to create an instance of a `ModuleActionCollection`. This is done in the `ModuleActions` property declaration.

```
Public ReadOnly Property ModuleActions() As _
DotNetNuke.Entities.Modules.Actions.ModuleActionCollection _
Implements DotNetNuke.Entities.Modules.IActionable.ModuleActions
    Get
    Dim Actions As New _
    Entities.Modules.Actions.ModuleActionCollection
```

We then use the `Add` method of this object to add and item to the menu.

```
        Actions.Add(GetNextActionID, _
        Localization.GetString( _
        Entities.Modules.Actions.ModuleActionType.AddContent, _
        LocalResourceFile), _
        Entities.Modules.Actions.ModuleActionType.AddContent, _
        "", _
        "", _
        EditUrl(), _
        False, _
        Security.SecurityAccessLevel.Edit, _
        True, _
        False)
        Return Actions
    End Get
End Property
```

The parameters of the `Actions.Add` method are:

Parameter	Type	Description
ID	Integer	The `GetNextActionID` function (found in the `ActionsBase.vb` file) will retrieve the next available ID for your `ModuleActionCollection`. This works like an auto-increment field, adding one to the previous action ID.
Title	String	The title is what is displayed in the context menu form your module.

Parameter	Type	Description
CmdName	String	If you want your menu item to call client-side code (JavaScript), then this is where you will place the name of the command. This is used for the delete action on the context menu. When the delete item is selected, a message asks you to confirm your choice before executing the command. For the menu items we are adding we will leave this blank.
CmdArg	String	This allows you to add additional arguments for the command.
Icon	String	This allows you to set a custom icon to appear next to your menu option.
URL	String	This is where the browser will be redirected to when your menu item is clicked. You can use a standard URL or use the EditURL function to direct it to another module. The EditURL function finds the module associated with your view module by looking at the key passed in. You will notice that the first example below passes in "Options" and the second one passes nothing. This is because the default key is "Edit". These keys are entered in the Module Definition. We will learn how to add these manually later.
ClientScript	String	As the name implies, this is where you would add the client-side script to be run when this item is selected. This is paired with the CmdName attribute above. We are leaving this blank for your actions.
UseActionEvent	Boolean	This determines if the user will receive notification when a script is being executed.
Secure	SecurityAccess Level	This is an Enum that determines the access level for this menu item.
Visible	Boolean	Determines whether this item will be visible.
New Window	Boolean	Determines whether information will be presented in a new window.

You will notice that the second parameter of the Add method asks for a title. This is the text that will show up on the menu item you create. In our code you will notice that instead of using a string, we use the Localization.GetString method to get the text from a local resource file.

```
Actions.Add(GetNextActionID, _
    Localization.GetString( _
    Entities.Modules.Actions.ModuleActionType.AddContent, _
    LocalResourceFile), _
    Entities.Modules.Actions.ModuleActionType.AddContent, _
    "", _
    "", _
    EditUrl(), _
    False, _
    Security.SecurityAccessLevel.Edit, _
    True, _
    False)
```

Localization is one of the many things that DotNetNuke 3.0 has brought us. This allows you to set the language seen on most sections of your portal to the language of your choice. Localization is somewhat beyond the scope of this chapter, but we will at least implement it for the actions menu.

To add a localization file, we first need to create a folder to place it in. Right-click on the EganEnterprises.CoffeeShopListing project in the Solution Explorer and select Add | New Folder. Name the folder App_LocalResources. This is where we will place our localization file. To add the file, right-click on the App_LocalResources folder and select Add | Add New Item from the menu. Select Assembly Resource File from the options and name it ShopList.ascx.resx. Click on Open when you are done.

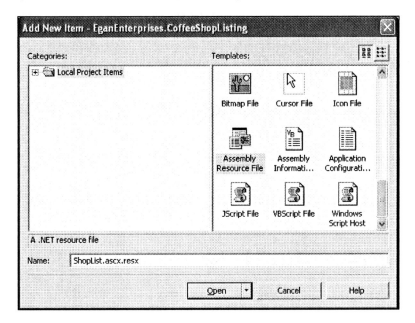

Under the name section add the resource key AddContent.Action and give it a value of
Add Coffee Shop. The action menu we implemented using the IActionable interface
earlier uses this key to place Add Coffee Shop on the context menu.

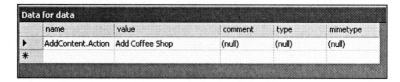

Data for data				
name	value	comment	type	mimetype
AddContent.Action	Add Coffee Shop	(null)	(null)	(null)

To learn more about how to implement localization in your DotNetNuke
modules, please see the DotNetNuke Localization white paper
(\DotNetNuke\Documentation\Public\DotNetNuke Localization.doc).

Now we can move on to the other interfaces. As we stated earlier, these interfaces only
need us to add the shell of the implemented functions into this file. These will only be
placed in this file to allow the framework to see, using reflection, if the module
implements the interfaces. We will write the code to implement these interfaces in the
CoffeeShopListingController class later.

```
Public Function ExportModule(ByVal ModuleID As Integer) _
As String Implements _
DotNetNuke.Entities.Modules.IPortable.ExportModule
    ' included as a stub only so that the core
    'knows this module Implements Entities.Modules.IPortable
End Function

Public Sub ImportModule(ByVal ModuleID As Integer, _
ByVal Content As String, _
ByVal Version As String, _
ByVal UserID As Integer) _
Implements DotNetNuke.Entities.Modules.IPortable.ImportModule
    ' included as a stub only so that the core
    'knows this module Implements Entities.Modules.IPortable
End Sub

Public Function GetSearchItems( _
ByVal ModInfo As DotNetNuke.Entities.Modules.ModuleInfo) _
As DotNetNuke.Services.Search.SearchItemInfoCollection _
Implements DotNetNuke.Entities.Modules.ISearchable.GetSearchItems
    ' included as a stub only so that the core
    'knows this module Implements Entities.Modules.IPortable
End Function
```

That is all the code we need at this time to set up our view module. Open up the display
portion of the control in Visual Studio, and by using Table | Insert | Table on Visual
Studio's main menu, add an HTML table to the form. Add the following text to the table:

Search Section
Results Sectoin

We add the table and text because we will be testing our modules to make sure that everything is in order before moving on the more advanced coding. Again, setting test points in your development allows you to pinpoint errors that may have been introduced into your code. Once we finish the setup for the Edit and Settings controls we will test the module to make sure we have not missed anything.

Module Edit Control

The Edit control is used by administrators to modify or change how your module functions. To set up the Edit control follow the steps we took to create the View control with the following exceptions:

- Do *not* implement the IPortable, IActionable, and ISearchable interfaces. The context menu only works with the View control. The control menu is used to navigate *to* the Edit control.

- Change the text in the table to say EditShopList RowOne and EditShopList RowTwo.

- Save the file as EditShopList.ascx.

Add the following in the HTML section:

```
<%@ Control language="vb" AutoEventWireup="false"
        Inherits="EganEnterprises.CoffeeShopListing.EditShopList"
        CodeBehind="EditShopList.ascx.vb"%>
```

and this to the code-behind page:

```
Imports DotNetNuke
Namespace EganEnterprises.CoffeeShopListing

    Public MustInherit Class EditShopList
        Inherits Entities.Modules.PortalModuleBase

        Private Sub Page_Load(ByVal sender As System.Object, _
        ByVal e As System.EventArgs) Handles MyBase.Load
            'Put user code to initialize the page here
        End Sub

    End Class

End Namespace
```

Again, add an HTML table to your control. When viewing your control in design mode it should look like the figure below.

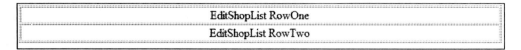

EditShopList RowOne
EditShopList RowTwo

Module Settings Control

The DotNetNuke framework allows you to add customized settings to the Module Settings Page. To do this you need to implement a Settings control.

To set up the Settings control follow the steps we took to create the View control with the following exceptions.

- Do *not* implement the IPortable, IActionable, and ISearchable interfaces.

- Change the text in the table to say OptionModule RowOne and OptionModule RowTwo.

- Save the file as Settings.ascx.

Add the following to the HTML section:

```
<%@ Control language="vb" AutoEventWireup="false"
Inherits="EganEnterprises.CoffeeShopListing.Settings"
CodeBehind="Settings.ascx.vb"%>
```

In the code-behind section it gets a little tricky. As opposed to the other two controls, this control inherits from ModuleSettingsBase instead of PortalModuleBase. This causes a problem in the Visual Studio designer when you attempt to view your form in design mode. The Visual Studio designer will show the following error.

This is because the ModuleSettingsBase has two abstract methods that we will need to implement: LoadSettings and UpdateSettings. So unless you want to design your control using only HTML, you will need to use the following workaround.

When you need to see this control in the designer, just comment out the Inherits ModuleSettingsBase declaration and both the public overrides methods (LoadSettings and UpdateSettings), and instead inherit from the PortalModuleBase. You can then drag and drop all the controls you would like to use from the toolbox and adjust them on your form. When you are happy with how it looks in the designer, simply switch over the `Inherits` statements. For now, the only code we need in the code-behind file for this control is the one below. We will add to this code once we have created the DAL (Data Access Layer)

```
Imports DotNetNuke

Namespace EganEnterprises.CoffeeShopListing

    Public Class Settings
        Inherits Entities.Modules.ModuleSettingsBase
        'Inherits Entities.Modules.PortalModuleBase

        Private Sub Page_Load(ByVal sender As System.Object, _
        ByVal e As System.EventArgs) Handles MyBase.Load
            'Put user code to initialize the page here
        End Sub

        Public Overrides Sub LoadSettings()
        End Sub

        Public Overrides Sub UpdateSettings()
        End Sub
    End Class

End Namespace
```

Just like the other controls, add an HTML table to the control so we can test our modules to this point.

| ShopListOptions RowOne |
| ShopListOptions RowTwo |

With all your controls complete, build your project and verify that it builds successfully. At this point, the module still cannot be viewed in a browser within the DotNetNuke framework. To do this you will first need to add module definitions to the portal.

Adding Module Definitions

When you upload a free or purchased module to your portal by using the host's file manager, the module definitions are added for you automatically. When developing modules, you will want to be able to debug them in the DotNetNuke environment using Visual Studio. This requires you to add module definitions manually.

Adding module definitions makes the module appear in the control panel module dropdown when you are signed on as host or admin. It connects your controls to the portal framework.

To add the module definitions needed for our project:

1. Hit *F5* to run the DotNetNuke solution, log in as host, and click on the Module Definitions option on the Host menu.

2. Under the Module Definition menu, select Add New Module Definition:

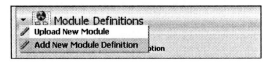

3. Enter the name for your module and a short description of what it does. When you are finished, click on the Update link:

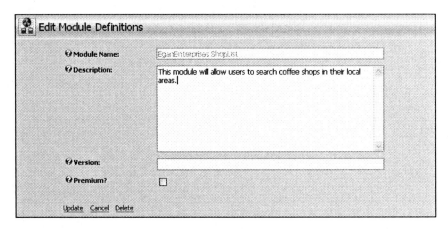

4. This will bring up a new section that allows you to add the definitions for the module. Enter the New Definition name and click on Add Definition. This will add the definition to the Definitions dropdown and will bring up a third section that will allow you to add the controls created in the previous section:

First, we will add the View control for the module.

1. Click on the Add Control link to start.

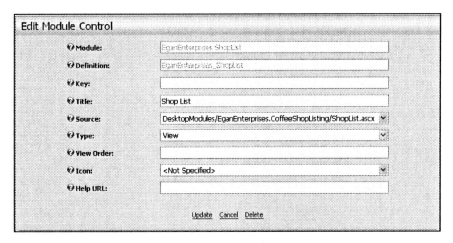

2. Enter the Title for the control. This is the default title when the control is added to a tab.

3. Select the Source for the control from the drop-down list. You will be selecting the file name of our control. This is the View control we created in the last section. Select the control from the dropdown.

4. Select the Type of control. This is the control that non-administrators will see when they view your module on the portal. Select View from the dropdown.

5. Click Update when done.

Next we want to add our Edit control.

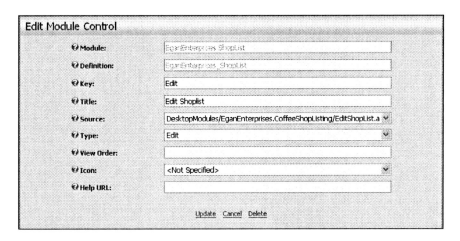

1. Enter Edit for the Key field. This is the key that the Actions Menu we created earlier will use to navigate to this control.

2. Enter a Title for the control.

3. Select the `ShopListEdit.ascx` control from the Source drop-down list.

4. Select Edit as in the Type dropdown.

5. Click Update when complete.

Finally we need to add our Settings control.

1. Click on Add Control to add the third control for this module.

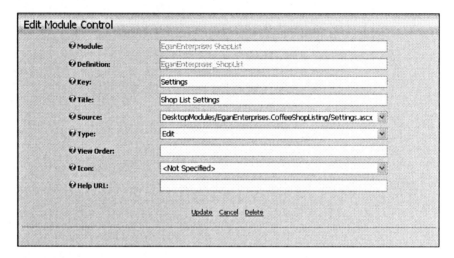

2. Enter Settings for the key field.

3. Enter a Title for the control.

4. Select the `Settings.ascx` control from the Source drop-down list.

5. Select Edit as in the Type dropdown.

6. Click Update when complete.

This will complete the module definition. Your control page will look like the following.

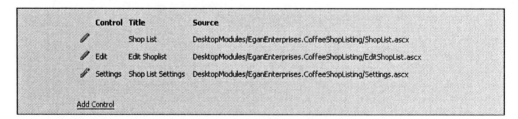

Click on the Home page menu item to exit the module definition section.

Adding Your Module to a Page

The last step before adding the real functionality to our module is to add the module to a page. I prefer to add a Testing Tab to the portal to test out my new modules. We add the modules to the site before adding any functionality to them to verify that we have set them up correctly. We'll do this in stages so that you can easily determine any errors you encountered, by ensuring each stage of development was completed successfully.

Create a tab called Testing Tab and select EganEnterprises ShopList (or the name you used) from the Module drop-down list on the control panel and click on the Add link to add it to a pane on the page.

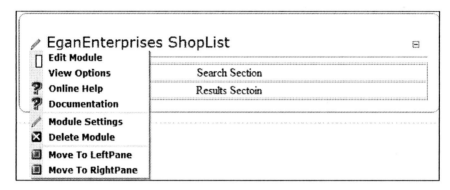

If all goes well you should see the module we created on the page. Verify that you can access the custom menu items from the context menu. When selected, they should bring you to the Edit and Settings controls that we created earlier.

> For your Module Settings section to appear correctly in the module settings page, make sure that you have it inheriting from ModuleSettingsBase, and not PortalModuleBase.

We now have a basic template for creating our module. Before we can give our controls the functionality they need we need to construct our data layers.

The Datastore Layer

The datastore layer consists of the table(s) needed to store our records and the stored procedures required to access them. We begin by creating our tables and stored procedures for SQL Server.

SQL Server

First, we need to create the tables needed to hold our coffee shop information. When naming your tables and stored procedures it is a good idea to prefix them with the name of your company (CompanyName_). This is done for two reasons:

- It helps to avoid your module overriding a table of the same name. Simple table names like options or tasks turn into EganEnterprises_options or EganEnterprises_tasks. The chances of another developer creating a table with the same name are low.

- Inside SQL Server Enterprise Manager, all of your tables and stored procedures are grouped together, making them easy to locate and work with.

Since we will be using Microsoft SQL Server, we will be displaying our table and stored procedure information in script format. The first thing we need to do is to create the table that will hold our coffee shop information. This is the specific information we want to collect about each coffee shop that we will store.

```
CREATE TABLE [EganEnterprises_CoffeeShopInfo] (
    [coffeeShopID] [int] IDENTITY (1, 1) NOT NULL ,
    [moduleID] [int] NOT NULL ,
    [coffeeShopName] [varchar] (100)  NOT NULL ,
    [coffeeShopAddress1] [varchar] (150)  NULL ,
    [coffeeShopAddress2] [varchar] (150)  NULL ,
    [coffeeShopCity] [varchar] (50)  NOT NULL ,
    [coffeeShopState] [char] (2)  NOT NULL ,
    [coffeeShopZip] [char] (11)  NOT NULL ,
    [coffeeShopWiFi] [smallint] NOT NULL ,
    [coffeeShopDetails] [varchar] (250)  NOT NULL
) ON [PRIMARY]
GO
```

Next we need to create a table that will hold our module option information. This simple table has only two fields, moduleID and AuthorizedRoles, and will be used to handle the customized security we will be using with our module. This information will be accessed through the Settings control we created and will be seen on the module settings page.

```
CREATE TABLE [EganEnterprises_CoffeeShopModuleOptions] (
    [moduleID] [int] NOT NULL ,
    [AuthorizedRoles] [varchar] (200) NOT NULL
) ON [PRIMARY]
GO
```

> When we create scripts that will be used to create the database tables automatically when the PA is uploaded to a site, we will be prefixing the scripts with the databaseOwner and objectQualifier variables as follows:
>
> CREATE TABLE databaseOwer {databaseOwner}{objectQualifier} [EganEnterprises_CoffeeShopInfo]

In this chapter, we are assuming that you use the SQL Server tools to create your database objects. If you are running these scripts from the SQL option on the host menu, you can add these variables to the script before you run them. Make sure that you have the Run As Script option checked.

We then need to create the stored procedures necessary to access our tables. Even though we can create stored procedures that combine functions like adding and updating records in the same stored procedure, we separate these out to make them easier to read and understand.

The following procedure adds new entries to our coffee shop listings:

```
CREATE PROCEDURE dbo.EganEnterprises_AddCoffeeShopInfo
@moduleID int,
@coffeeShopName              varchar(100)  ,
@coffeeShopAddress1          varchar(150),
@coffeeShopAddress2          varchar(150),
@coffeeShopCity              varchar(50) ,
@coffeeShopState             char(2),
@coffeeShopZip               char(11),
@coffeeShopWiFi              int,
@coffeeShopDetails           varchar(250)

AS

INSERT INTO EganEnterprises_CoffeeShopInfo (
    moduleID,
    coffeeShopName,
    coffeeShopAddress1,
    coffeeShopAddress2,
    coffeeShopCity,
    coffeeShopState,
    coffeeShopZip,
    coffeeShopWiFi,
    coffeeShopDetails
)
VALUES (
    @moduleID,
    @coffeeShopName,
    @coffeeShopAddress1,
    @coffeeShopAddress2,
    @coffeeShopCity,
    @coffeeShopState,
    @coffeeShopZip,
    @coffeeShopWiFi,
    @coffeeShopDetails
)
```

The following procedure adds roles to the CoffeeShopModuleOptions table:

```
CREATE PROCEDURE dbo.EganEnterprises_AddCoffeeShopModuleOptions
@moduleID                    int,
@authorizedRoles varchar(250)
```

```
      AS

      INSERT INTO  EganEnterprises_CoffeeShopModuleOptions
        (moduleId, AuthorizedRoles)
      VALUES
        (@moduleID, @authorizedRoles)
```

The following procedure deletes a shop listing:

```
      CREATE PROCEDURE dbo.EganEnterprises_DeleteCoffeeShop
      @coffeeShopID  int

      AS

      DELETE
      FROM    EganEnterprises_CoffeeShopInfo
      WHERE   coffeeShopID = @coffeeShopID
```

The following procedure retrieves the users authorized to add shops:

```
      CREATE PROCEDURE dbo.EganEnterprises_GetCoffeeShopModuleOptions
      @moduleId int

      AS

      SELECT  *
      FROM    EganEnterprises_CoffeeShopModuleOptions
      WHERE
              moduleID = @moduleID
```

The following procedure retrieves all coffee shops:

```
      CREATE PROCEDURE dbo.EganEnterprises_GetCoffeeShops
      @moduleId int

      AS

      SELECT coffeeShopID,
             coffeeShopName,
             coffeeShopAddress1,
             coffeeShopAddress2,
             coffeeShopCity,
             coffeeShopState,
             coffeeShopZip,
             coffeeShopWiFi,
             coffeeShopDetails
      FROM    EganEnterprises_CoffeeShopInfo
      WHERE
              moduleID = @moduleID
```

The following procedure retrieves one shop for editing:

```
      CREATE PROCEDURE dbo.EganEnterprises_GetCoffeeShopsByID
      @coffeeShopID int

      AS

      SELECT coffeeShopID,
             coffeeShopName,
             coffeeShopAddress1,
```

```
        coffeeShopAddress2,
        coffeeShopCity,
        coffeeShopState,
        coffeeShopZip,
        coffeeShopWiFi,
        coffeeShopDetails
FROM    EganEnterprises_CoffeeShopInfo
WHERE
        coffeeShopID = @coffeeShopID
```

The following procedure retrieves shops by zip code:

```
CREATE PROCEDURE dbo.EganEnterprises_GetCoffeeShopsByZip
@moduleID int,
@coffeeShopZip          char(11)

AS

SELECT coffeeShopID,
        coffeeShopName,
        coffeeShopAddress1,
        coffeeShopAddress2,
        coffeeShopCity,
        coffeeShopState,
        coffeeShopZip,
        coffeeShopWiFi,
        coffeeShopDetails
FROM    EganEnterprises_CoffeeShopInfo
WHERE
        coffeeShopZip = @coffeeShopZip AND moduleID = @moduleID
```

The following procedure updates a coffee shop listing:

```
CREATE PROCEDURE dbo.EganEnterprises_UpdateCoffeeShopInfo
@coffeeShopID            int,
@coffeeShopName          varchar(100),
@coffeeShopAddress1      varchar(150),
@coffeeShopAddress2      varchar(150),
@coffeeShopCity          varchar(50),
@coffeeShopState         char(2),
@coffeeShopZip           char(11),
@coffeeShopWiFi          int ,
@coffeeShopDetails       varchar(250)

AS

UPDATE EganEnterprises_CoffeeShopInfo
SET     coffeeShopName = isnull(@coffeeShopName,coffeeShopName),
        coffeeShopAddress1 = isnull(@coffeeShopAddress1,
        coffeeShopAddress1),
        coffeeShopAddress2 = isnull(@coffeeShopAddress2,
        coffeeShopAddress2),
        coffeeShopCity = isnull(@coffeeShopCity,coffeeShopCity),
        coffeeShopState = isnull(@coffeeShopState,coffeeShopState),
        coffeeShopZip = isnull(@coffeeShopZip,coffeeShopZip),
        coffeeShopWiFi = isnull(@coffeeShopWiFi,coffeeShopWiFi),
        coffeeShopDetails = isnull(@coffeeShopDetails,
        coffeeShopDetails)
WHERE   coffeeShopID = @coffeeShopID
```

The following procedure updates who can add coffee shop listings:

```
CREATE PROCEDURE dbo.EganEnterprises_UpdateCoffeeShopModuleOptions
@moduleID        int,
@authorizedRoles varchar(250)

AS

UPDATE EganEnterprises_CoffeeShopModuleOptions
SET    AuthorizedRoles = @AuthorizedRoles
WHERE  moduleID = @moduleID
```

The Data Access Layer (DAL)

The provider model that DotNetNuke uses allows you to connect to the database of your choice. It is designed so that switching the datastore used by both the core and the modules can be done by simply changing the default provider. The DAL is where we place the code necessary for each provider we wish to support.

Before building our DAL, we need to create a few folders to organize our project. Right-click on your PA project and select Add Folder. Create two new folders in addition to the App_LocalResources folder created earlier: Providers and Installation.

The Providers folder will be used to hold the provider that we are going to create, and the Installation folder will be used to organize our installation files when we get to that section.

To begin building the DAL for our module, right-click on the EganEnterprises.CoffeeShopListing project and select Add Class. Name the class DataProvider.vb. This is the base provider class that will be used for the module. We will walk through and discuss each section of this file.

The first thing we need to do is to add a few import statements that we need for our class. We will be using both caching and reflection in our provider:

```
Imports System
Imports DotNetNuke
```

Just as we did for our controls, we want to place this class inside our CompanyName.ModuleName namespace:

```
Namespace EganEnterprises.CoffeeShopListing
```

This class will be used as the base class for our provider so we declare this as MustInherit. This means we will not be able to instantiate this class; it can only be used as the base class for our provider:

```
Public MustInherit Class DataProvider
```

Next, we need to declare the object that will serve as the singleton object for this class:

```
Private Shared objProvider As DataProvider = Nothing
```

We use a singleton object to ensure that only one instance of the data provider is created at any given time. The constructor is used to instantiate the object. In the constructor, we call the CreateProvider method to ensure that only one instance is created.

```
Shared Sub New()
    CreateProvider()
End Sub
```

The CreateProvider method uses reflection to create an instance of the data provider being created. We pass it the provider type, the namespace, and the assembly name.

```
Private Shared Sub CreateProvider()
    objProvider = _
    CType(Framework.Reflection.CreateObject _
    ("data", "EganEnterprises.CoffeeShopListing", _
    "EganEnterprises.CoffeeShopListing"), DataProvider)
End Sub
```

Finally, the Instance method is used to actually create the instance of our data provider.

```
Public Shared Shadows Function Instance() As DataProvider
    Return objProvider
End Function
```

At the bottom of the DataProvider class we need to define all the abstract methods that will correspond to the stored procedures we have already created. The methods are created as MustOverride because we will need to implement them in our provider object.

Since the provider module allows any datastore to be used, the implementation of these methods will reside in the provider. Here we will only create the signature of the methods. The parameter names match those in our stored procedures (minus the @).

As you can see, when implemented, these methods will be responsible for all the inserts, updates, and deletions for or module tables.

```
' all core methods defined below
Public MustOverride Function EganEnterprises_GetCoffeeShops _
    (ByVal ModuleId As Integer) As IDataReader

Public MustOverride Function EganEnterprises_GetCoffeeShopsByZip _
    (ByVal ModuleId As Integer, ByVal coffeeShopZip As String) _
    As IDataReader

Public MustOverride Function EganEnterprises_GetCoffeeShopsByID _
    (ByVal coffeeShopID As Integer) As IDataReader

Public MustOverride Function EganEnterprises_AddCoffeeShopInfo _
    (ByVal ModuleId As Integer, _
     ByVal coffeeShopName As String, _
     ByVal coffeeShopAddress1 As String, _
     ByVal coffeeShopAddress2 As String, _
     ByVal coffeeShopCity As String, _
     ByVal coffeeShopState As String, _
     ByVal coffeeShopZip As String, _
     ByVal coffeeShopWiFi As System.Int16, _
     ByVal coffeeShopDetails As String) As Integer

Public MustOverride Sub EganEnterprises_UpdateCoffeeShopInfo _
    (ByVal coffeeShopID As Integer, _
     ByVal coffeeShopName As String, _
     ByVal coffeeShopAddress1 As String, _
     ByVal coffeeShopAddress2 As String, _
     ByVal coffeeShopCity As String, _
     ByVal coffeeShopState As String, _
     ByVal coffeeShopZip As String, _
     ByVal coffeeShopWiFi As System.Int16, _
     ByVal coffeeShopDetails As String)

Public MustOverride Sub EganEnterprises_DeleteCoffeeShop _
    (ByVal coffeeShopID As Integer)

Public MustOverride Function _
    EganEnterprises_AddCoffeeShopModuleOptions _
    (ByVal ModuleID As Integer, _
     ByVal authorizedRoles As String) As Integer
```

We have a separate table that will hold the options for our module. The definitions for the options table are placed here.

```
'Options info
Public MustOverride Function _
    EganEnterprises_GetCoffeeShopModuleOptions _
    (ByVal ModuleID As Integer) As IDataReader

Public MustOverride Function _
    EganEnterprises_UpdateCoffeeShopModuleOptions _
    (ByVal ModuleID As Integer, ByVal authorizedRoles As String) _
    As Integer
```

```
Public MustOverride Function _
EganEnterprises_AddCoffeeShopModuleOptions _
(ByVal ModuleID As Integer, ByVal authorizedRoles As String) _
As Integer

End Class
End Namespace
```

After this class is created, we need to create the `SqlDataProvider` project that our module will use.

The SQLDataProvider Project

The `SqlDataProvider` project is built as a separate private assembly. We will again be creating a **Class Library** type project. Name the project with a `CompanyName` `.ModuleName.SqlProvider` syntax (its location should be the `Providers` folder). In our case, the project will be called `EganEnterprises.CoffeeShopListing.SqlProvider`, and will be created in the `C:\DotNetNuke\DesktopModules\EganEnterprises.Coff eeshopListing\Providers` folder.

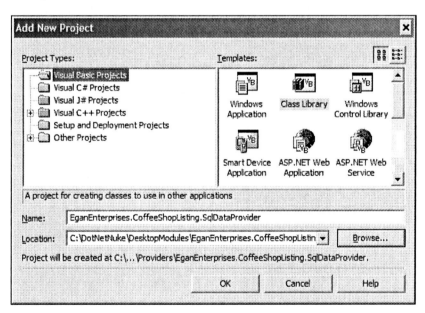

Just as we did for your module project, we will need to modify a few properties for the project. Right-click on the new project and select **Properties**. This will bring up the property pages.

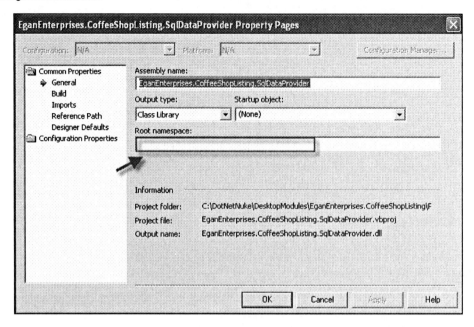

Under the General section of the Common Properties folder, clear out the Root namespace.

We also want the project to build into the bin directory of the DotNetNuke project. This is where DotNetNuke will look for the assembly when it tries to load the provider. To allow the BuildSupport project to add our DLL, we need to add a reference to the SqlDataProvider project.

1. Right-click on the reference folder located below the BuildSupport project and select Add Reference.
2. Select the Projects tab.
3. Double-click on the EganEnterprises.CoffeeShopListing .SqlDataProvider project to place it in the Selected Components box.
4. Click OK to add the reference.

Finally, we want to be able to use all of the objects available to us in DotNetNuke in our private assembly, so we need to add a reference to the DotNetNuke project.

1. Right-click on the reference folder located below the EganEnterprises .CoffeeShopListing.SqlDataProvider private assembly project we just created and select Add Reference.
2. Select the Projects tab.
3. Double-click on the DotNetNuke project to place it in the Selected Components box.

4. Click OK to add the reference.

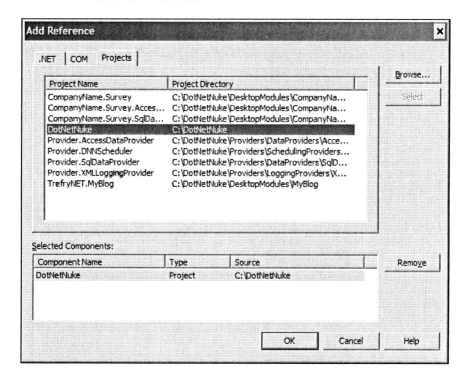

The Provider File

After you are finished setting up the project, it is time to create the `SqlDataProvider` class. First delete the `Class1.vb` file that was created with the project, then right-click on the project and select **Add Class**. Name the file `SqlDataProvider.vb` and click OK. This will provide you with the shell needed to create the provider. We will walk through the modifications needed to create the provider.

The first thing you need to do is to pull in a few imports. Most of these you should be quite used to seeing but the one that stands out is `Microsoft.ApplicationBlocks.Data`. This is a class created by Microsoft to help with the connections and commands needed to work with SQL Server. It is used to facilitate calls to the database without having to create all of the ADO.NET code manually. You will find this class in the `C:\DotNetNuke\Providers\DataProviders\SqlDataProvider\SQLHelper` folder of the DotNetNuke project. Take time to look it over; its methods are quite easy to understand. We will be using methods from this class in our data provider. To start, we add the imports we need for our class.

```
Imports System
Imports System.Data
Imports System.Data.SqlClient
```

```
Imports Microsoft.ApplicationBlocks.Data
Imports DotNetNuke
Imports DotNetNuke.Common.Utilities
Imports DotNetNuke.Framework.Providers
```

After adding the import statements, we need to wrap our class in the namespace for our module. As you can see, we will also be inheriting from the DataProvider base class created earlier. We also need to declare a constant variable that will hold the type of the provider. There are many different providers used in DotNetNuke so we need to specify the type. This is done by assigning it the simple lowercase string data.

```
Namespace EganEnterprises.CoffeeShopListing
    Public Class SqlDataProvider
        Inherits EganEnterprises.CoffeeShopListing.DataProvider
        Private Const ProviderType As String = "data"
```

We then use this type to instantiate a data provider configuration:

```
        Private _providerConfiguration As _
        ProviderConfiguration = _
        ProviderConfiguration.GetProviderConfiguration _
        (ProviderType)
```

Then we declare a few variables that will hold the information necessary for us to connect to the database:

```
        Private _connectionString As String
        Private _providerPath As String
        Private _objectQualifier As String
        Private _databaseOwner As String
```

In the constructor for the class we read the attributes that we set in the web.config file to fill the database specific information like connection string, database owner, etc.

```
Public Sub New()

    Dim objProvider As Provider = _
    CType(_providerConfiguration.Providers _
    (_providerConfiguration.DefaultProvider), _
        Provider)
If objProvider.Attributes("connectionStringName") <> "" AndAlso _
    System.Configuration.ConfigurationSettings.AppSettings _
    (objProvider.Attributes("connectionStringName")) <> "" Then
    _connectionString = _
    System.Configuration.ConfigurationSettings.AppSettings _
    (objProvider.Attributes("connectionStringName"))
Else
    _connectionString = _
    objProvider.Attributes("connectionString")
End If

    _providerPath = objProvider.Attributes("providerPath")
    _objectQualifier = _
    objProvider.Attributes("objectQualifier")
    If _objectQualifier <> "" And _
        _objectQualifier.EndsWith("_") = False Then
        _objectQualifier += "_"
    End If
```

```
            _databaseOwner = objProvider.Attributes("databaseOwner")
            If _databaseOwner <> "" And _
            _databaseOwner.EndsWith(".") = False Then

                _databaseOwner += "."

            End If

    End Sub

        Public ReadOnly Property ConnectionString() As String
            Get
                Return _connectionString
            End Get
        End Property

        Public ReadOnly Property ProviderPath() As String
            Get
                Return _providerPath
            End Get
        End Property

        Public ReadOnly Property ObjectQualifier() As String
            Get
                Return _objectQualifier
            End Get
        End Property

        Public ReadOnly Property DatabaseOwner() As String
            Get
                Return _databaseOwner
            End Get
        End Property
```

As you recall, in the base provider class we declared our methods as MustOverride. In this section, we are doing just that. We override the methods from the base class and use the Microsoft.ApplicationBlocks.Data class to make the calls to the database.

The GetNull function is used to convert an application-encoded null value to a database null value that is defined for the datatype expected. We will be utilizing this throughout the rest of this section.

```
        ' general
        Private Function GetNull(ByVal Field As Object) As Object
            Return Null.GetNull(Field, DBNull.Value)
        End Function
    Public Overrides Function EganEnterprises_GetCoffeeShops( _
        ByVal ModuleId As Integer) _
        As IDataReader
        Return CType(SqlHelper.ExecuteReader(ConnectionString, _
            DatabaseOwner & _
            ObjectQualifier & _
            "EganEnterprises_GetCoffeeShops", _
            ModuleId), _
            IDataReader)
    End Function
```

```
Public Overrides Function EganEnterprises_GetCoffeeShopsByZip( _
    ByVal ModuleId As Integer, _
    ByVal coffeeShopZip As String) _
    As IDataReader
     Return CType(SqlHelper.ExecuteReader(ConnectionString, _
        DatabaseOwner & _
        ObjectQualifier & _
        "EganEnterprises_GetCoffeeShopsByZip", _
        ModuleId, _
        coffeeShopZip), _
        IDataReader)
End Function

Public Overrides Function EganEnterprises_GetCoffeeShopsByID( _
    ByVal coffeeShopID As Integer) _
    As IDataReader
     Return CType(SqlHelper.ExecuteReader(ConnectionString, _
        DatabaseOwner & _
        ObjectQualifier & _
        "EganEnterprises_GetCoffeeShopsByID", _
        coffeeShopID), _
        IDataReader)
End Function

Public Overrides Function EganEnterprises_AddCoffeeShopInfo( _
    ByVal ModuleId As Integer, _
    ByVal coffeeShopName As String, _
    ByVal coffeeShopAddress1 As String, _
    ByVal coffeeShopAddress2 As String, _
    ByVal coffeeShopCity As String, _
    ByVal coffeeShopState As String, _
    ByVal coffeeShopZip As String, _
    ByVal coffeeShopWiFi As System.Int16, _
    ByVal coffeeShopDetails As String) _
    As Integer
     Return CType(SqlHelper.ExecuteScalar(ConnectionString, _
        DatabaseOwner & _
        ObjectQualifier & _
        "EganEnterprises_AddCoffeeShopInfo", _
        ModuleId, _
        coffeeShopName, _
        GetNull(coffeeShopAddress1), _
        GetNull(coffeeShopAddress2), _
        coffeeShopCity, _
        coffeeShopState, _
        coffeeShopZip, _
        coffeeShopWiFi, _
        coffeeShopDetails), _
        Integer)
End Function

Public Overrides Sub EganEnterprises_UpdateCoffeeShopInfo( _
    ByVal coffeeShopID As Integer, _
    ByVal coffeeShopName As String, _
    ByVal coffeeShopAddress1 As String, _
    ByVal coffeeShopAddress2 As String, _
    ByVal coffeeShopCity As String, _
    ByVal coffeeShopState As String, _
    ByVal coffeeShopZip As String, _
```

```
        ByVal coffeeShopWiFi As System.Int16, _
        ByVal coffeeShopDetails As String)
          SqlHelper.ExecuteNonQuery(ConnectionString, _
             DatabaseOwner & _
             ObjectQualifier & _
             "EganEnterprises_UpdateCoffeeShopInfo", _
             coffeeShopID, _
             coffeeShopName, _
             GetNull(coffeeShopAddress1), _
             GetNull(coffeeShopAddress2), _
             coffeeShopCity, _
             coffeeShopState, _
             coffeeShopZip, _
             coffeeShopWiFi, _
             coffeeShopDetails)
End Sub

Public Overrides Sub EganEnterprises_DeleteCoffeeShop( _
    ByVal coffeeShopID As Integer)
      SqlHelper.ExecuteNonQuery(ConnectionString, _
         DatabaseOwner & _
         ObjectQualifier & _
         "EganEnterprises_DeleteCoffeeShop", _
         coffeeShopID)
End Sub

Public Overrides Function EganEnterprises_GetCoffeeShopModuleOptions( _
    ByVal ModuleId As Integer) _
    As IDataReader
      Return CType(SqlHelper.ExecuteReader(ConnectionString, _
         DatabaseOwner & _
         ObjectQualifier & _
         "EganEnterprises_GetCoffeeShopModuleOptions", _
         ModuleId), _
         IDataReader)
End Function

Public Overrides Function
EganEnterprises_UpdateCoffeeShopModuleOptions( _
    ByVal ModuleID As Integer, _
    ByVal AuthorizedRoles As String) _
    As Integer
      Return CType(SqlHelper.ExecuteNonQuery(ConnectionString, _
         DatabaseOwner & _
         ObjectQualifier & _
         "EganEnterprises_UpdateCoffeeShopModuleOptions", _
         ModuleID, _
         AuthorizedRoles), _
         Integer)
End Function

Public Overrides Function EganEnterprises_AddCoffeeShopModuleOptions( _
    ByVal ModuleID As Integer, _
    ByVal AuthorizedRoles As String) _
    As Integer
      Return CType(SqlHelper.ExecuteNonQuery(ConnectionString, _
         DatabaseOwner & _
         ObjectQualifier & _
         "EganEnterprises_AddCoffeeShopModuleOptions", _
```

```
        ModuleID, _
        AuthorizedRoles), _
        Integer)
    End Function
    End Class
    End Namespace
```

The Business Logic Layer (BLL)

The third piece in this provider puzzle is the **Business Logic Layer** (BLL). The BLL connects the data-access sections we just completed with the presentation layer. Since we will have a Settings control, we will need to create four different classes:

- CoffeeShopListingInfo
- CoffeeShopListingController
- CoffeeShopListingOptionsInfo
- CoffeeShopListingOptionsController

CoffeeShopListingInfo and CoffeeShopListingOptionsInfo

The CoffeeShopListingInfo and CoffeeShopListingOptionsInfo classes are very simple classes that hold the information we need to pass to our database layer. These are used to pass hydrated objects instead of individual pieces of information. Each class will hold all the information associated with each object.

We start by adding our Imports statements and Namespace declarations.

```
Imports System
Imports System.Configuration
Imports System.Data
Namespace EganEnterprises.CoffeeShopListing
```

The next region of the code consists of private variables to hold the data and public properties to allow the setting and getting of the variables. Both classes are shown below.

```
Public Class CoffeeShopListingInfo

#Region "Private Members"
        Private m_moduleID As Integer
        Private m_coffeeShopID As Integer
        Private m_coffeeShopName As String
        Private m_coffeeShopAddress1 As String
        Private m_coffeeShopAddress2 As String
        Private m_coffeeShopCity As String
        Private m_coffeeShopState As String
        Private m_coffeeShopZip As String
        Private m_coffeeShopWiFi As System.Int16
        Private m_coffeeShopDetails As String
#End Region

#Region "Constructors"
    Public Sub New()
    End Sub
#End Region
```

```vbnet
#Region "Public Properties"
        Public Property moduleID() As Integer
            Get
                Return m_moduleID
            End Get
            Set(ByVal Value As Integer)
                m_moduleID = Value
            End Set
        End Property
        Public Property coffeeShopID() As Integer
            Get
                Return m_coffeeShopID
            End Get
            Set(ByVal Value As Integer)
                m_coffeeShopID = Value
            End Set
        End Property
        Public Property coffeeShopName() As String
            Get
                Return m_coffeeShopName
            End Get
            Set(ByVal Value As String)
                m_coffeeShopName = Value
            End Set
        End Property
        Public Property coffeeShopAddress1() As String
            Get
                Return m_coffeeShopAddress1
            End Get
            Set(ByVal Value As String)
                m_coffeeShopAddress1 = Value
            End Set
        End Property
        Public Property coffeeShopAddress2() As String
            Get
                Return m_coffeeShopAddress2
            End Get
            Set(ByVal Value As String)
                m_coffeeShopAddress2 = Value
            End Set
        End Property
        Public Property coffeeShopCity() As String
            Get
                Return m_coffeeShopCity
            End Get
            Set(ByVal Value As String)
                m_coffeeShopCity = Value
            End Set
        End Property
        Public Property coffeeShopState() As String
            Get
                Return m_coffeeShopState
            End Get
            Set(ByVal Value As String)
                m_coffeeShopState = Value
            End Set
        End Property
        Public Property coffeeShopZip() As String
            Get
```

```
                          Return m_coffeeShopZip
                    End Get
                    Set(ByVal Value As String)
                          m_coffeeShopZip = Value
                    End Set
            End Property
            Public Property coffeeShopWiFi() As System.Int16
                    Get
                          Return m_coffeeShopWiFi
                    End Get
                    Set(ByVal Value As System.Int16)
                          m_coffeeShopWiFi = Value
                    End Set
            End Property
            Public Property coffeeShopDetails() As String
                    Get
                          Return m_coffeeShopDetails
                    End Get
                    Set(ByVal Value As String)
                          m_coffeeShopDetails = Value
                    End Set
            End Property
      #End Region
      End Class

      Namespace EganEnterprises.CoffeeShopListing
      Public Class CoffeeShopListingOptionsInfo
            Private m_moduleID As Integer
            Private m_AuthorizedRoles As String

            Public Property moduleID() As Integer
                    Get
                          Return m_moduleID
                    End Get
                    Set(ByVal Value As Integer)
                          m_moduleID = Value
                    End Set
            End Property
            Public Property AuthorizedRoles() As String
                    Get
                          Return m_AuthorizedRoles
                    End Get
                    Set(ByVal Value As String)
                          m_AuthorizedRoles = Value
                    End Set
            End Property
      End Class
      End Namespace
```

Once these classes have been completed, we then create the controller classes. As the name suggests, these are in charge of controlling the data flow to our module.

CoffeeShopListingController and CoffeeShopListingOptionsController

The CoffeeShopListingController class is paired with the CoffeeShopListingInfo class and is used to pass the CoffeeShopListingInfo objects to the dataprovider.

To help minimize the task of populating custom business objects from the data layer, the DotNetNuke core team has created a generic utility class to help hydrate your business objects, the CBO class. This class contains two public functions—one for hydrating a single object instance and one for hydrating a collection of objects.

For more information on custom business objects refer to DotNetNuke Data Access.doc under C:\DotNetNuke\Documentation\Public.

When looking at the classes CoffeeShopListingController and CoffeeShopListingOptionsController, there are a few things you'll notice:

- For functions like EganEnterprises_AddCoffeeShopInfo, the parameters for module-specific information are not passed individually but as a CoffeeShopListingInfo object.

- The functions used to hydrate your data are found in the CBO class. This class uses database-neutral objects to fill your data so that it can be passed to the database of your choice.

- We will be implementing the ISearchable and IPortable interfaces.

First, we will look at the CoffeeShopListingController class. We begin by adding our namespace to the class.

```
Namespace EganEnterprises.CoffeeShopListing
```

This is followed by the actual class declaration and the declarations for the interfaces.

```
Public Class CoffeeShopListingController
    Implements Entities.Modules.ISearchable
    Implements Entities.Modules.IPortable
```

We will break our code up into two different regions. In the Public Methods region, we create the functions that will make our calls to the database. We use the CBO object that calls the implemented DataProvider methods. Notice that we pass the detailed information about the coffee shop in a CoffeeShopListInfo object and then the function breaks out all of the individual items needed to call the DataProvider methods.

```
#Region "Public Methods"
    Public Function EganEnterprises_GetCoffeeShops( _
        ByVal ModuleId As Integer) As ArrayList
        Return CBO.FillCollection _
        (DataProvider.Instance(). _
        EganEnterprises_GetCoffeeShops _
        (ModuleId), GetType(CoffeeShopListingInfo))
    End Function

    Public Function EganEnterprises_GetCoffeeShopsByZip( _
    ByVal ModuleId As Integer, _
    ByVal coffeeShopZip As String) _
    As ArrayList
```

```
            Return CBO.FillCollection _
            (DataProvider.Instance(). _
            EganEnterprises_GetCoffeeShopsByZip _
            (ModuleId, coffeeShopZip), _
            GetType(CoffeeShopListingInfo))
      End Function

      Public Function EganEnterprises_GetCoffeeShopsByID( _
      ByVal coffeeShopID As Integer) As CoffeeShopListingInfo
            Return CType(CBO.FillObject _
            (EganEnterprises.CoffeeShopListing. _
            DataProvider.Instance(). _
            EganEnterprises_GetCoffeeShopsByID( _
            coffeeShopID), GetType(CoffeeShopListingInfo)), _
            CoffeeShopListingInfo)
      End Function

      Public Function EganEnterprises_AddCoffeeShopInfo( _
      ByVal objShopList As _
      EganEnterprises.CoffeeShopListing.CoffeeShopListingInfo) _
      As Integer
            Return CType(EganEnterprises.CoffeeShopListing. _
            DataProvider.Instance(). _
            EganEnterprises_AddCoffeeShopInfo( _
            objShopList.moduleID, _
            objShopList.coffeeShopName, _
            objShopList.coffeeShopAddress1, _
            objShopList.coffeeShopAddress2, _
            objShopList.coffeeShopCity, _
            objShopList.coffeeShopState, _
            objShopList.coffeeShopZip, _
            objShopList.coffeeShopWiFi, _
            objShopList.coffeeShopDetails), Integer)
      End Function

      Public Sub EganEnterprises_UpdateCoffeeShopInfo( _
      ByVal objShopList As _
      EganEnterprises.CoffeeShopListing.CoffeeShopListingInfo)
            EganEnterprises.CoffeeShopListing. _
            DataProvider.Instance(). _
            EganEnterprises_UpdateCoffeeShopInfo( _
            objShopList.coffeeShopID, _
            objShopList.coffeeShopName, _
            objShopList.coffeeShopAddress1, _
            objShopList.coffeeShopAddress2, _
            objShopList.coffeeShopCity, _
            objShopList.coffeeShopState, _
            objShopList.coffeeShopZip, _
            objShopList.coffeeShopWiFi, _
            objShopList.coffeeShopDetails)
      End Sub

      Public Sub EganEnterprises_DeleteCoffeeShop( _
      ByVal coffeeShopID As Integer)
            EganEnterprises.CoffeeShopListing. _
            DataProvider.Instance(). _
            EganEnterprises_DeleteCoffeeShop(coffeeShopID)
      End Sub
   #End Region
```

Remember that when we created our ShopList.ascx.vb file we only created the shells needed for our interfaces. In our controller class, we will be coding the implementation of these interfaces.

Implementing IPortable

The IPortable interface can be implemented to allow a user to transfer data from one module instance to another. This is accessed on the context menu of the module.

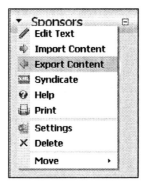

To use this interface, you will need to implement two different methods, ExportModule and ImportModule. The implementation of these methods will be slightly different depending on the data that is stored in the module. Since we will be holding information about certain coffee shops in our module this is the information we need to import and export. This is accomplished using the System.XML namespace built into .NET.

The ExportModule method uses our EganEnterprises_GetCoffeeShops stored procedure to build an ArrayList of CoffeeShopListingInfo objects. The objects are then converted to XML nodes and returned to the caller. We don't need to call the ExportModule function ourselves; the DotNetNuke framework takes this when the Export link is clicked, and the data is exported to a physical file.

```
Public Function ExportModule(ByVal ModuleID As Integer) _
As String Implements _
DotNetNuke.Entities.Modules.IPortable.ExportModule

  Dim strXML As String
  Dim arrCoffeeShops As ArrayList = _
  EganEnterprises_GetCoffeeShops(ModuleID)
```

```
    If arrCoffeeShops.Count <> 0 Then
      strXML += "<coffeeshops>"
      Dim objCoffeeShop As CoffeeShopListingInfo
      For Each objCoffeeShop In arrCoffeeShops
        strXML += "<coffeeshop>"
        strXML += "<name>" & _
        XMLEncode(objCoffeeShop.coffeeShopName) & "</name>"
        strXML += "<address1>" & _
        XMLEncode(objCoffeeShop.coffeeShopAddress1) & "</address1>"
        strXML += "<address2>" & _
        XMLEncode(objCoffeeShop.coffeeShopAddress2) & "</address2>"
        strXML += "<city>" & _
        XMLEncode(objCoffeeShop.coffeeShopCity) & "</city>"
        strXML += "<state>" & _
        XMLEncode(objCoffeeShop.coffeeShopState) & "</state>"
        strXML += "<zip>" & _
        XMLEncode(objCoffeeShop.coffeeShopZip.ToString) & "</zip>"
        strXML += "<wifi>" & _
        XMLEncode(objCoffeeShop.coffeeShopWiFi.ToString) & "</wifi>"
            strXML += "<details>" & _
    XMLEncode(objCoffeeShop.coffeeShopDetails) & "</details>"
        strXML += "</coffeeshop>"
      Next
      strXML += "</coffeeshops>"
    End If
    Return strXML
  End Sub
```

The `ImportModule` method does just the opposite; it takes the XML file created by the `ExportModule` method and creates `CoffeeShopListingInfo` items. Then it uses the `EganEnterprises_AddCoffeeShopInfo` method to add them to the database, thus filling the module with transferred data.

```
Public Sub ImportModule(ByVal ModuleID As Integer, _
ByVal Content As String, ByVal Version As String, _
ByVal UserID As Integer) _
Implements DotNetNuke.Entities.Modules.IPortable.ImportModule

  Dim xmlCoffeeShop As XmlNode
  Dim xmlCoffeeShops As XmlNode = _
  GetContent(Content, "coffeeshops")

  For Each xmlCoffeeShop In xmlCoffeeShops
    Dim objCoffeeShop As New CoffeeShopListingInfo
    objCoffeeShop.moduleID = ModuleID
    objCoffeeShop.coffeeShopName = _
    xmlCoffeeShop.Item("name").InnerText
    objCoffeeShop.coffeeShopAddress1 = _
    xmlCoffeeShop.Item("address1").InnerText
```

```
        objCoffeeShop.coffeeShopAddress2 = _
        xmlCoffeeShop.Item("address2").InnerText
        objCoffeeShop.coffeeShopCity = _
        xmlCoffeeShop.Item("city").InnerText
        objCoffeeShop.coffeeShopState = _
        xmlCoffeeShop.Item("state").InnerText
        objCoffeeShop.coffeeShopZip = _
        xmlCoffeeShop.Item("zip").InnerText
        objCoffeeShop.coffeeShopWiFi = _
        xmlCoffeeShop.Item("wifi").InnerText
        objCoffeeShop.coffeeShopDetails = _
        xmlCoffeeShop.Item("details").InnerText
        EganEnterprises_AddCoffeeShopInfo(objCoffeeShop)
    Next
End Sub
```

Implementing ISearchable

With DotNetNuke 3.0 came the ability to search the portal for content. To allow your modules to be searched, you need to implement the ISearchable interface. This interface has only one method you need to implement: GetSearchItems.

This method uses a SearchItemCollection, which can be found in the DotNetNuke .Services.Search namespace, to hold a list of the items available in the search. In our implementation, we use the EganEnterprises_GetCoffeeShops method to fill an ArrayList with the coffee shops in our database. We then use the objects returned to the ArrayList to add to a SearchItemInfo object. The constructor for this object is overloaded and it holds items like Title, Descrption, Author, and SearchKey. What you place in these properties depends on your data. For our coffee shop items we will be using coffeeShopName, coffeeShopID, and coffeeShopCity to fill the object.

```
Public Function GetSearchItems _
(ByVal ModInfo As DotNetNuke.Entities.Modules.ModuleInfo) _
As DotNetNuke.Services.Search.SearchItemInfoCollection _
Implements DotNetNuke.Entities.Modules.ISearchable.GetSearchItems

    Dim SearchItemCollection As New SearchItemInfoCollection
    Dim CoffeeShops As ArrayList = _
    EganEnterprises_GetCoffeeShops(ModInfo.ModuleID)
    Dim objCoffeeShop As Object

    For Each objCoffeeShop In CoffeeShops
        Dim SearchItem As SearchItemInfo
        With CType(objCoffeeShop, CoffeeShopListingInfo)
            SearchItem = New SearchItemInfo _
            (ModInfo.ModuleTitle & " - " & .coffeeShopName, _
            .coffeeShopName, _
            Convert.ToInt32(10), _
            DateTime.Now, ModInfo.ModuleID, _
            .coffeeShopID.ToString, _
            .coffeeShopName & " - " & .coffeeShopCity)
            SearchItemCollection.Add(SearchItem)
        End With
    Next
    Return SearchItemCollection
End Function
```

Each time it loops through the arraylist it will add a search item to the SearchItemCollection. The core framework takes care of all the other things needed to implement this on your portal.

Since we only need to implement the interfaces for the CoffeeShopListingController class, the code for the CoffeeShopListingOptionsController class is much simpler.

```
Imports System
Imports System.Data
Imports DotNetNuke

Namespace EganEnterprises.CoffeeShopListing
    Public Class CoffeeShopListingOptionsController
        Public Function EganEnterprises_GetCoffeeShopModuleOptions( _
            ByVal ModuleId As Integer) _
            As ArrayList
              Return CBO.FillCollection(DataProvider.Instance(). _
              EganEnterprises_GetCoffeeShopModuleOptions(ModuleId), _
                GetType(CoffeeShopListingOptionsInfo))
        End Function
        Public Function EganEnterprises_UpdateCoffeeShopModuleOptions( _
            ByVal objShopListOptions As EganEnterprises. _
            CoffeeShopListing.CoffeeShopListingOptionsInfo) _
            As Integer
              Return CType(DataProvider.Instance(). _
              EganEnterprises_UpdateCoffeeShopModuleOptions( _
              objShopListOptions.moduleID, _
                objShopListOptions.AuthorizedRoles), _
                Integer)
        End Function
        Public Function EganEnterprises_AddCoffeeShopModuleOptions( _
            ByVal objShopListOptions As EganEnterprises. _
            CoffeeShopListing.CoffeeShopListingOptionsInfo) _
            As Integer
              Return CType(DataProvider.Instance(). _
              EganEnterprises_AddCoffeeShopModuleOptions( _
              objShopListOptions.moduleID, _
              objShopListOptions.AuthorizedRoles), Integer)
        End Function
    End Class
End Namespace
```

The Presentation Layer

We can now get back to the View, Edit, and Settings controls we created in our private assembly project. Now we can write code to interact with the data store.

ShopList.aspx

Our View control will consist of two panels, of which only one will be shown at any given moment. The first panel will be used to search and view coffee shops by zip code.

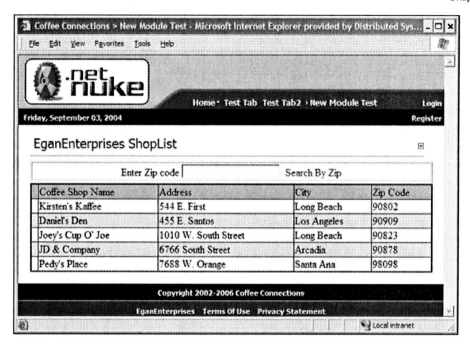

The second panel will allow users to add coffee shops to the database.

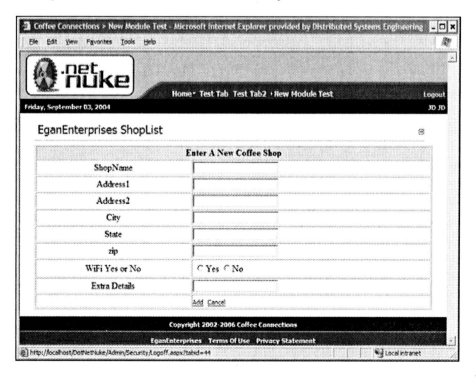

Since leaving fields blank when submitting this form could cause various runtime errors, in a real-world application it would be necessary to add validation to all user input. You could use ASP.NET validation controls to accomplish this task.

```
<%@ Control language="vb" AutoEventWireup="false"
Inherits="EganEnterprises.CoffeeShopListing.ShopList"
CodeBehind="ShopList.ascx.vb"%>
<asp:Panel id="pnlGrid" runat="server">
    <TABLE id="Table1" cellSpacing="1" cellPadding="1" width="100%"
     border="1">
      <TR>
        <TD>
            <P align="center">Enter Zip code
              <asp:TextBox id="txtZipSearch" runat="server">
              </asp:TextBox> 
              <asp:LinkButton id="lbSearch" runat="server">Search
               By Zip</asp:LinkButton></P>
        </TD>
      </TR>
      <TR>
        <TD>
            <P align="center">
              <asp:linkbutton id="lbAddNewShop" runat="server">
              Add New Shop</asp:linkbutton></P>
        </TD>
      </TR>
    </TABLE>

    <asp:datagrid id="dgShopLists" runat="server" Width="100%"
    BorderWidth="2px" BorderColor="Blue" AutoGenerateColumns="False">
        <AlternatingItemStyle BackColor="Lavender">
        </AlternatingItemStyle>
        <HeaderStyle BackColor="Silver"></HeaderStyle>
        <Columns>
            <asp:TemplateColumn>
                <ItemTemplate>
                    <asp:HyperLink id=hlcoffeeShopID runat="server"
Visible="<%# IsEditable %>" NavigateUrl='<%#
EditURL("coffeeShopID",DataBinder.Eval(Container.DataItem,"coffeeShopID
")) %>' ImageUrl="~/images/edit.gif">
                    </asp:HyperLink>
                </ItemTemplate>
            </asp:TemplateColumn>

            <asp:BoundColumn DataField="coffeeShopName" ReadOnly="True"
              HeaderText="Coffee Shop Name"></asp:BoundColumn>
            <asp:BoundColumn DataField="coffeeShopAddress1"
              ReadOnly="True" HeaderText="Address"></asp:BoundColumn>
            <asp:BoundColumn DataField="coffeeShopCity" ReadOnly="True"
              HeaderText="City"></asp:BoundColumn>
            <asp:BoundColumn DataField="coffeeShopZip" ReadOnly="True"
              HeaderText="Zip Code"></asp:BoundColumn>
        </Columns>
    </asp:datagrid>
</asp:Panel>
```

```
<asp:Panel id="pnlAdd" runat="server">
    <TABLE id="Table2" cellSpacing="1" cellPadding="1"
      width="100%" border="1">
        <TR>
            <TD align="center" bgColor="lavender" colSpan="2">
                <STRONG><FONT color="#000000">Enter A New Coffee Shop
                </FONT></STRONG></TD>
        </TR>
        <TR>
            <TD>
                <P align="center">ShopName</P>
            </TD>
            <TD>
                <asp:textbox id="txtcoffeeShopName" runat="server">
                </asp:textbox></TD>
        </TR>
        <TR>
            <TD>
                <P align="center">Address1</P>
            </TD>
            <TD>
                <asp:textbox id="txtCoffeeShopAddress1" runat="server">
                </asp:textbox></TD>
        </TR>
        <TR>
            <TD>
                <P align="center">Address2</P>
            </TD>
            <TD>
                <asp:textbox id="txtCoffeeShopAddress2" runat="server">
                </asp:textbox></TD>
        </TR>
        <TR>
            <TD>
                <P align="center">City</P>
            </TD>
            <TD>
                <asp:textbox id="txtcoffeeShopCity" runat="server">
                </asp:textbox></TD>
        </TR>
        <TR>
            <TD>
                <P align="center">State</P>
            </TD>
            <TD>
                <asp:textbox id="txtcoffeeShopState" runat="server">
                </asp:textbox></TD>
        </TR>
        <TR>
            <TD>
                <P align="center">zip</P>
            </TD>
            <TD>
                <asp:textbox id="txtcoffeeShopZip" runat="server">
                </asp:textbox></TD>
        </TR>
        <TR>
            <TD height="31">
```

```
                <P align="center">WiFi Yes or No</P>
            </TD>
            <TD height="31">
                <asp:RadioButtonList id="rblWiFi" runat="server"
                            RepeatDirection="Horizontal">
                    <asp:ListItem Value="1">Yes</asp:ListItem>
                    <asp:ListItem Value="0">No</asp:ListItem>
                </asp:RadioButtonList></TD>
        </TR>
        <TR>
            <TD>
                <P align="center">Extra Details</P>
            </TD>
            <TD>
                <asp:TextBox id="txtcoffeeShopDetails" runat="server">
                </asp:TextBox></TD>
        </TR>
        <TR>
            <TD>
                <P align="center"> </P>
            </TD>
            <TD>
                <P>
                    <asp:LinkButton id="cmdAdd" runat="server"
                        CssClass="CommandButton" BorderStyle="none"
                        Text="Update">Add</asp:LinkButton> 
                    <asp:LinkButton id="cmdCancel" runat="server"
                        CssClass="CommandButton" BorderStyle="none"
                        Text="Cancel" CausesValidation="False">
                    </asp:LinkButton> 
                </P>
            </TD>
        </TR>
    </TABLE>
</asp:Panel>
```

We are going to start our look into the code-behind file by looking at the code that is fired when the search button is clicked. This event, of course, expects a zip code to be placed in the textbox before it is executed.

The first line instantiates a CoffeeShopListingController object. This is the class we created in the last section that handles the interface to our data provider. Next we create an ArrayList to hold the data that is returned when we call the EganEnterprises_GetC offeeShopsByZip function. This function takes only ModuleID and Zipcode as parameters. You notice that we just typed in ModuleID without ever declaring the variable. ModuleID is a variable that we inherit from the PortalModuleControl class. It will hold the unique ModuleID for this module. This will, of course fill our ArrayList, which we then bind to our datagrid.

```
Private Sub lbSearch_click( _
    ByVal sender As System.Object, _
    ByVal e As System.EventArgs)

    Dim objCoffeeShops As New CoffeeShopListingController
    Dim myList As ArrayList
```

```
    myList = _
    objCoffeeShops.EganEnterprises_GetCoffeeShopsByZip _
    (ModuleId, txtZipSearch.Text)
    Me.dgShopLists.DataSource = myList
    Me.dgShopLists.DataBind()

End Sub
```

The next method we will look at is the AddNewShop link button's Click event-handler. As we will see when we look at the Page_Load event, this button is only available to certain security roles. This button click simply redirects the page back to itself and adds a querystring to the end. Then NavigateURL function is used to work in conjunction with the URL rewriting.

```
Private Sub lbAddNewShop_Click( _
    ByVal sender As System.Object, _
    ByVal e As System.EventArgs)

    Response.Redirect(NavigateURL(TabId, "", "Add=YES"), True)

End Sub
```

Now we will look at the Page_Load method. The first thing the event looks for is whether or not the Add querystring exists. Based on this, the control will show either the panel with the datagrid, or the panel with the form to allow users to add coffee shops to the list. If we are showing the grid, we will fill it using the same technique as we used in the search method.

```
Private Sub Page_Load(ByVal sender As System.Object, _
ByVal e As System.EventArgs) Handles MyBase.Load
    'If we are not adding show the grid
    If (Request.Params("Add") Is Nothing) Then
        'Grid panel is visible
        pnlAdd.Visible = False
        pnlGrid.Visible = True

        'Then fill the grid
        If Not Page.IsPostBack Then
            Dim objCoffeeShops As New CoffeeShopListingController
            Dim myList As ArrayList

            myList = objCoffeeShops.EganEnterprises_GetCoffeeShops _
            (ModuleId)
            Me.dgShopLists.DataSource = myList
            Me.dgShopLists.DataBind()

        End If
```

We will now be looking at the security roles set up for the portal. We wanted to be able to tie into security roles to allow only certain users the ability to add a new coffee shop. We did not want to use the module settings because that would give the role the ability to modify more of the module than we want. We will be saving the security roles that can add a coffee shop into the options table we created earlier. This will be done on the ShopListOptions control. In this section we will be reading that table.

We use the `CoffeeShopListingOptionsController` class we created to put roles that are authorized to add a coffee shop into a delimited string.

```
'Check roles to see if the user can add items to the listing
'String of roles for shoplist
Dim objShopRoles As New CoffeeShopListingOptionsController
Dim objShopRole As CoffeeShopListingOptionsInfo
Dim arrShopRoles As ArrayList = _
objShopRoles.EganEnterprises_GetCoffeeShopModuleOptions _
(ModuleId)

'Put roles into a string
Dim shopRoles As String = ""
For Each objShopRole In arrShopRoles
    shopRoles = objShopRole.AuthorizedRoles.ToString
Next
```

We then use the portal settings and the role controller to find the security roles the user possesses. These are placed in an array and compared against the roles allowed to add a coffee shop.

The `RoleController` class works similarly to the controller classes we created for our module.

```
Dim bAuth = False
If UserInfo.UserID <> -1 Then
    If UserInfo.IsSuperUser = True Then
        bAuth = True
    Else

        Dim objRoles As New RoleController
        Dim Roles As String() = objRoles.GetPortalRolesByUser _
        (UserInfo.UserID, PortalSettings.PortalId)
        Dim maxRows As Integer = UBound(Roles)

        Dim i As Integer
        For i = 0 To maxRows
            Dim objRoleInfo As RoleInfo
            objRoleInfo = objRoles.GetRoleByName(PortalId, Roles(i))

            If shopRoles.IndexOf(objRoleInfo.RoleID & ";") <> -1 Then
                bAuth = True
                Exit For
            End If
        Next
    End If
End If
```

If the user is authorized, the Add New Shop link button is visible.

```
If bAuth Then
    lbAddNewShop.Visible = True
Else
    lbAddNewShop.Visible = False
End If
```

If the Add querystring exists then we want to show the Add panel and hide the grid panel.

```
    Else ' If we are adding...

        'Add panel is visible
        pnlAdd.Visible = True
        pnlGrid.Visible = False
    End If
End Sub
```

The next section we will look at is the Add button click event. Remember that this is only visible if the user has the authority to add a coffee shop. This is what adds the information typed into the add coffee shop form.

The first thing we do is create an instance of our CoffeeShopListingInfo class and fill it with the information filled out in the textboxes:

```
Private Sub cmdAdd_Click( _
    ByVal sender As System.Object, _
    ByVal e As System.EventArgs)

    Dim objShopList As New CoffeeShopListingInfo
    With objShopList
        .moduleID = ModuleId
        .coffeeShopID = coffeeShopID
        .coffeeShopName = txtcoffeeShopName.Text
        .coffeeShopAddress1 = txtCoffeeShopAddress1.Text
        .coffeeShopAddress2 = txtCoffeeShopAddress2.Text
        .coffeeShopCity = txtcoffeeShopCity.Text
        .coffeeShopState = txtcoffeeShopState.Text
        .coffeeShopZip = txtcoffeeShopZip.Text
        .coffeeShopDetails = txtcoffeeShopDetails.Text
        .coffeeShopWiFi = rblWiFi.SelectedValue
    End With
```

We then create an instance of our controller class and pass the objShopList to the EganEnterprises_AddCoffeeShopInfo function. When complete we are redirected back to the grid view of the control.

```
    Dim objShopLists As New CoffeeShopListingController

    coffeeShopID = _
    objShopLists.EganEnterprises_AddCoffeeShopInfo(objShopList)

    ' Redirect back to the portal
        Response.Redirect(NavigateURL())
End Sub
```

We then finish up by adding redirect code to the Cancel button-click event.

```
Private Sub cmdCancel_Click( _
    ByVal sender As System.Object, _
    ByVal e As System.EventArgs)
    ' Redirect back to the portal
    Response.Redirect(NavigateURL())
End Sub
```

EditShopList.ascx

The EditShopList control is designed similarly to the Add Coffee Shops form on the View control. The only difference is that administrators of the module are able to not only add new shops but also modify and delete them. The first thing we need to do is to build the form that the administrators will be working with.

Since leaving fields blank when submitting this form could cause various runtime errors, it would be necessary in a real-world application to add validation to all user input. You could use ASP.NET validation controls to accomplish this task.

```
<%@ Control language="vb" AutoEventWireup="false"
Inherits="EganEnterprises.CoffeeShopListing.EditShopList"
CodeBehind="EditShopList.ascx.vb"%>
<TABLE id="Table1" cellSpacing="1" cellPadding="1" width="100%"
border="1">
    <TR>
        <TD>
            <P align="center">ShopName</P>
        </TD>
        <TD><asp:textbox id="txtcoffeeShopName" runat="server">
            </asp:textbox></TD>
    </TR>
    <TR>
        <TD>
            <P align="center">Address1</P>
        </TD>
        <TD><asp:textbox id="txtCoffeeShopAddress1" runat="server">
            </asp:textbox></TD>
    </TR>
```

```
<TR>
    <TD>
        <P align="center">Address2</P>
    </TD>
    <TD><asp:textbox id="txtCoffeeShopAddress2" runat="server">
        </asp:textbox></TD>
</TR>
<TR>
    <TD>
        <P align="center">City</P>
    </TD>
    <TD><asp:textbox id="txtcoffeeShopCity" runat="server">
        </asp:textbox></TD>
</TR>
<TR>
    <TD>
        <P align="center">State</P>
    </TD>
    <TD><asp:textbox id="txtcoffeeShopState" runat="server">
        </asp:textbox></TD>
</TR>
<TR>
    <TD>
        <P align="center">zip</P>
    </TD>
    <TD><asp:textbox id="txtcoffeeShopZip" runat="server">
        </asp:textbox></TD>
</TR>
<TR>
    <TD height="31">
        <P align="center">WiFi Yes or No</P>
    </TD>
    <TD height="31">
        <asp:RadioButtonList id="rblWiFi" runat="server"
                        RepeatDirection="Horizontal">
            <asp:ListItem Value="1">Yes</asp:ListItem>
            <asp:ListItem Value="0">No</asp:ListItem>
        </asp:RadioButtonList></TD>
</TR>
<TR>
    <TD>
        <P align="center">Extra Details</P>
    </TD>
    <TD>
        <asp:TextBox id="txtcoffeeShopDetails" runat="server">
        </asp:TextBox></TD>
</TR>
<TR>
    <TD>
        <P align="center"> </P>
    </TD>
    <TD>
        <P>
            <asp:LinkButton id="cmdUpdate" runat="server"
                Text="Update" BorderStyle="none"
                CssClass="CommandButton"></asp:LinkButton> 
```

```
                    <asp:LinkButton id="cmdCancel" runat="server"
                        Text="Cancel" BorderStyle="none"
                        CssClass="CommandButton"
                        CausesValidation="False"></asp:LinkButton> 
                    <asp:LinkButton id="cmdDelete" runat="server"
                        Text="Delete" BorderStyle="none"
                        CssClass="CommandButton"
                        CausesValidation="False"></asp:LinkButton>
                </P>
            </TD>
        </TR>
</TABLE>
```

We are going to start our look into the code-behind file by seeing the code executed when the `Page_Load` event is fired. The first thing we do is check to see if there is a `coffeeShopID` in the querystring. This will be used to determine whether this is a update or a new record.

```
Imports DotNetNuke

Namespace EganEnterprises.CoffeeShopListing

    Public MustInherit Class EditShopList
        Inherits Entities.Modules.PortalModuleBase
        Dim coffeeShopID As Integer = -1

Private Sub Page_Load(ByVal sender As System.Object, _
        ByVal e As System.EventArgs) Handles MyBase.Load
            ' get parameter
            If Not (Request.Params("coffeeShopID") Is Nothing) Then
                coffeeShopID = _
                Integer.Parse(Request.Params("coffeeShopID"))
            Else
                coffeeShopID = Null.NullInteger
            End If
```

Then, if this is not a post back to the page, we add some JavaScript to the `cmdDelete` button that will make them confirm their action before a deletion takes place. Although this code is shown on the server-side, this action will be used client-side.

```
If Page.IsPostBack = False Then

    cmdDelete.Attributes.Add("onClick", _
        "javascript:return confirm('Are You Sure You Wish To Delete This
Item ?');")
```

Next, we check the `coffeeShopID` value to determine whether it is an update or a new record. If `coffeeShopID` is `Not Null` then it is an existing record.

```
    If Not DotNetNuke.Common.Utilities.Null.IsNull(coffeeShopID) Then
```

Since the record exists, we need to create a `CoffeeShopListingController` and use it to obtain the information from the database.

This information is loaded into a `CoffeeShopListingInfo` object and used to populate the textboxes located on the form.

```
If Not objCoffeeShop Is Nothing Then

    txtcoffeeShopName.Text = objCoffeeShop.coffeeShopName
    txtCoffeeShopAddress1.Text = objCoffeeShop.coffeeShopAddress1
    txtCoffeeShopAddress2.Text = objCoffeeShop.coffeeShopAddress2
    txtcoffeeShopCity.Text = objCoffeeShop.coffeeShopCity
    txtcoffeeShopState.Text = objCoffeeShop.coffeeShopState
    txtcoffeeShopZip.Text = objCoffeeShop.coffeeShopZip
    If objCoffeeShop.coffeeShopWiFi Then
        rblWiFi.Items(0).Selected = True
    Else
        rblWiFi.Items(1).Selected = True
    End If
    txtcoffeeShopDetails.Text = objCoffeeShop.coffeeShopDetails

Else ' If object has no data we want to go back
    Response.Redirect(NavigateURL())
End If
```

If this is a new record, then all we need to do is remove the **Delete** link from the form.

```
Else
    ' This is new item
    cmdDelete.Visible = False
End If
```

Once we have determined that it is a new record, we want to look at the code that is called when the **Update** button is clicked. Again, we will make use of both the `CoffeeShopListingInfo` object and the `CoffeeShopListingController` object. We fill the first one with the data found in the form, and use the last one to call the update or insert code.

```
Private Sub cmdUpdate_Click( _
    ByVal sender As System.Object, _
    ByVal e As System.EventArgs)
    Try
        Dim objShopList As New CoffeeShopListingInfo

        objShopList.moduleID = ModuleId
        objShopList.coffeeShopID = coffeeShopID
        objShopList.coffeeShopName = txtcoffeeShopName.Text
        objShopList.coffeeShopAddress1 = txtCoffeeShopAddress1.Text
        objShopList.coffeeShopAddress2 = txtCoffeeShopAddress2.Text
        objShopList.coffeeShopCity = txtcoffeeShopCity.Text
        objShopList.coffeeShopState = txtcoffeeShopState.Text
        objShopList.coffeeShopZip = txtcoffeeShopZip.Text
        objShopList.coffeeShopDetails = txtcoffeeShopDetails.Text
        objShopList.coffeeShopWiFi = rblWiFi.SelectedValue
```

```
        Dim objShopLists As New CoffeeShopListingController

        If Null.IsNull(coffeeShopID) Then
            coffeeShopID = _
    objShopLists.EganEnterprises_AddCoffeeShopInfo(objShopList)
        Else
    objShopLists.EganEnterprises_UpdateCoffeeShopInfo(objShopList)
        End If

        ' Redirect back to the portal
        Response.Redirect(NavigateURL())
    Catch ex As Exception
        ProcessModuleLoadException(Me, ex)
    End Try
End Sub
```

The final section that we will look at is called when the Delete button is clicked. This
code uses the coffeeShopID and calls the EganEnterprises_DeleteCoffeeShop stored
procedure.

```
Private Sub cmdDelete_Click( _
    ByVal sender As System.Object, _
    ByVal e As System.EventArgs)
    If Not Null.IsNull(coffeeShopID) Then
        Dim objShopLists As New CoffeeShopListingController
        objShopLists.EganEnterprises_DeleteCoffeeShop(coffeeShopID)
    End If

    ' Redirect back to the portal
    Response.Redirect(NavigateURL())
End Sub
```

This completes our Edit control and leaves us with our Settings control.

Settings.ascx

The Settings control allows you to set additional properties for your module that will
appear in the module settings page. We are currently only saving one property but it is a
unique one. We want to be able to tie into the built-in security roles in DotNetNuke and
use them to decide what users can add items with out giving them access to the context
menu. To accomplish this we use the DualList control that is found in the DotNetNuke
controls folder.

> To be able to work with this control in design mode, you will first need to change
> the class to inherit from PortalModuleBase instead of ModuleSettingsBase.
> Make sure you changes this back when you are done or it will not work properly.

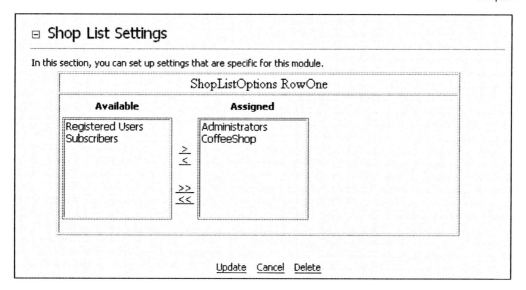

We will be adding a dual list control to our HTML textbox. Here is the code for the Settings control:

```
<%@ Register TagPrefix="Portal" TagName="DualList"
Src="~/controls/DualListControl.ascx" %>
<%@ Control language="vb" AutoEventWireup="false"
     Inherits="EganEnterprises.CoffeeShopListing.Settings"
     CodeBehind="Settings.ascx.vb"%>
<TABLE id="Table1" cellSpacing="1" cellPadding="1" width="100%"
     border="1">
   <TR>
      <TD>
         <P align="center">ShopListOptions RowOne</P>
      </TD>
   </TR>
   <TR>
      <TD><portal:duallist id="ctlAuthRoles" runat="server"
            ListBoxWidth="130" ListBoxHeight="130"
            DataValueField="Value" DataTextField="Text" /></TD>
   </TR>
</TABLE>
<asp:LinkButton id="lbUpdate" runat="server">Update</asp:LinkButton>
```

In order for this control to integrate into the module settings page, we need to override two methods in our base class: LoadSettings and UpdateSettings. LoadSettings is called when the module settings page is accessed, and UpdateSettings is called when the update button is clicked on the module settings page.

We will be using the options section of the module settings page to hold security settings for this module that are outside the normal module security settings. We want to give users the ability to add a coffee shop without giving them access to the context menu and we also want to read and store the Assigned Roles in our EganEnterprises_ShopListOptions table.

We will start with the LoadSettings method by declaring ArrayList objects to hold both our available roles and our authorized roles.

```
' declare roles
Dim arrAvailableAuthRoles As New ArrayList
Dim arrAssignedAuthRoles As New ArrayList
```

The available roles are retrieved from the portal and are tied into the portal security.

```
' Get list of possible roles
Dim objRoles As New RoleController
Dim objRole As RoleInfo
Dim arrRoles As ArrayList = _
objRoles.GetPortalRoles(PortalId)
```

The authorized roles are obtained from our EganEnterprises_ShopListOptions table.

```
'String of roles for shoplist
Dim objShopRoles As New CoffeeShopListingOptionsController
Dim objShopRole As CoffeeShopListingOptionsInfo
Dim arrShopRoles As ArrayList = _
objShopRoles.EganEnterprises_GetCoffeeShopModuleOptions _
(ModuleId)
```

This passes back a single semicolon-delimited string corresponding to this module only.

```
'Put roles into a string
Dim shopRoles As String = ""

For Each objShopRole In arrShopRoles
    'If it makes it here then we will be updating
    shopRoles = objShopRole.AuthorizedRoles.ToString
Next
```

We then loop through all roles available in the portal and place them in the correct list.

```
'Now loop through all available roles in portal
For Each objRole In arrRoles
    Dim objListItem As New ListItem

    objListItem.Value = objRole.RoleID.ToString
    objListItem.Text = objRole.RoleName

    'If it matches a role in the ShopRoles string put
    'it in the assigned box
    If shopRoles.IndexOf(objRole.RoleID & ";") _
    <> -1 Or objRole.RoleID = _
    PortalSettings.AdministratorRoleId Then
        arrAssignedAuthRoles.Add(objListItem)
```

```
      Else ' put it in the available box
          arrAvailableAuthRoles.Add(objListItem)

      End If
Next

' assign to duallist controls
ctlAuthRoles.Available = arrAvailableAuthRoles
ctlAuthRoles.Assigned = arrAssignedAuthRoles
```

The dual lists' built-in functionality allows you to move roles between the lists to give or remove the rights of your users.

The UpdateSettings method will save the authorized list to our table. We build a semicolon-delimited list from the listbox and use our CoffeeShopListingOptionsInfo and CoffeeShopListingOptionsController classes to add it to the table.

```
Dim objShopRoles As New CoffeeShopListingOptionsController
Dim objShopRole As New CoffeeShopListingOptionsInfo
Dim item As ListItem
Dim strAuthorizedRoles As String = ""
For Each item In ctlAuthRoles.Assigned
    strAuthorizedRoles += item.Value & ";"
Next item

objShopRole.AuthorizedRoles = strAuthorizedRoles
objShopRole.moduleID = ModuleId
Dim intExists As Integer
intExists = objShopRoles. _
EganEnterprises_UpdateCoffeeShopModuleOptions(objShopRole)
If intExists = 0 Then 'New record
    objShopRoles.EganEnterprises_AddCoffeeShopModuleOptions _
    (objShopRole)
End If
```

This completes all three of the controls needed for our module. All that's left for us to do is to test our work.

Testing Your Module

Throughout the development process you should use all of Visual Studio's debugging capabilities to make sure that your code is working correctly. Since we set up our module as a private assembly within the DotNetNuke solution, you will be able to set breakpoints and view your code in the various watch windows. Make sure that your project is set up to allow debugging.

Your project's Properties configuration should be set to Active(Debug) and your ASP.NET debugger should be enabled. You will also need to make sure that debug is set to true in your web.config file. When you have finished debugging your module, you are ready to package it and get it ready for distribution.

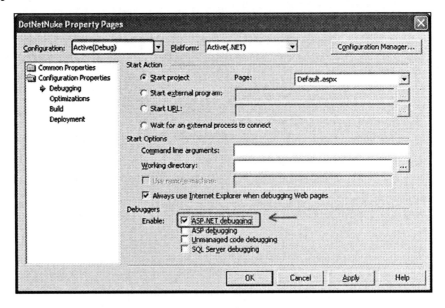

Creating Your Installation Scripts

The first step in preparing your module for distribution is to create the installation scripts needed to create the tables and procedures required by your module. There should be two files: an installation script and an uninstallation script. You should name your scripts in the following manner.

Type of Script	Description	Example

Uninstallation Script	Concatenate the word uninstall with the type of provider the script represents.	`Uninstall.AccessDataProvider`
		
		`Uninstall.SqlDataProvider`

Installation Script	Concatenate the version number of your module with the type of provider the script represents.	`01.00.00.SqlDataProvider`
		
		`01.00.00.AccessDataProvider`

These scripts are similar to the code run for creating your tables in the beginning of this chapter. The scripts for your PA installation should use the databaseOwner and objectQualifier variables as well as including code to check if the database objects you are creating already exist in the database. This will help to ensure that uploading your module will not overwrite previous data. The full scripts can be found in the code download for this chapter.

The version number for your scripts is very important. If a version of the module is already installed on your portal, the framework checks the version number on the script file to determine whether to run the script. If the number on the file matches the number in the database then the script will not be run. In this way, you can have one package work as an installation and upgrade package.

Packaging Your Module for Distribution

To get our module package ready for the masses, we will first need to create a manifest for our module. DotNetNuke uses a XML-based file with a .dnn extension to accomplish this. Since this is an XML file, it is important to note that it needs to be well formed. This means that all opening tags <mytag> need to have associated closing tags </mytag>.

To begin setting up our manifest, right-click on the Installation folder we created earlier and select Add | Add New Item. Select XML File from the list and name the file CoffeeShopListing.dnn. The .dnn extension is used by DotNetNuke to designate this file as a module installation file. Below you will see the file itself.

The outside tags <dotnetnuke> and </dotnetnuke> are used to tell the uploader the version and type of item that is being uploaded. The <folder> element then starts to map out where it is going to place all the files for our module.

```
<?xml version="1.0" encoding="utf-8" ?>
<dotnetnuke version="3.0" type="Module">
  <folders>
    <folder>
```

The <name> element is the name of the folder that will be created for your module. This folder will be created under the DotNetNuke\DesktopModules folder. It is important that you follow the CompanyName.ModuleName format when creating your modules to avoid naming collisions with other module developers. The <version> element then determines the version of your module that is being uploaded. This is followed by the <businesscontrollerclass> element. If you implement any of the interfaces we discussed earlier in your module, you will need this element to allow the import, export, and search to work. This element holds the full class name of the module (including the namespace), followed by your module's assembly name.

Since our controller class is called CoffeeShopListingController, that's what we will use inside this node.

```
<name>EganEnterprises.CoffeeShopListing</name>
<description>Listing of Coffee Shops</description>
<version>01.00.00</version>
<businesscontrollerclass>
EganEnterprises.CoffeeShopListing.CoffeeShopListingController,EganEnter
prises.CoffeeShopListing</businesscontrollerclass>
```

We then start describing the controls themselves. We follow the same process when we created controls manually when building our private assembly. The <key> is how your context menu is connected to your control. This is left out for the view control. The <title> is what will show up in the module definition form. The <src> is the physical file name for the control, and the <type> determines whether this is a view control or an edit control. Both our Edit and Options controls use this element.

```
<modules>
    <module>
    <friendlyname>Coffee Shop Listing</friendlyname>
        <controls>
        <control>
            <title>View Coffee Shops</title>
            <src>ShopList.ascx</src>
            <type>View</type>
        </control>
        <control>
            <key>Edit</key>
            <title>Edit CoffeeShop Listing</title>
            <src>EditShopList.ascx</src>
            <type>Edit</type>
        </control>
        <control>
            <key>Settings</key>
            <title>Shop List Settings</title>
            <src>Settings.ascx</src>
            <type>Edit</type>
        </control>
        </controls>
        </module>
</modules>
```

After creating the <module> tags, we need to declare the physical files for our module. Be sure to include the controls and DLLs, as well as the installation and uninstall scripts for your module.

```
<files>
    <file>
    <name>ShopList.ascx</name>
    </file>
    <file>
    <name>EditShopList.ascx</name>
    </file>
    <file>
    <name>Settings.ascx</name>
    </file>
    <file>
    <name>01.00.00.SqlDataProvider</name>
    </file>
    <file>
    <name>Uninstall.SqlDataProvider</name>
    </file>
    <file>
    <name>EganEnterprises.CoffeeShopListing.dll</name>
    </file>
```

```
    <file>
        <name>EganEnterprises.CoffeeShopListing
.SqlDataProvider.dll</name>
        </file>
    </files>
    </folder>
</folders>
</dotnetnuke>
```

The Install ZIP file

Now it is time to package all of the files into a ZIP file to enable them to be uploaded and installed on your portal. Do not just drag the folder containing these files into a ZIP file. Make sure that they all in the main ZIP folder. The DNN framework will take care of placing the files in the correct folders.

The files you need to place in your ZIP file are:

- EganEnterprises.CoffeeShopListing.dll
- EganEnterprises.CoffeeShopListing.SqlDataProvider.dll
- ShopList.ascx
- EditShopList.ascx
- Settings.ascx
- CoffeeShopListing.dnn
- 01.00.00.SqlDataProvider
- uninstall.SqlDataProvider

Testing Your Installation

This is the final step. At this stage, all of your coding should work fine because you have tested it in your Visual Studio .NET environment. Now you need to test if uploading your module will work for you. You have a couple of options. Since you have already set up this module manually in your visual studio environment you would have to remove the private assembly and delete the tables in your database to fully test whether your upload file works. I don't like this method. I like my PA to stay just the way it is to make it easy to do further development. What I do for testing is to set up a separate instance of DotNetNuke on my development computer that is only used for testing uploads of modules. You can decide what works best for you.

Uploading the module is simple. Sign in as Host and navigate to the module definitions item on the host menu. Hover the cursor over the context menu and select Upload New Module. Browse to your ZIP file and add it to the file download box. Click on Upload New File to load your module.

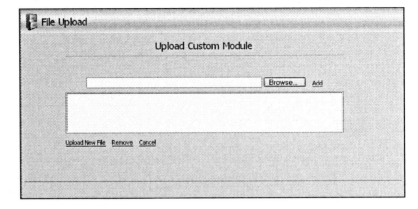

This will create a file-upload log, which will only be displayed on the screen below the upload box.

Search the log for any errors that may have occurred during the upload process and fix the errors. Since we have done our testing in Visual Studio, any errors encountered here should be related to the ZIP or DNN file.

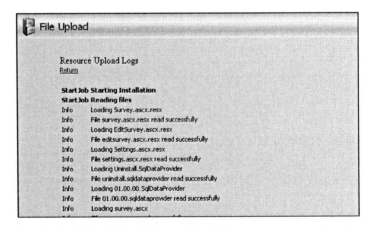

Add your module to a tab and put it through its paces. Make sure to try out all the features. It is a good idea to have others try to break it. You will be surprised at the things that users will do with your module. When all features have been tested, you are ready to distribute it to the DotNetNuke world.

Summary

We have covered a lot of code in this chapter. Starting from creating a private assembly and setting up our project, to creating the controls, business logic layer, and the data access layer. We then saw how to package the module so it can be shared.

Since this code was very extensive, we broke it into sections and advised you to build your project at regular intervals. Doing this should give the ability to solve any issues you come across while building your module. We then took things a bit further and showed you how to use a few extra items like the settings page, the dual-list box, and the optional interfaces. This should give you a sound understanding of how all the different parts work together.

It is important to note that once you are familiar with how all of the different parts work together, there are a few tools available that can help to automate the processes of building your modules. Visual Studio DNN Project Templates can be found at DNNJungle (`http://dnnjungle.vmasanas.net/Default.aspx?PageContentID=5&tabid=32`) and CodeSmith templates to help you design you data architecture can be found at Smcculloch.Net (`http://www.smcculloch.net/`). These two tools can help speed up you module development tremendously. As with any code wizard, if you don't understand the underlying code then you will spend more time trying to figure out what the wizard created and will lose any advantage gained. Hopefully this chapter has given you a rich foundation on which to build your knowledge.

8

Creating DotNetNuke Skins

One of the major drawbacks to the previous versions of DotNetNuke was that even though you could add different modules, colors, and icons, all of the sites still had that "DNN Feel". Well, no more. With the release of DotNetNuke 2.0 came one of the most exciting advancements in the development of DotNetNuke, skinning. Simply put, a "skin" is the outer shell of an application. It is what the users see when they browse to your portal. With the ability to skin a DotNetNuke portal, what your site looks like is entirely up to you. In this chapter, we will cover:

- A general overview of the skinning architecture
- How to create your own skin using an HTML Editor
- How to package your skin files
- How to upload your skin files
- Changing skins

What Are Skins?

In general terms, a skin is the outward appearance of your portal. The colors, images, and layout of your modules all make up the outer skin of your portal. In previous chapters we have talked extensively about the core functionality of DotNetNuke, the detailed explanation of the nuts and bolts of how the portal works. Visitors to your portal will never see the inner workings of your portal; they will only see how it is presented on a web page.

I have heard many analogies used to try to explain skinning; from a sandwich (the meat is the core and the bread is the skin) to a car (the engine is the core and the body is the skin) to Mr. Potato Head (the potato is the core and the items you place on compose the skin). While Mr. Potato Head is probably the best analogy for its sheer comical value, I believe the best analogy is that of a person. Think of a normal person who works in an office environment. When they go to work they dress in a suit and tie and their presentation is very pressed and professional.

On the weekend, this same person can throw on sweat pants and a baseball cap and present a completely different appearance. The person inside has not changed—what they know or who they are—only the outward appearance has. Skins work in a similar way for your portal. They separate the "engine" of your portal from its outward appearance.

As we have discovered from previous chapters, DotNetNuke uses a single ASPX page (`Default.aspx`) for rendering all of its content. This simplifies the act of skinning the portal because you only need to worry about skinning one page. In addition, each module that you place on the page can itself be skinned. These types of skins are called **container skins**. While page skins take care of the headers, footers, menus, panes, and backgrounds, the container skins cover each individual module.

So now we know what "skinning" means. But what makes up a DotNetNuke skin? What are the physical parts we need to create to put this all together?

There are two different ways to create a skin for your DotNetNuke portal. You can use an HTML editor to create an HTML page that contains the **images**, **colors**, and **tokens** (which we will discuss later) that will make up your skin. Since we have been working with Visual Studio for most of this book, we will use it to create our skin as well. Using this method, we create a skin as a `.aspx` page combined with the images, colors, and controls needed for your site.

What Are Containers?

Skins can be applied at host, portal, page, or module levels. When specified at the module level, they are referred to as container skins or **containers**. Containers allow you to separately customize the look and feel of the modules that you place on your site.

Below is an example of *one* module with *two* different container skins applied to it.

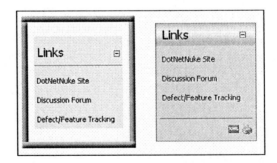

Container skins are usually created along with a **portal skin** so as to give a site a consistent look.

Uploading Skins and Containers

There are many free skins available for you to use on your DotNetNuke portal. The main DotNetNuke site held a skinning contest and freely distributes the contest winners (`http://www.dotnetnuke.com/Default.aspx?tabid=648`); you must be registered and signed in to both view and download the skins. It is also important to read any copyright notices that may accompany the skins.

There are also great DotNetNuke sites dedicated to skinning. Nina's Skinning Magic (`http://www.skinningmagic.com/`) and DNNSkins (`http://www.dnnskins.com/`) are two of the many sites that offer skins that are free for you to download. Both of these sites along with Snowcovered (`http://www.Snowcovered.com`) also provide skins that can be purchased. Often, the download is a single ZIP file containing separate ZIP files for container skins and portal skins. In most cases it may be necessary to extract the individual ZIP files before uploading them to your site. In addition, you will not always get container skins with the portal skins you receive. In this instance you will be expected to use the default containers that come with DotNetNuke.

Uploading as a Host

The act of uploading a new skin or container file is simple but it may depend on the ability of the role that you are signed on as. The default implementation of DotNetNuke allows only the Host sign-on the ability to upload new skins. If signed on as host, you can upload skins from more than one location. For your first option, you need to navigate to Host Settings on the host menu. Under the Basic Settings section you will find an Appearance sub-section. At the bottom of this section, you can upload your skins or containers by clicking on the corresponding links.

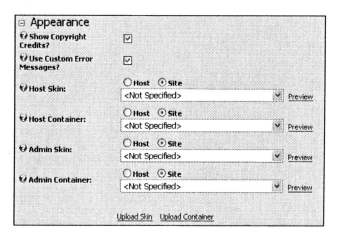

This will take you to the Upload Skin Package section. Browse to the location of your ZIP file, click on Add to place it in the upload box, and click on Upload New File to upload the skin to your site.

This will produce Resource Upload Logs. Read this log to determine if any errors occurred during the upload process. Click on the Return link to exit this screen and go back to the Host Settings page.

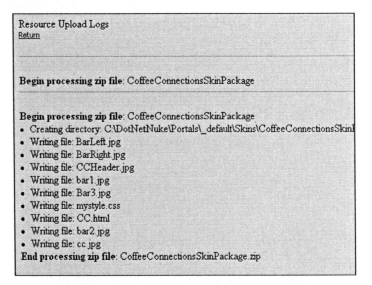

Uploading as Admin

To give administrators the ability to upload skins to the portal, sign in as Host and navigate to Host Settings on the host menu. Under the Advanced Settings section you will find an Other Settings sub-section. In this section, you will see where you can set the Skin Upload Permissions.

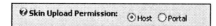

You will need to select Portal and click on the Update link to save your settings. Once you have done this, sign on as Admin and navigate to Skins on the admin menu.

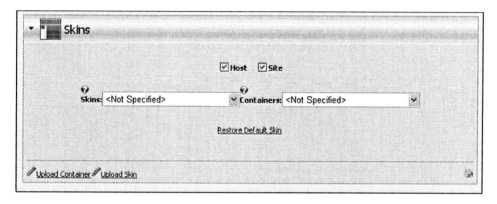

From here you will be able to upload new skins as well as manage the skins and containers that you have already uploaded to your site. To upload a skin, just click on the Upload Skin link and you will be presented with the same dialog box as you saw in the last section. Follow the same instructions to upload your skin.

Applying Skins

As you saw earlier, skins can be applied at host, portal, page, or module level. In addition to this, there is more than one way to apply the skins. This section will cover all the ways in which this can be done.

Applying a Skin at Host and Portal Levels

Having a consistent look to you portal plays an integral part in how people feel when they browse your site. If all of the pages on your site looked different, with the menu in different places, and the colors and images changing as the users navigate, it would be very easy for them to get disorientated. Giving your site a consistent look helps to build a level of comfort for your users. In this section, we will show you how to apply the skin you have selected to your entire site.

Using the Skins Manager

Once uploaded, the skins can be managed from the Skins section on the Admin menu. To get started, select the skin you would like to apply from the Skins dropdown.

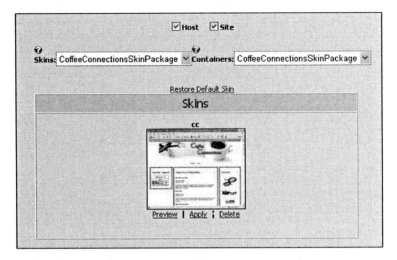

If the skin developer included an image of the skin in the skin package, you will be able to see a thumbnail of the skin. From this screen, you can preview, delete, or apply the skin by clicking on the appropriate link. The checkboxes at the top of the screen determine if whether the skin will be applied at host and/or site level. If you select the Host checkbox, you will apply the skin to all the parent and child portals that are associated with your DotNetNuke installation. The Site checkbox will apply the skin to the current site only.

Using Host and Site Settings

You can also apply skins to your site using both the Site and Host Settings sections.

Once the skin has been uploaded, you can apply it to your portal by signing in as Host or Admin and navigating to Admin | Site Settings or Host | Host Settings on the main menu.

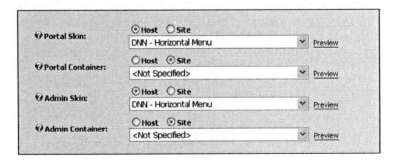

In the Appearance section, you can change the skin by selecting it from the dropdown. If you are signed on as a superuser (host), you again will be able to apply the skin at a host or site level. You can apply Portal Skin/Containers and Admin Skin/Containers to your portal. The Admin Skin will be seen when accessing the admin or host pages. The Portal Skin will be seen on all other pages. You can see a preview of what the skin will look like, by clicking on the Preview link. When you are satisfied with your choice, just click on the Update link to apply the changes.

Applying a Skin at Page Level

There may be times when you will want one page to stand out from the rest. You might want a page that does something completely different from all the other pages on your site. A great example of this is the home page. This page welcomes users to your site. You might want to put a larger header or fewer panes on this page to use it more aesthetically than functionally. In such a case, you can apply a custom skin to this page.

To modify the skin for only one page you will first need to sign on as an admin or a super-user. This will bring up the control panel pane on the top of your portal.

If you have your control panel set to ICONBAR, you can click on the Settings link in the Page Functions pane, if the control panel is set to CLASSIC, click on the Edit link. This will bring you to the page management pane. You will find the Page Skin dropdown under the Advanced Settings | Appearance section.

Depending on how the skins were uploaded, you will need to select either Host or Site, and then the skin you would like to apply from the Page Skin dropdown. This will override the host- or site-level skin, and will apply the selected skin to this page.

Applying a Skin at Module Level

As we discussed earlier, when a skin is applied at the module level, it is referred to as a container. This skin can be applied to all modules by applying it at a host or site level as we have done for the page skins, and can also be applied on a page level. All of these locations have a dropdown for the container skins. However, the lowest level of applying a container skin is at the module level. This will change the container skin for only one particular module.

To modify the skin for only one module you will first need to sign on as an Admin (or super-user). Hover the cursor over the module menu icon and select Settings.

This will bring you to the Module Settings page. You will find the Module Container dropdown under the Page Settings | Appearance section.

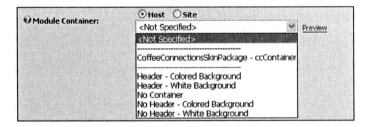

Depending on how the container skins were uploaded, you will need to select Host or Site, and then select the container skin you would like to apply from the Module Container dropdown. This skin will override the container skin applied at a host, site, or page level, and will be applied to only this module.

Creating Custom Skins

In addition to downloading and using free or purchased skins you can also create your own unique skin for your site. The skinning solution incorporated into DotNetNuke gives you great flexibility when designing your skin. Skins can be defined using ASCX user controls or simple HTML files. In addition, you can employ any number of additional techniques such as CSS or XML to further enhance you skin. We will discuss both of these techniques as we walk through creating a custom skin for Coffee Connections.

File Structure and Setup

Before we begin to create our skin, we will first take a moment to discuss the basic file structure for the skin itself. A basic skin will contain an HTML table with, at the least, a row for the header, a row for the menu, a row for the login controls, a row for the panes where the modules will be placed, and finally a row for the footer. The border for the table should be set to 0 (zero). As you will see when we begin to design our skin, this basic construct is only limited by the talent of the designer. This is by no means the structure for every skin, but only the format we will use in this discussion. The image below depicts the basic table design we will be using.

Row For Header		
Row For Menu		
Row	For	Login
Row	For	Modules
Row For Footer		

How this table is created will depend on which method you decide to use: ASCX user controls, or HTML page. The path you decide to take depends more on your comfort level with the technology rather than on any advantage either would provide. If you are very familiar with Visual Studio and have created Web User controls in the past, you might want to select this method. On the other hand, if you have worked with HTML design and are comfortable with web page designers like Microsoft's Front Page or Macromedia's Dreamweaver, you may select this method. While we discuss each method, we will focus on the differences between the two.

> If you create a skin using the HTML method and upload it to the portal, the DotNetNuke framework converts the HTML file into a .NET Web User control.

Skin Images

During the construction of skins using both methods, we will be using images that we created using both Adobe Photoshop and Macromedia Fireworks MX. We will not be discussing how these have been created since this subject could very easily fill a book itself. We have deliberately kept the structure of the skin simple to discuss how the skin architecture works within DotNetNuke. Once you have this basic knowledge, you can use many other design techniques that may be available to you.

Creating a Skin Using Visual Studio

Most tutorials on DotNetNuke skinning show you how to create a skin using an HTML editor. Since we have been using Visual Studio throughout this book, we will use this environment while we create our custom skin.

As we have learned in previous chapters, the default download of DotNetNuke has been broken up into many different solutions. Deciding which one to use depends on the section of the code you would like to work with. For our discussions of skins, we have created a new solution called DotNetNuke skins. To this blank solution we have added the DotNetNuke project (C:\DotNetNuke.proj), a new class library project, and a build-support project.

> For more information on how to create private assemblies and solutions, please refer to Chapter 7, which discusses creating custom modules.

When your setup is complete, your solution should look like the following image:

Creating the Skin Web User Control

You will notice that if you select your Class Library project and attempt to add a Web User control, it will not be an option for you. For this reason, and others that will become apparent in a few moments, we will create our user control in the DotNetNuke project. To do this, right-click on the DotNetNuke project and select Add | Add Web User control from the context menu. Give your control a name and click OK to create it.

Creating Your Skin Table

Next, we want to create the table structure that we discussed earlier in this chapter. To do this, go to Table | Insert | Table from the main menu. Make the table width 100%, with a border size 0, 5 rows, and 3 columns. Click OK to create the table.

We then need to modify the first, second, and last rows so that they have only one column. To do this, move your cursor to the left end of the first row until your cursor turns into a black arrow. Now right-click and highlight the entire row. To merge the cells, go to Table | Merge Cells on the main menu. Repeat this procedure for the second and last rows. When you are finished, your table should look like the following image:

Setting Up Your Module Panes

As explained in Chapter 4, when you add a module to a page you need to select the pane in which you would like to place the module. In a standard skin, you will need a Left Pane, a Content Pane, and a Right Pane. You are not limited to these three panes, but this is the norm for most skins.

The panes are represented by cells in the table that we have just created. To set this in Visual Studio, select the cell and set the Property IDs to LeftPane, ContentPane, and RightPane respectively. Place no spaces between the words. The image below has labels in the cells you will need to add IDs for. Your table will *not* look like this. This is only to help you determine the cells to be modified.

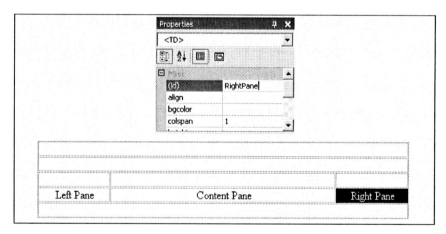

Now since we used the top menu item to add a table to our Web User control, we added an HTML table. The cells we have added IDs to will need to communicate with our web server in order to work with the DotNetNuke architecture. To do this, we will click on the HTML tab at the bottom of the screen and modify the code directly. Find the code for the cells that you just added the IDs to and modify it to look like the following:

```
<tr>
    <td valign="top" width="150" id="LeftPane"
        runat="Server"> </td>
    <td valign="top" width="500" id="ContentPane"
        runat="Server"> </td>
    <td valign="top" width="150" id="RightPane"
        runat="Server"> </td>
</tr>
```

In this step, we are accomplishing two things: firstly, we add the `runat="Server"` attribute to the cells, and secondly, we set the width of the cells so that the content pane is larger than the other two panes. The `runat="Server"` attribute will allow these cells to communicate with the server when the page is requested. The table is now complete. We now are ready to add the DotNetNuke functionality to the skin.

Adding Skin Objects

There are certain items in a DotNetNuke portal that will remain relatively the same no matter what skin is used for your site. For example, you will need to integrate certain items like the menu, registration, and login capabilities to your site. This is accomplished by using **skin objects**. Skin objects are Web User controls that encapsulate all the required functionality for any specific action your portal possesses. All you need to do is drag the object onto your skin and place it in the cell you would like it to appear in.

These objects can be found in the Solution Explorer inside the Admin/Skins folder.

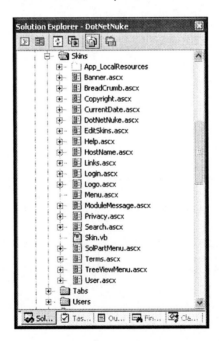

For our skin, we will be keeping it simple. We will use the SolPartMenu control, Login control, User control, Terms control, and Copyright control. Place them inside your table as shown opposite, by dragging them from the Solution Explorer.

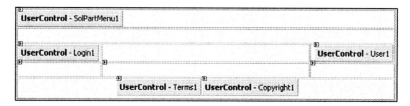

When we created the Web User control for our skin, we did so inside the DotNetNuke project. We did this for a few reasons. First, a Class Library project did not allow us to add a Web User control directly, and second, with our skin control inside the DotNetNuke project, we could easily drag the needed Skin User controls onto our form. Now that we have finished both of these tasks, we want to move the Skin control into the Class Library project that we initially set up.

To do this, we click on our Skin User control in the Solution Explorer and drag it to the CCSkin project. We move our control because with DotNetNuke always changing, we don't want to add extra items into the DotNetNuke core project. Also, we want to keep all of the items we will use for our skin (ASCX file, CSS file, images) in their own directory.

Adding Images to the Skin

This step is fairly simple for our demonstration. Simply add the images you are going to use with your skin to the folder that holds your project. Then, using the Solution Explorer, select the Show All Files icon and right-click each image and select Include in Project. After this is done, you can add an image control to the form and set its src property to the name of your image.

Creating Your CSS File

Our final step is to create a **Cascading Style Sheet (CSS)** to define the font types, colors, and sizes to use on our site. If you have never worked with CSS before, don't worry; all of the styles are already defined for DotNetNuke. All you need to do is to copy the default style sheet from the skin folder of your DotNetNuke installation and place it in the same folder as the skin you just created.

You can find this file in the `C:\DotNetNuke\Portals\_default\Skins\_default` folder. You can modify any of the attributes in this file to match the look and feel of your skin. We will modify a few of the items found in the `skins.css` file. We first want to change the background of the menu to match our skin. To do this we add an item to the `.MainMenu_MenuContainer` section of the file.

```
/*  Add background-image: : url(bar2.jpg)*/
.MainMenu_MenuContainer
{
    background-color: transparent;
    background-image: url(bar2.jpg);
}
```

We want an image that we created to serve as the background for our menu, so we add a `background-image` tag to this section, passing it the URL of the image that we will include in our package.

The only other change we will make is to have the menu-item color change from black to white when the menu item is selected. To accomplish this, we change the `color` tag under the `.MainMenu_MenuItemSel` section from `Black` to `White`:

```
/*  Change color: from black to White*/
.MainMenu_MenuItemSel {
    cursor: pointer;
    cursor: hand;
    color: White;
    font-family: Tahoma, Arial, Helvetica;
    font-size: 9pt;
    font-weight: bold;
    font-style: normal;
    background-color: #C1D2EE;
}
```

The `skin.css` file contains many different sections that allow you to customize your skin even further. The top of the file, for example, has sections that allow you to change the colors of the control panel when signed on as an administrator. When you are done modifying the `skin.css` file, save your changes and put it aside. We will be including this file when we package our skin.

Modifying the HTML Code

The last thing we need to do to our skin is to modify some of the attributes in the HTML. When we created the Web User control for our skin in Visual Studio, it created a code-behind file for us. When we package up our skin we will not need this file. As a matter of fact, if you include it you will get a file error when you try to upload it. We need to modify our CodeBehind attribute to read ~/admin/Skins/skin.vb, and our Inherits attribute to read DotNetNuke.Skin as shown in the code on the facing page. In addition, we also need to change the Src attributes that point to our controls to have a relative path. This is done by placing a *tilde + backslash* (~/).

```
<%@ Control Language="vb" AutoEventWireup="false"
CodeBehind="~/admin/Skins/skin.vb" Inherits="DotNetNuke.Skin"  %>
<%@ Register TagPrefix="uc1" TagName="Terms"
Src="~/admin/Skins/Terms.ascx" %>
<%@ Register TagPrefix="uc1" TagName="SolPartMenu"
Src="~/admin/Skins/SolPartMenu.ascx" %>
<%@ Register TagPrefix="uc1" TagName="Copyright"
Src="~/admin/Skins/Copyright.ascx" %>
<%@ Register TagPrefix="uc1" TagName="Login"
Src="~/admin/Skins/Login.ascx" %>
<%@ Register TagPrefix="uc1" TagName="User"
Src="~/admin/Skins/User.ascx" %>
```

When we are finished making these changes, we can save our files to get them ready to package for uploading.

Creating a Skin Using HTML

The procedure for creating a skin using HTML is strikingly similar to how we created the skin using Visual Studio. Because of this, we will not be walking through this step by step. We will instead hit on the main highlights and differences between the two. In the HTML Editor of your choice, create a table with the following specifications. Make the table width 100%, border size 0, with 5 rows, and 3 columns. Then modify the first, second, and last rows so that they only have one column each. Your table should resemble the image below:

Now you need to place your skin objects as you did while using Visual Studio. Only this time since you are using HTML to create your skin, you will be using tokens to determine the location of your skin objects. Tokens are a popular technique used in many different scripting languages and are used as placeholders by the DotNetNuke framework to represent *where* the corresponding controls should be placed on the skin. The following image shows an example of using tokens on our HTML skin.

When an HTML skin is uploaded to the portal, the DotNetNuke framework converts the HTML page into a Web User control and replaces the tokens with the corresponding skin objects.

> To find a complete list of tokens and skin objects available to you when creating a skin, refer to the Skinning white paper in the C:\DotNetNuke\Documentation\ Public folder.

Adding Panes to the Skin

As we have discussed earlier, the DotNetNuke portal page is divided into different panes. You will also need to declare the cells that represent the Left, Content, and Right panes. This is done by first adding the id attribute followed by the runat="Server" attribute as shown below. We made the same modifications to our ASPX control.

```
<td valign="top" width="150" id="LeftPane" runat="Server"> </td>
<td valign="top" width="500"
id="ContentPane"runat="Server"><p> </p></td>
<td valign="top" width="150" id="RightPane"
runat="Server"> </td>
```

That is all that is needed to create a simple HTML skin for your portal. Once you place the images and tokens where you would like them to be, you can then turn your attention to creating a container to match your skin.

Creating Custom Containers

Container skins are best thought of as picture frames for your modules. They surround your modules and should complement the skin applied to the page. It is not required that you create a container to match every skin you create, but it does help to keep a consistent look and feel.

First let's take a look at what our finished container will look like.

Around our module, we will be placing a bar that matches the color and appearance of our skin. Again, the images used for the container can be created in the editor of your choice. Just like our skin, the container is a collection of tables that we use to place the elements of the module in the position we would like.

There are two important things to note here.

- Make sure that when you build your container, it does not have any <html> or <body> tags. Modules are inserted into a page that will already have these tags, and additional tags could cause unexpected results.

- The images are separated from the tokens by being placed in different cells. This is done to give a boundary between the information inside the module and the module walls.

Below you will find the complete HTML needed to create the container shown above. Since it is just a collection of tables with tokens added, we will not cover this in detail.

```
<table border="0" cellspacing="0" cellpadding="0" width="100%">
  <tr>
    <td width="23"><img border="0" src="topleft.jpg"
      WIDTH="23" HEIGHT="31" Alt="Module Border"></td>
    <td background="Topbar2.jpg"></td>
    <td width="23" valign="top"><img  border="0" src="topright.jpg"
      WIDTH="23" HEIGHT="31" Alt="Module Border"></td>
  </tr>
  <tr>
    <td  background="lefttile.jpg" width="23"></td>
    <td runat="server" id="ContentPane">
      <table cellSpacing="0" cellPadding="0" width="98%"
        summary="Module Title Table">
        <tr>
          <td vAlign="bottom" noWrap align="left" height="34">
```

```
                [SOLPARTACTIONS]
              </td>
              <td vAlign="bottom" nowrap align="left" height="34">
                [ICON] 
              </td>
              <td vAlign="bottom" nowrap align="left" width="100%"
                height="34">
                [TITLE] 
              </td>
              <td vAlign="bottom" nowrap align="right" height="34">
                [VISIBILITY]
              </td>
            </tr>
            <tr>
              <td colspan="3" width="100%">
              </td>
            </tr>
          </table>
          <hr noshade size="1">
        </td>
        <td  background="righttile.jpg" width="23"></td>
      </tr>
      <tr>
        <td width="23"><img  border="0" src="bottomleft.jpg" WIDTH="23"
          HEIGHT="31" Alt="Module Border"></td>
        <td  background="bottombar.jpg"></td>
        <td width="23"><img  border="0" src="bottomright.jpg" WIDTH="23"
          HEIGHT="31" Alt="Module Border"></td>
      </tr>
    </table>
```

Just like skins, the containers also use tokens to place controls from DotNetNuke into your custom container. These differ from skin tokens because the functionalities of modules differ from the functionality of the page itself. The most important token is the [SOLPARTACTIONS] token, which places the module context menu in your module. Without this token you will not be able to manage your modules. The following table lists the tokens available for your container.

Token	Description
[SOLPARTACTIONS]	Popup module actions menu (formerly [ACTIONS])
[DROPDOWNACTIONS]	Simple drop-down combo box for module actions
[LINKACTIONS]	Links list of module actions
[ICON]	Displays the icon related to the module
[TITLE]	Displays the title of the module
[VISIBILITY]	Displays an icon representing the minimized or maximized state of a module
[PRINTMODULE]	Displays a new window with only the module content displayed

Once your container is finished, it is time to package both your skin and container to enable them to be uploaded to your portal.

Adding Thumbnail Images

Within the DotNetNuke skin-management interface covered earlier, you saw that if an image is available, the administration panel will display thumbnails of the skins or containers you have installed. Though it is not necessary for your skin to work properly, you should create a full-size, high-quality screenshot in JPEG image format. The name of your image is important; it needs to match the name of your skin for the manager to be able to see it. In our case, we have a skin called CCSkin.ascx and a container called ccContainer.html, so we must create screenshots called CCSkin.jpg and ccContainer.jpg. The thumbnail will be created for you by the Management module.

Packaging Your Custom Skins and Containers

Packaging your skins and containers requires that you package the HTML or ASPX skin files as well as all graphics into a ZIP file. There are two ways to accomplish this. If you would like to keep your skins and containers together, you would package them in one ZIP file that contains both packages. Although this would seem to be the most logical method when you have both skins and containers, it does not seem to be the norm. A more common occurrence is to package your skin and container files separately. Since we created both a page skin and a container skin, we will demonstrate the first method.

We will begin by packaging up both our page skin and our container skin into separate ZIP files. Place all of your graphics files, your skin.css file, and your HTML or ASCX file into the corresponding ZIP file. For this method, the ZIP files that are created will need to be named skins.zip and containers.zip.

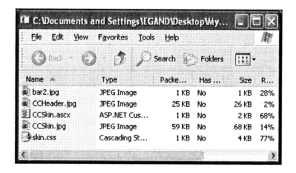

When you are zipping up your files, you do not just zip up the folder that they are in. If you zip up the folder instead of the individual files, the skins and containers will not work properly.

You will not see an error when uploading, but they will not be seen in the site settings skin dropdowns. This is because when you upload your skin, an additional embedded folder is created and so your skin package will not be seen.

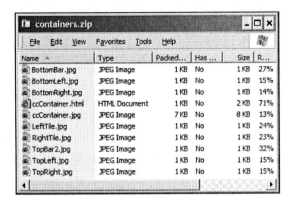

We then want to package the ZIP files we just created into a master ZIP file. This ZIP file should be given a descriptive name.

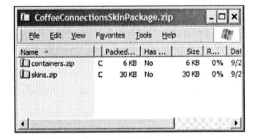

When DotNetNuke uploads this package, it will use the name of this file as the name of both the skin and the container. It will append the name with the name of your skin file. The following image shows how this skin package will be named when uploaded.

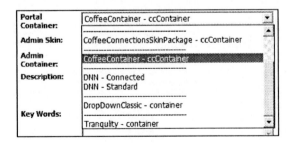

Summary

In the preceding chapters, you learned how to administer your portal, create custom modules, and finally how to create custom skins and containers to give your portal a unique look. The wonderful part of DotNetNuke is that you don't have to create everything on your own. In the next chapter, we will explore a number of freely available modules that will greatly enhance the usability of your portal.

9
Enhancing Your Portal

Up until now in the book, we have had to work alone when creating custom modules and skins and diving deeply into the core of DotNetNuke. But what if you do not have either the time or expertise to make these modifications yourself? Not to worry; DotNetNuke has a very large open-source community, and there are many free custom modules out there that can give your portal not only the look you are searching for but also the custom functionality that will separate your portal from the rest. The trick is to be able to find the resources that are spread out across the Web. This chapter will:

- Introduce you to free "must-have" modules
- Tell you where and how to find modules on the Internet
- Tell you about sites that offer modules for a price

Must-Have Modules to Enhance Your Portal

Even though DotNetNuke is jam-packed with many modules, there are a few modules that are needed to really make your portal come alive. Most of the modules that we will cover here can be found for no cost. Although these modules are free, their quality and usefulness are outstanding.

All the modules listed here have been upgraded to 3.0 or are being upgraded. The following are the modules that we will be covering in this chapter:

- **YetAnotherForum**: Portal forum
- **ActiveForums**: Portal forum
- **AIS-EC**: DotNetNuke e-Commerce module
- **DNNelearn**: Online classroom-based module
- **Spohn Software security modules**: A group of modules that helps secure your site
- **MyBlog**: DotNetNuke weblog module

Adding a Forum to Your Portal

Whether your site is designed to help programmers with their coding problems or is a sports-related site that allows fans to comment on their favorite teams, one of the most useful additions to your site is a community forum. It allows users to ask questions, communicate with each other, or just express their thoughts.

YetAnotherForum

The first forum we will look at is YetAnotherForum (YAF). YetAnotherForums is an open-source project using C# that has been converted to a module in order to work with DotNetNuke. Since it is open source, it can be added to your portal at no cost. YAF comes with the following features.

- User-configurable cultures (see dates and numbers in the way that you are used to)
- Unlimited number of categories, forums, and messages
- Private messaging
- Polls
- Active topics' list
- Active users' list
- Print topics
- Watch forums or topics for new posts
- Support for smileys/emoticons
- IP banning

Unlike other modules we will look at, YAF takes a little more work than a simple upload using the file uploader. We will walk through the steps necessary to get this forum working on your portal. The first thing you will need to do is to download the files from the YetAnotherForum site (http://www.yetanotherforum.net). The site's download section has a stand-alone version, a version for Rainbow Portal, and one for the DotNetNuke portal. Make sure that you download the DotNetNuke module.

Once you have downloaded the ZIP file, unzip it to your DotNetNuke directory. In our case, this would be C:\DotNetNuke. It will place a folder inside the DesktopModules folder, and a DLL file inside the bin folder.

Next you will need to make some updates to the web.config file. A sample file is shipped with the forum. It is called web.config.old and you can find it in C:\DotNetNuke\DesktopModules\YetAnotherForumDotNet. You will need to take this template and merge it into the web.config file found in the root of DotNetNuke. Now we will go over the changes that need to be made.

The configuration section of the web.config file in your DotNetNuke directory already has a section for DotNetNuke; we need to add an additional section for YAF.

```
<configSections>

  <sectionGroup name="dotnetnuke">
        <section name="data"
        type="DotNetNuke.ProviderConfigurationHandler, DotNetNuke" />

        <section name="logging"
        type="DotNetNuke.ProviderConfigurationHandler, DotNetNuke" />

        <section name="scheduling"
        type="DotNetNuke.ProviderConfigurationHandler, DotNetNuke" />

        <section name="htmlEditor"
        type="DotNetNuke.ProviderConfigurationHandler, DotNetNuke" />

        <section name="searchIndex"
        type=
        "DotNetNuke.Framework.Providers.ProviderConfigurationHandler,
         DotNetNuke" />

        <section name="searchDataStore"
        type=
        "DotNetNuke.Framework.Providers.ProviderConfigurationHandler,
         DotNetNuke" />

        <section name="friendlyUrl"
        type=
        "DotNetNuke.Framework.Providers.ProviderConfigurationHandler,
         DotNetNuke" />
  </sectionGroup>

        <section name="yafnet" type="yaf.SectionHandler,yaf" />

</configSections>
```

Next we need to add the configuration handler section. This can be copied from the web.config.old file and placed under the closing </dotnetnuke> tag. You will need to make a few changes to this information after you add it to the web.config file:

- Change the <connstr> element to match your database information.

- Change the root directory to match your configuration.

- Change the upload directory to match your configuration.

```
<yafnet>
        <dataprovider>yaf.MsSql,yaf</dataprovider>
<connstr>
 user id=YourServerID;password=YourPassword;data
source=YourServerName;
initial catalog=DotNetNuke;timeout=90
</connstr>
        <root>/DotNetNuke/DesktopModules/yetanotherforumdotnet</root>
        <language>english.xml</language>
        <theme>standard.xml</theme>
```

```
<uploaddir>
/DotNetNuke/DesktopModules/yetanotherforumdotnet/upload/
</uploaddir>
<!--logtomail>email=;server=;user=;pass=;</logtomail-->
</yafnet>
```

The last change is to be made to the `<authentication>` section of the `web.config` file. You just need to add an additional node to handle authentication on the forums.

```
<authentication mode="Forms">
<forms name=".DOTNETNUKE" protection="All" timeout="60" />
<forms name="YetAnotherForum" slidingExpiration="true"/>
</authentication>
```

Save the `web.config` file when you are finished with your changes.

Now we need to add the forum modules to the site. Adding module definitions allows the module to be added from the module dropdown when you are signed on as host or admin. To add the module definitions needed for YAF, log in as host, and click on the Module Definitions option on the host menu. Select Add New Module Definition.

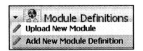

Enter the name for your module and a short description of what it does. When you are finished, click on the Update link.

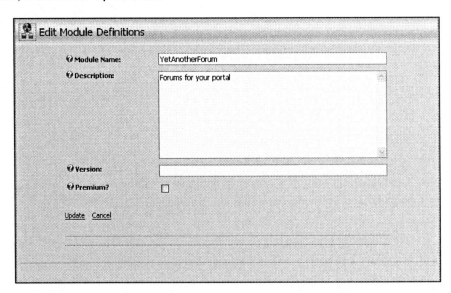

This will bring up a new section that allows you to add the definitions for the module.
Enter the New Definition name and click on Add Definition.

Now we can finally add the controls to the definition. First we will add the View control
for the forums. Click on the Add Control link to start.

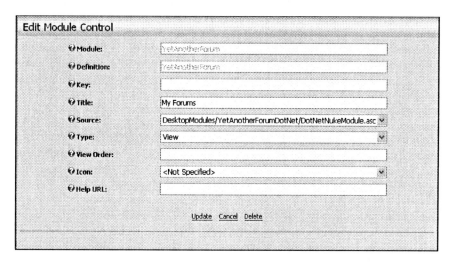

1. Enter the Title for the control. This will be the default title when the control is
   added to a tab.
2. Enter the source for the control. This is the view control we that we have
   previously unzipped into our DesktopModules/YetAnotherForumDotNet
   folder. Select the DotNetNukeModule.ascx control from the source
   dropdown.
3. Select the Type of control. This is the public interface for our control so we
   want to select View from the dropdown.
4. Click Update when done.

Next we want to add our Edit control.

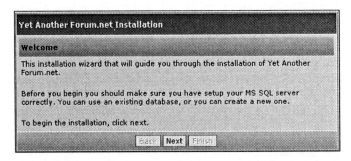

1. Enter Edit for the Key field. This is the key that the Actions Menu will use to navigate to this control.

2. Enter a Title for the control.

3. Select the DotNetNukeModuleEdit.acsx control from the Source dropdown.

4. Select Edit in the Type dropdown.

5. Click Update when complete.

When you are finished adding the module definition, create a tab and place the YetAnotherForums module on the new tab. The module will then attempt to set up the forum using a wizard.

First, the installation needs to check whether you have a working web.config file.

Click Next to begin this process:

The wizard will then try to verify your web.config file. Do not get confused when the text refers to a web.config file inside the YetAnotherForumDotNet folder. The config file that we modified earlier is all that is needed for the forum:

This message may tell you have to set it up manually. Ignore this message because it is looking in the wrong place for the web.config file. Click Next to proceed.

The installation now needs to set up the tables and stored procedures that work with the forum. Click on Next to continue. When it is finished updating your database you will then need to configure the administration of the forum. When asked for an admin username, use the admin name and password that you use for DotNetNuke:

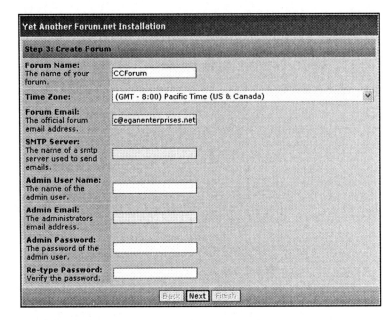

Complete the setup by clicking on the Finish button on the confirmation screen that appears after clicking on Next in the above screenshot. Your forum is now ready to run:

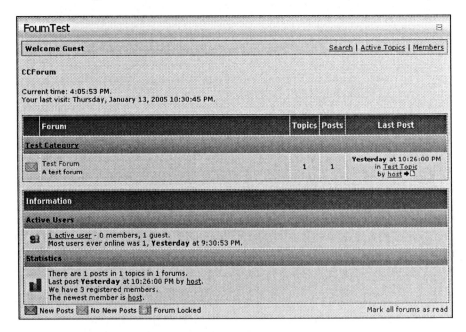

This module integrates with the users you already have in your DotNetNuke portal. There is no need for them to register a second time. If you need help administering your forum refer to the discussion forums located at `http://forum.yetanotherforum.net`.

ActiveForums

As an alternative way to place a forum on your site, I suggest ActiveForums. It has been specifically designed for use with DotNetNuke, so no extra modifications need to be made to get it working. It can be uploaded just like any other DotNetNuke module.

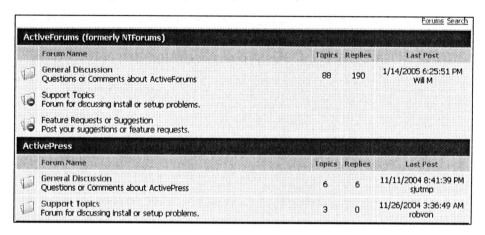

ActiveForums is packed with many of the features you see in stand-alone forum systems.

- Unlimited forum groups
- Unlimited forums
- Expanded user profile, allowing your visitors to share information
- Built-in e-mail sending to protect e-mail addresses: No need to worry about spam spiders picking up your users, e-mail addresses
- Manage look and feel with CSS: Customize the look and feel for the forums for each portal
- Create moderated or open forums
- Users can subscribe to topics and forums: Users will be sent an e-mail with details of the posts
- Supports SQL Server: Optimized for SQL Server using Stored Procedures
- Rank user based upon number of posts: Reward and encourage forum members for participation
- Display users' online status

- Users can upload or link to Avatars: Avatars allow forum members to add their own sense of personalization to each post they make
- Three input options for posts: Plain text, ActiveEditor, and DNN HTML Editor Provider

In addition to these features and ease of installation, ActiveForums comes with a "Latest Discussion" module, which allows you to place on your home page the last five posts that have occurred in the forum. The price for this forum module is minimal while giving you look and feel of full forum applications. ActiveForums is available from `http://www.activemodules.com/Default.aspx?tabid=518`.

Adding e-Commerce to Your DotNetNuke Portal

Whether you are planning on creating a full-blown store or just selling a few things on your portal, AIS-EC for DNN is a feature-rich e-commerce solution for the DotNetNuke portal framework. This solution consists of several integrated modules that provide clear, concise user and administrative functionality. AIS-EC for DNN is developed in VB.NET and requires no modification of the basic the DotNetNuke framework.

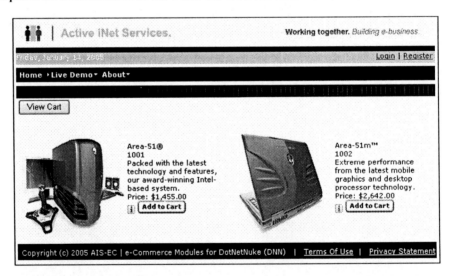

AIS-EC provides advanced features such as:

- Real-time credit card processing (Authorize.NET with many more to come)
- Custom shipping calculations
- Customer management
- Custom tax management

246

- Order management
- Four alternative product views
- SSL Support
- User friendliness

While there are a few other e-commerce modules available for DotNetNuke, this is the only one that is free. It is also the easiest to install. To install, just register and login to Active iNet Services (`http://www.activeinetservices.net`). You will find the module by navigating to Services | Projects | AIS-EC 2.0 from the main menu. When you navigate to AIS-EC 2.0, you will also see four demo sub-menus. Do not navigate to these; click on the AIS-EC 2.0 menu item. You will find the link to download the module at the bottom of the page. You will need to be registered and logged in to be able see it.

Once the module is downloaded, you can upload the module like any other using the file-upload option on the Host menu. There is also a demo store set up on the site for you to work with. With this module, you can upgrade your portal from an information portal to an e-commerce portal in just minutes.

Adding Classroom Management to Your Portal

As web technology continues to advance, so does the use of the Web in the education environment. Whether you are teaching a class completely online or just supplementing your classroom activity with easy-to-find information for your students, DNNeLearn fits the bill.

DNNeLearn provides high-quality delivery of distance-learning content over the Web. The system, as a module of DotNetNuke, is designed to be self-sufficient and only requires the DotNetNuke portal to run. The initial focus of the project is for course management. It contains several modules that can be easily dropped into the DotNetNuke framework to deliver course content online.

DNNeLearn provides features such as:

- Online grades for students and teachers
- Online document and file downloads
- Online quizzes
- Student assignment uploads
- Class announcements
- Bulk e-mail functionality

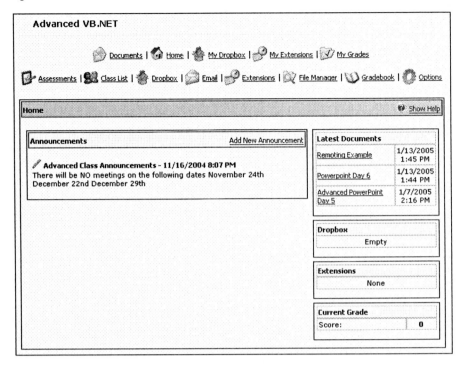

If you have to manage any type of classroom environment, you will find this module indispensable. It is easy to install using the file upload found on the host menu, and can be downloaded from (http://www.DNNeLearn.com). The download includes the source files and the PA, as well as a well-presented DnneLearn manual that demonstrates many of the features.

Adding Security to Your DotNetNuke Portal

The next must-have is actually three different modules found at the same site. One of the problems encountered by DotNetNuke users is remembering the username they used for signing up on a portal. To help this situation, Spohn Software has created the "Forgotten Username" module. This module is a nice addition to any sign-in screen.

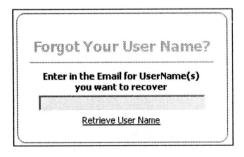

This control will search for a sign-on based on the e-mail address of the user. If it is found, the username will be e-mailed to the e-mail address on record.

The second module helps to enhance the security of your portal by requiring the user to create a strong password when registering for a user account on your portal. You decide on the password requirements on your portal

Options include:

- Minimum password length
- Require upper and lower case characters in password
- Require numeric
- Require special characters
- Provide the special characters allowed

Adding this module and configuring the options coupled with the password encryption settings available on the host settings page can greatly increase the security of your user information. These first two modules can be downloaded from the Spohn Software site (http://www.spohnsoftware.com) in the Freebies section. You will need to click on the link at the top of the page that says Freebies.

The third module in this section is called Watch Dog. Protecting the integrity of your portal and keeping it safe from attacks can be a daunting task. This module can help you with this task.

DNN Watch Dog will help you monitor invalid sign-on attempts and access denied messages as they occur. Keep unwanted people out, while keeping your site safe for those you do want in. You can view all of the features of Watch Dog by accessing the DNN Modules menu item on the Spohn Software site (http://www.spohnsoftware.com).

Adding a Blog to Your Site

One of the biggest booms on the Internet in recent years is the weblog (blog for short). The blog is basically an online diary of your thoughts and ideas, and whether you use it to share your views on politics in the world or simply to share code ideas with the rest of the community, your site would not be complete without one. There are a couple of blog modules that are available for DotNetNuke, but we have chosen MyBlog for a few reasons. It is free, easy to install, and was written specifically for DotNetNuke.

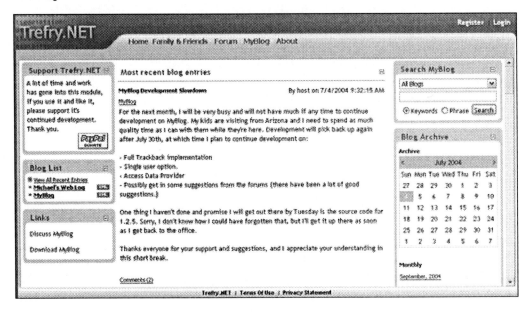

MyBlog comes with the following features:

- Multiple blog administration
- Blog search
- Blog archives
- Trackbacks
- Comments
- Blog listings

MyBlog, which was originally started by Michael Trefry (http://www.trefry.net) is open source and is now being enhanced and distributed by Crisafulli (http://www.crisafulli.org/Default.aspx?tabid=33). You can use MyBlog for your own commentary or give your users the ability to start their own blog on your site. This is a great way to give your site dynamic content with minimal effort.

Finding Custom Modules

The DotNetNuke community is over 100,000 strong and many members have created custom modules for use by the community. The trick is finding these modules on the Web. Finding the modules you need to make your site complete is not as difficult as you might think. There are a couple of key places that you need to look when searching for that perfect module.

The most comprehensive listing of free DotNetNuke modules has been compiled by DotNetNuke core team member Cathal Connolly and can be found at (`http://www.cathal.co.uk/`). Cathal consistently updates this list with the latest and greatest free modules.

Another place to find a large collection of DNN modules is at Snowcovered.com (`http://www.snowcovered.com`). As opposed to Cathal's site, Snowcoverd has modules for sale and contact with the author of the module is done through the site. The modules at this site range from $9.99 to $500.00 and the number of modules available grows by the day.

The DotNetNuke main site has a listing of free modules that can be found by navigating to Community | Modules from the main menu. The listing here is not as comprehensive as the offerings found at either of the above sites.

Summary

We have now discovered the modules that come pre-packaged with DNN, worked on creating our own custom module, found the must-have modules, and finally learned where to find modules that others have created. With all of these resources, we can build a portal to fit any need.

Up to this point we have been refining our site and working on it locally. Now it is time to deploy all of our hard work to the Web. The next few chapters will take you through this process and guide you away from possible pitfalls that may be waiting.

10
Deploying Your DNN Portal

Once your portal is looking the way you want it to, it is time to share your creation with the rest of the world. We want to transfer our site from our local computer and set it up on the World Wide Web.

When you are done with this chapter, you will know the following:

- How to obtain a domain name for your site
- What to look for in a hosting provider
- How to modify your files to prepare for moving to a host
- How to set up your database on a hosted site
- What file permissions are needed for your site to run

Acquiring a Domain Name

One of the most exciting parts of starting a website is acquiring a domain name. When selecting the perfect name there are a few things that you need to keep in mind:

- **Keep it brief**: The more letters that a user has to type in to get to your site the more difficult it is going to be for them to remember your site. The name you select will help to brand your site. If it is catchy then people will remember it more readily.

- **Have alternative names in mind**: As time goes on, great domain names are becoming fewer and fewer. Make sure you have a few alternatives to choose from. The first domain name you had in mind may already be taken so having a backup plan will help when you decide to purchase a name.

- **Consider buying additional top-level domain names**: Say you've already bought www.DanielsDoughnuts.com. You might want to purchase www.DanielsDoughnuts.net as well to protect your name.

Once you have decided on the name you want for your domain, you will need to register it. There are dozens of different sites that allow you to register your domain name as well

as search to see if it is available. Some of the better-known domain-registration sites are
Register.com and NetworkSolutions.com. Both of these have been around a long time
and have good reputations. You can also look into some of the discount registers like
BulkRegister (http://www.BulkRegister.com) or Enom (http://www.enom.com).

After deciding on your domain name and having it registered, you will need to find a
place to physically host your portal. Most registration services will also give the ability to
host your site with them but it is best to search for a provider that fits your site's needs.

Finding a Hosting Provider

When deciding on a provider to host your portal, you will need to consider a few things:

- **Cost**: This is of course one of the most important things to look at when
  looking for a provider. There are usually a few plans to select from. The
  basic plan usually allows you a certain amount of disk space for a very small
  price but has you share the server with numerous other websites. Most
  providers also offer dedicated (you get the server all to yourself) and semi-
  dedicated (you share with a few others). It is usually best to start with the
  basic plan and move up if the traffic on your site requires it.

- **Windows servers**: The provider you select needs to have Windows Server
  200/2003 running IIS (Internet Information Services). Some hosts run
  alternatives to Microsoft like Linux and Apache web server.

- **.NET framework**: The provider's servers need to have the .NET framework
  version 1.1 installed. Most hosts have installed the framework on their
  servers, but not all. Make sure this is available because DotNetNuke needs
  this to run.

- **Database availability**: You will need database server availability to run
  DotNetNuke and Microsoft SQL Server is the preferred back-end. It is
  possible to run your site off Microsoft Access or MySQL (with a purchased
  provider), but I would not suggest it. Access does not hold up well in a multi-
  user platform and will slow down considerably when your traffic increases.
  Also, since most module developers target MS SQL, MySQL, while able to
  handle multiple users, does not have the module support.

- **FTP access**: You will need a way to post your DotNetNuke portal files to
  your site and the easiest way is to use FTP. Make sure that your host
  provides this option.

- **E-mail server**: A great deal of functionality associated with the DotNetNuke
  portal relies on being able to send out e-mails to users. Make sure that you
  will have the availability of an e-mail server.

- **Folder rights**: The ASPNET or NetworkService Account (depending on server) will need to have full permissions to the root and subfolders for your DotNetNuke application to run correctly. Make sure that your host either provides you with the ability to set this or is willing to set this up for you. We will discuss the exact steps later in this chapter.

The good news is that you will have plenty of hosting providers to choose from and it should not break the bank. Try to find one that fits all of your needs. There are even some hosts (www.WebHost4life.com) that will install DotNetNuke for you free of charge. They host many DotNetNuke sites and are familiar with the needs of the portal.

Preparing Your Local Site

Once you have your domain name and a provider to host your portal, you will need to get your local site ready to be uploaded to your remote server. This is not difficult, but make sure you cover all of the following steps for a smooth transition.

1. Modify the compilation debug setting in the web.config file:
   You will need to modify your web.config file to match the configuration of the server to which you will be sending your files. The first item that needs to be changed is the debug configuration. This should be set to false. You should also rebuild your application in release mode before uploading. This will remove the debug tokens, perform optimizations in the code, and help the site to run faster:

```
<!-- set debugmode to false for running application -->
    <compilation debug="false" />
```

2. Modify the data-provider information in the web.config file:
   You will need to change the information for connecting to the database so that it will now point to the server on your host. There are three things to look out for in this section (changes shown overleaf):

- First, if you are using MS SQL, make sure SqlDataProvider is set up as the default provider.

- Second, change the connection string to reflect the database server address, the database name (if *not* DotNetNuke), as well as the user ID and password for the database that you received from your provider.

- Third, if you will be using an existing database to run the DotNetNuke portal, add an objectQualifier. This will append whatever you place in the quotations to the beginning of all of the tables and procedures that are created for your database.

```
<data defaultProvider=" SqlDataProvider" >
  <providers>
    <clear/>
      <add name = "SqlDataProvider"
        type = "DotNetNuke.Data.SqlDataProvider,
          DotNetNuke.SqlDataProvider"
        connectionStringname =
          "Server=MyServerIP;Database=DotNetNuke;
            uid=myID;pwd=myPWD;"
        providerPath =
          "~\Providers\DataProviders\SqlDataProvider\"
        objectQualifier = "DE"
        databaseOwner = "dbo"
        upgradeConnectionString = ""
      />
```

3. Modify any custom changes in the web.config file:

    Since you set up YetAnotherForum for use on our site, we will need to make the modifications necessary to ensure that the forums connect to the hosted database. Change the <connstr> to point to the database on the server:

```
<yafnet>
    <dataprovider>yaf.MsSql,yaf</dataprovider>
    <connstr>
      user id=myID;password=myPwd;data
      source=myServerIP;initial catalog=DotNetNuke;timeout=90
    </connstr>
    <root>/DotNetNuke/DesktopModules/YetAnotherForumDotNet/</root>
    <language>english.xml</language>
    <theme>standard.xml</theme>
    <uploaddir>/DotNetNuke/DesktopModules/yetanotherforum.net
              /upload/</uploaddir>
    <!--logtomail>email=;server=;user=;pass=;</logtomail-->
</yafnet>
```

4. Add your new domain name to your portal alias:

    Since DotNetNuke has the ability to run multiple portals we need to tell it which domain name is associated with our current portal. To do this we need to sign on as host (not admin) and navigate to Admin | Site Settings on the main menu. If signed on as host, you will see a Portal Aliases section on the bottom of the page. Click on the Add New HTTP Alias link:

5. Add your site alias into the HTTP Alias box and click on Update to finish:

6. Build your portal in release mode:
    The DotNetNuke project when downloaded is set up to be used and debugged in Visual Studio. In order to remove the debug tokens and speed up the response time for each page request, you will need to compile the project in release mode. For this, open up the DotNetNuke solution in Visual Studio, change the build type in the Solutions Configurations dropdown, and build the solution by going to Build Solution on the Build menu:

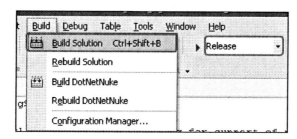

7. Configure your application to work with the .NET framework 1.1:
    If you enter HTML into a textbox while using the 1.1 version of the .NET framework, you may get an error message "A potentially dangerous Request.Form value was detected...". To stop this from occurring, set the `validateRequest` attribute in the `web.config` file to `false`:
    `<pages enableViewStateMac="true" validateRequest="false" />`

Now the code files for your DotNetNuke installation are ready to post to your hosted server. Before that can happen, you need to set up the database on the server.

Setting Up the Database

There are a few ways to get your database set up on the remote server. It all depends on how you want to start your site on the hosted server. If you have set up your localhost site by applying skins, adding modules, and installing forums, generally setting it up how you want to see it on the Web, you probably do not want to have to recreate this information when you post it to your hosted account. On the other hand, you may want to just get DotNetNuke up and running on the hosted server and then set it up how you want it.

We will cover both methods. We covered this when we set up our site locally, but if you set up a fresh install of DotNetNuke on the hosted server, it is important that you change the default admin and host passwords as soon as you have it running.

Backup and Restore Database

We will be using Microsoft's Enterprise Manager to accomplish this task. If you do not have access to these tools or if you have been using MSDE for you local server there are tools that you can use to accomplish the same tasks. You can use free tools such as DbaMgr (`http://www.asql.biz/DbaMgr.shtm`) or the command-line interface with Microsoft's osql utility (`http://msdn.microsoft.com/library/default.asp?url =/library/en-us/coprompt/cp_osql_1wx1.asp`). Either way, the basic concepts of this procedure will be the same.

If you want to keep the information and setup that is located in your local database, you will need to make a backup copy of the database. To begin, open Enterprise Manager, drill down on the (local) server, and open up the Databases folder. Look for DotNetNuke and right-click on it to bring up the menu. Select All Tasks and Backup Database to begin the back-up procedure.

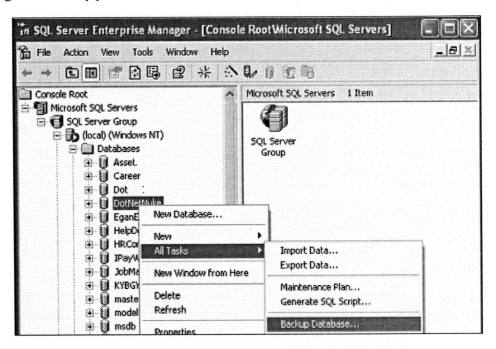

On the General tab, leave all the default settings and click on Add. In the File Name box, enter the location where you would like the backup saved and fill in a name for your backup. It is common to put an extension of .bak at the end of the file name, but it is not necessary. Click on the OK button on the Select Backup Destination dialog and then click on OK again on the General tab. You will receive a message when the backup completes successfully.

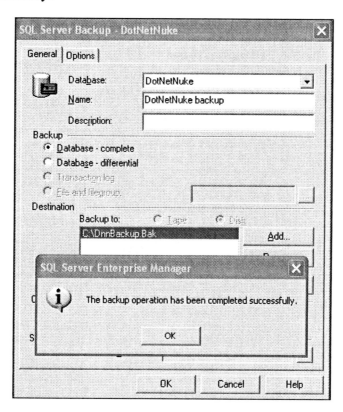

What you do with the backup file will depend on your hosting provider. Some providers give you the ability to do backup and restore operations on your own; other providers will do the restore for you. Contact your provider to find out how you can restore the database on their server.

Build New Database

If you would like to start your site from scratch on your hosted web server, you will need to manually create the database that will hold the tables and stored procedures needed to run DotNetNuke. This procedure will differ depending on your provider. Some may give you web access to your database; others will allow you to use Enterprise Manager to connect to your database server. We will be using the Enterprise Manager to accomplish this task. To get to Enterprise Manager, click on the Start button, go to Programs | Microsoft SQL Server | Enterprise Manager. Drill down on the (local) server by clicking on the plus (+) signs, right-click on Databases, and select New Database.

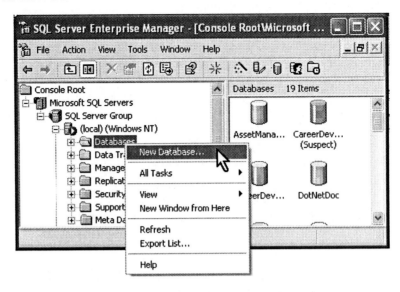

Type DotNetNuke into the name field and click OK.

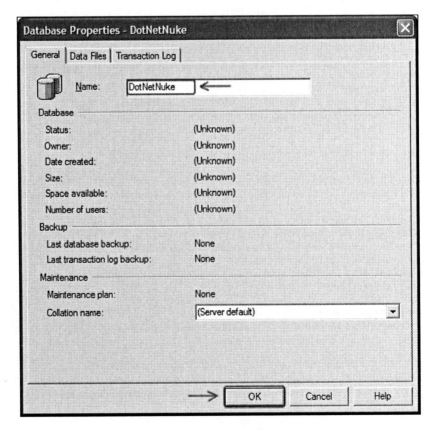

It will take a few moments for your database to be created. This will generate the system tables and stored procedures. The actual tables and procedures needed to run DotNetNuke will be created when you navigate to your portal for the first time.

> Note that the `web.config` connection strings that we discussed earlier will need to be set properly for this to work.

FTP Your Files

The easiest way to transfer your files from your local computer to the hosted server is to use File Transfer Protocol (FTP). You will need to obtain the location of your FTP account from your hosting provider. Once you have this information, you can use any number of tools to send your files. FrontPage XP and Macromedia Dreamweaver both have tools available to FTP files. You can also find free FTP programs such as FTP Commander (`http://www.vista.ru/2inter.htm`) or SmartFTP (`http://www.smartftp.com/download/`), which will also help you transfer your files. Once you have uploaded your files to the server, you need to give the appropriate file permissions for your portal to work correctly.

> Not all files need to be uploaded to the hosted site. Files with extensions of `.vb`, `.resx` , `.vbproj`, `.vbproj.webinfo`, `.sln`, `.doc`, `.bat`, and `.rsp` do not need to be uploaded. There have been discussions of creating a "hosted" version of the code so that unneeded files could be left behind, but as of now, no "hosted" version has been created.
>
> My suggestion would be that if you understand enough to remove the unneeded files, do so; if not, leave them there.

The file permissions needed for your portal will differ slightly depending on the type of server on which your account will be hosted.

If your portal will be hosted on a Windows 2000 server using IIS5, the {NameOfServer}/ASPNET user account must have read, write, and change control of the root application directory (this allows the application to create files and folders). This will be the directory that holds all of your files. Your provider will know the folder that needs permissions as it'll be setting up the virtual directory.

If your portal will be hosted on a Windows 2003 server using IIS6, the {NameOfServer}/NetworkService user account must have read, write, and change control of the root application directory.

Some providers give you the ability to set these permissions yourself; others will need to set the permissions for you.

Once the file permissions are set, all that is needed to complete the setup is to navigate to your site. If you are starting from scratch, your database tables and stored procedures will be created and you are ready to start adding content to your portal. As with any software installation, we have not covered all the issues that can arise. If you run into any issues during installation, make a descriptive post in the DotNetNuke forums for additional help (`http://www.asp.net/forums/showforum.aspx?forumid=90`).

Summary

In this chapter, we covered the steps necessary to take the site you created from your local machine and post it for everyone to see on the World Wide Web. The tasks needed to accomplish this are not difficult, but may require the assistance of your host provider. With our portal up and running, we will discuss how to run multiple portals from one DotNetNuke installation.

11

Creating Multiple Portals

One of the more compelling reasons to use DotNetNuke is the capability to create multiple portals off one installation of DotNetNuke. All of the portals will share one database, which makes portal backup easy. In this chapter, you will learn the following:

- Why you would want to create multiple portals
- How child portals differ from parent portals
- How to set up multiple portals
- How to create a portal template
- How to use the Site Wizard to update your site

Multiple Portals

Before we get into how to set up multiple portals, let's understand what is meant by multiple portals and why they are important. In a typical web-hosting environment, you purchase a domain name and contact a hosting provider to host your site. In normal situations, this is a one-to-one arrangement. If you then want to host another website, you follow the process again, creating another hosting account, with additional fees, and set up your site.

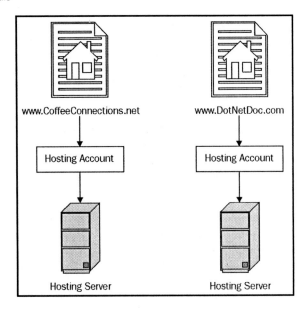

This can become time-consuming and expensive. Although this can be avoided by either spending more money to get a dedicated hosting account (you have full access to the server) or by creating sub-domains and pointing to subfolders on your site, it will take some technical knowledge on your part, and, if you use sub-domains, could get kind of messy. DotNetNuke solves this dilemma by allowing you to create multiple portals easily using a single hosting account.

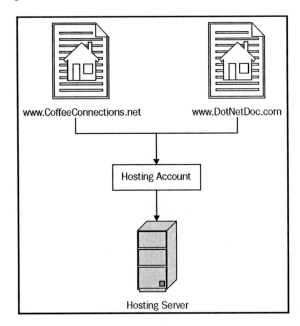

So why would you need multiple portals? Well let's say that you have your portal up and running, and then get a great idea for a second site dedicated to the "World of Chocolate". And then your spouse decides to sell hand-made crafts and needs a website to do it. Finally, during a family dinner you decide you want to put up a website dedicated to your family tree.

Normally you would need to create separate hosting accounts, build the site, design the look and feel, add the needed functionality, set up the database, and finally post your site on the Web. This could take you weeks or months to set up, and the costs would be proportional to the number of sites you needed.

When you have a DotNetNuke portal up and running, there are no additional costs to create additional portals, and with the help of wizards and templates in DotNetNuke, you could have these sites up in a matter of hours or days.

> It is important to note that when considering the costs of multiple portals, you need to take into account the amount of traffic each one will have. Most web-hosting services sell plans based on the disk usage of your site. This may require you to purchase a plan that accommodates more traffic.

In this chapter, you will see what different types of portals are available to you, how to use the wizard to set up your portal, and how to create templates so you never have to duplicate your work.

Parent Portals Versus Child Portals

Parent portals are sites that are defined by a unique URL (`www.CoffeeConnections.net`, `www.e-coffeehouse.com`, etc.). Parent portals allow you to run multiple sites from the same host and same DotNetNuke installation. This means that each domain name is unique but points to the same location. DotNetNuke handles how to route the requests depending on which domain name is entered.

Child portals, on the other hand, are sub-portals related to your main portal and share the domain name of their parent. A directory is created on your web server allowing the portal to be accessed through a URL address that includes a parent name and the directory name combined (say `www.CoffeeConnections.net/TestingPortal`).

Setting Up a Parent Portal

The first thing that needs to be done before you attempt to set up a parent portal is to purchase a domain name. As discussed in the previous chapter, this can be done through many different providers. In working with `CoffeeConnections.net`, we have realized that the sale of coffee-unique coffee beans has grown into a nice-sized side business.

To help this part of the company grow without overshadowing the original concept, we have decided to have a companion portal called e-Coffeehouse.com.

Registering Your Domain and Setting the DNS

Setting up multiple portals on a DNN site does not mean that we have to share the same name as the original portal. So, to give our new portal its own name, we need to purchase a domain name. When you purchase the domain name, you will need to tell it *which* domain name server (DNS) to point to. You will need to set up a primary and secondary DNS. The following screenshot shows an example of this when registering a domain name on the Network Solutions website.

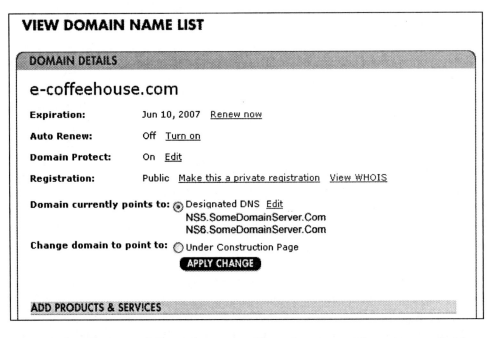

To get your domain server information, you will need to contact the company that is hosting your site to find out the name of your DNS server as well as adding your new domain name to your hosting account.

Most hosting providers will have a control panel that will allow you to add your domain names and find your DNS. The next screenshot shows an example of this type of screen.

Account Details & Info *(dotnetdoc)*

Domain Name(s):
eganenterprises.net
DotNetDoc.com
coffeeconnections.net
eganenterprises.com
e-coffeehouse.com
dotnetclassroom.com
(view all subdomain names)

Domain IP:

Temp URL:

Hosting Plan: Semi Basic

Hosting Length: 1 Year

Status: Normal

Disk Usage: 49.2395 MB out of 2000 MB

ASP.NET Status: ON

FTP Address:
FTP IP:

POP3:

SMTP:

DNS SERVER INFO
eganenterprises.net
Get DNS Info

Home Directory:
c:\webhost4life_aspnet

Perl Path:

Once you set the DNS, you will need to wait a few days for it to propagate. On completing these tasks, you will be ready to set up your portal within DotNetNuke.

Creating a Parent Portal

In the last chapter, we moved our local implementation of DotNetNuke to our hosting provider. Now we are going to create a parent portal from this installation. For this, log in as host and navigate to Host | Portals. This will bring up a list of the portals that have already been set up. To add another portal, access the context menu next to the Portals icon and select Add New Portal.

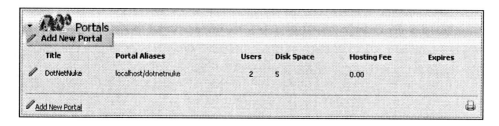

Title	Portal Aliases	Users	Disk Space	Hosting Fee	Expires
DotNetNuke	localhost/dotnetnuke	2	5	0.00	

Add New Portal

You will then be presented with the Portal Setup dialog box.

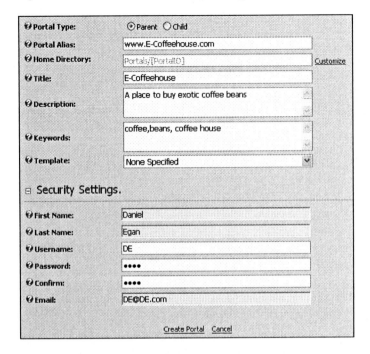

- Select the type of portal you want to create: In this instance we will, of course, be creating a Parent portal.

- Enter the portal alias: This is the website address of your portal (excluding the http://).

- Home directory: If desired, you can change the location where the framework will save portal-specific information. This includes skin and container files.

- Enter the name for your portal.

- Select a template for your portal: You can create templates for your portal so that when they are created, all the skins, containers, modules, and tabs will be created for you. You will find a sample file under the portals/default folder of your installation. Select DotNetNuke, which will create an empty shell for you.

- Enter the administrator information for this portal. This will create a user that will act as the administrator for this new portal.

- When finished, click on Create Portal.

This will create a new empty portal all ready for you to modify.

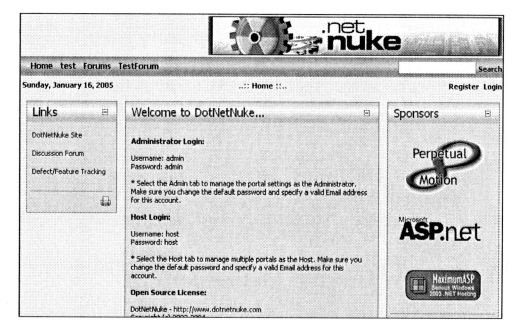

It is important to note that your new portal will use the default properties defined in the Host Settings module. Once the portal is created, these settings can be modified in the Admin Site Settings module.

Setting Up a Child Portal

Child portals, as opposed to parent portals, give you a way to create separate portals without having to set up separate domain names. For this, log in as host and navigate to Host | Portals. This will bring up a list of the portals that have already been set up. To add another portal, hover the cursor over the pencil icon next to the Portals icon and select Add New Portal.

Title	Portal Aliases	Users	Disk Space	Hosting Fee	Expires
DotNetNuke	localhost/dotnetnuke	2	5	0.00	

Add New Portal

You will be presented with the Portal Setup dialog box:

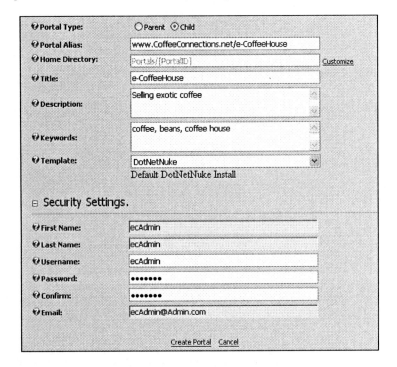

- Select the type of portal you want to create. In this instance, we will be creating a Child portal.

- Enter the portal alias. Since this is a child portal, it is run off a directory on you main site. When you select Child portal, it will fill in the name of your domain with a forward slash(/). Just add the directory name for your portal.

- Enter a title for your portal.

- Enter a description and key words for your portal.

- Select a template for your portal. You can create templates for your portals so that when they are created, all of the skins, containers, modules, and tabs will be created for you. You will find a sample file under the portals/default folder of your installation. Select DotNetNuke, which will create an empty shell for you.

- Enter the administrator information for this portal. This will create a user that will act as the administrator for this new portal.

- When finished click on Create Portal.

This will create a new empty portal all ready for you to modify.

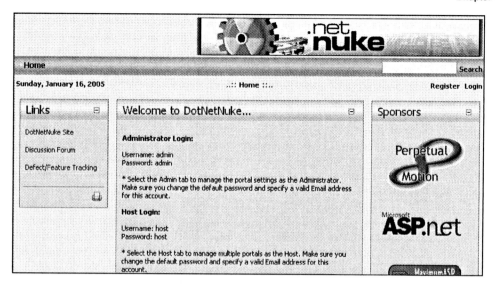

The new portal will use the default properties defined in the Host Settings module. Once the portal is created, these settings can be modified in the Admin Site Settings module.

Creating Portal Templates

In the previous examples, we created our sites using the default DotNetNuke template. While this is helpful if you want to create a site from scratch, you usually wouldn't want to have to add all of the common functionality you would like on your portal each and every time you create a new one. Fortunately, DotNetNuke makes creating a portal template easy.

When you previously created new portals by going to Host | Portals, you may have noticed a section called Export Template at the bottom.

This section allows you to save your portal configuration into a template. This includes your menu navigation, modules, and module content.

- Portal: Just select the portal you would like to export.
- Template File Name: Enter a file name for this template.
- Template Description: Enter a description on the kind of information this template contains.
- Include Content: If you would like the content of the modules to be saved, check this box.

Click on the Export Template link to save your template.

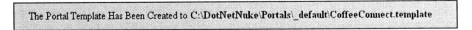

The Portal Template Has Been Created to C:\DotNetNuke\Portals_default\CoffeeConnect.template

This will save your template into an XML-formatted file. If you would like to see the file that is created, navigate to the location presented on the screen. When setting up future portals, you can use this portal as a template.

Using the Site Wizard

The site wizard will allow you to customize your site by walking you through an easy-to-understand step-by-step process. To access this wizard, sign-on as host and click on the Wizard icon in the top panel of the screen:

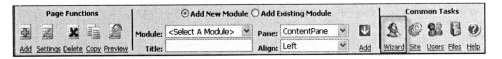

This will bring you to the first step in the site wizard. The first page asks you if you would like to apply a template to your site. If you did not do this when the site was set up, you can accomplish this now. If you already have content on your site, it will ask you how you want to deal with duplicate entries. For example, if you already have a Home page with modules and the template has a Home page with modules, how would you like to resolve this conflict? You have three choices:

- Ignore: This will ignore any items that already exist on your site.
- Replace: This will replace anything on your site with what is contained in the template.
- Merge: This will merge the content in the template with what is already on your site. This may produce multiple menu items or modules, but these can be deleted later.

Click on Next to proceed to the next screen in the wizard.

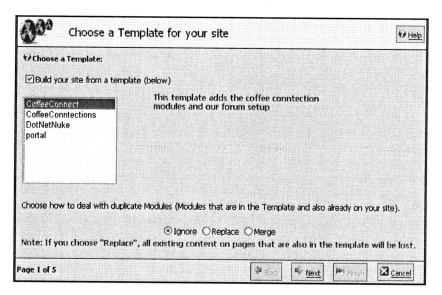

The following screen allows you to apply any skin that you have available to your portal. If you would like to apply a certain skin, select the radio button next to the skin and click on the Next button.

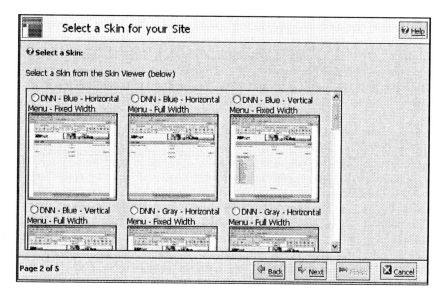

The following screen allows you to set any container that you have available to your portal as the default. If you would like to set a container skin, select the radio button next to the container and click on the Next button.

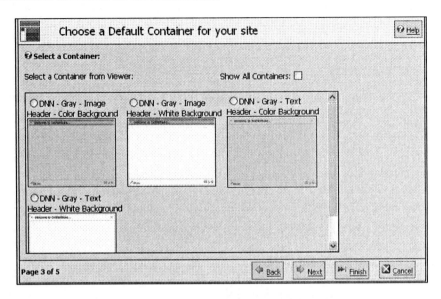

The following screen allows you to add a description and keywords for your portal. Click on the Next button to continue.

The last screen allows you to select the logo you would like to use for your site. In the default DotNetNuke skin, this would show up in the header of your portal.

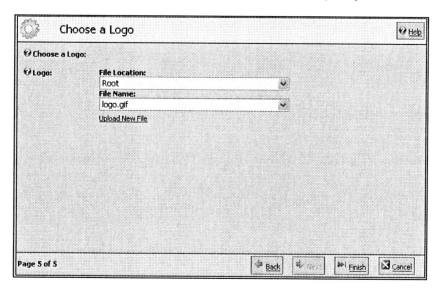

Click on the Finish button to save your settings.

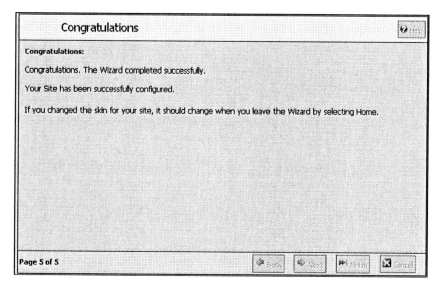

To view the changes, click on the Home menu item. Any changes that you made will now be reflected on your site.

Managing Multiple Portals

As the host user, you will have access to every portal you create. To manage your portals, you just need to navigate to the Portals page by going to Host | Portals from the main menu.

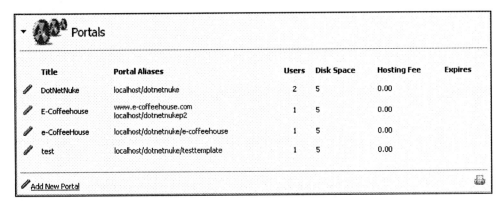

Title	Portal Aliases	Users	Disk Space	Hosting Fee	Expires
DotNetNuke	localhost/dotnetnuke	2	5	0.00	
E-Coffeehouse	www.e-coffeehouse.com localhost/dotnetnukep2	1	5	0.00	
e-CoffeeHouse	localhost/dotnetnuke/e-coffeehouse	1	5	0.00	
test	localhost/dotnetnuke/testtemplate	1	5	0.00	

Add New Portal

You can access each site by clicking on the Portal Aliases link or edit each site by clicking on the pencil icon next to the portal. You will notice that next to each portal there are columns for the following:

- **Users**: The number of users registered for the particular portal.
- **Disk Space**: Since each separate portal shares the same hosting environment, you can set the disk space allowed to each. This will limit the amount each admin will be able to upload to their particular site.
- **Hosting Fee**: If you are charging a hosting fee for each site, you can place that fee in this section.
- **Expires**: You can enforce the fees that you charge for each portal.

It is important to note that even though users of each portal are kept in the same database, they are only assigned to the portal that they registered on. In a default implementation of DotNetNuke, a user would have to register for *each* portal they would like to be a part of. If you need to manage users in a multi-portal environment, I suggest the ITSCS Manage Users PRO available on Snowcovered.com. It allows you to manage users from all portals as well as replicate user credential to multiple portals.

All of these items can be accessed by clicking on the pencil icon next to the portal name. This will bring up the portal settings page. We have seen most of these in the administration chapter of this book. We will just look at the Host Settings section:

This is where you can set the information found on the Portals page. Only the superuser (host) sign-on is able to see all of the portals that have been created. The administrators of each portal will only be able to see the information related to their portal.

Summary

In this chapter, we learned how to create multiple portals that can all be hosted from one account. We have seen how to create and use templates, and how to use the Site Wizard to upgrade your site. We then finished this off by showing you how to manage these portals once they have been set up. Not only will this functionality allow you to create multiple portals, but since all of the information is stored in one database, backing them up is simple. In the next chapter, we will be diving into the world of design patterns and will see how they are integrated into DotNetNuke.

12

Implementing the Provider Model in DotNetNuke

The next version of Visual Studio.NET and the .NET framework (VS 2005, codenamed Whidbey) will come with many new features that are bound to change the way that we program. One of these features is the provider-model design pattern. In this chapter we will:

- Discover what a design pattern is
- Be introduced to the Provider design pattern
- Find out how DotNetNuke uses this pattern
- Create our own HTML Editor provider

What Is an HTML Editor?

An HTML Editor gives the DotNetNuke portal users the ability to design webpages on the fly using an online web-based ASP.NET WYSIWYG control. This replaces a standard textbox with a RichTextBox. For an example of a HTML textbox, sign on as host or admin and select Edit from the context menu of any HTML/Text module.

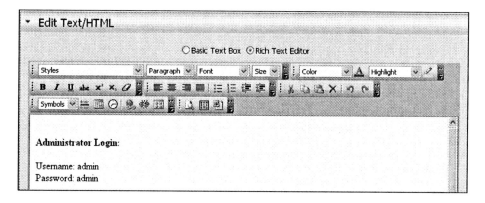

This will give you the ability to edit the HTML/Text area with a control that is similar in functionality to Microsoft Word. The default provider packaged with DotNetNuke is the FreeTextBox (http://www.FreeTextBox.com).

What Is an HTML Editor Provider?

While the FreeTextBox Editor control can be hard-coded into each module that needs to use this functionality, the HTML Editor provider uses the Provider design pattern to extract this functionality outside of the core code. This leads us to a question: What exactly is a design pattern?

Patterns in programming have been around for quite a while, but it was only after a group of authors—Erich Gamma, Richard Helm, Ralph Johnson, and John Vlissides, named the Gang of Four (GOF) affectionately—collaborated, that they were all combined into one body of work. Their groundbreaking book *Design Patterns Elements of Reusable Object-Oriented Software (*Addison-Wesley, 1995*)* took what were at the time scattered ideas, and brought them to the forefront of object-oriented programming.

Probably the simplest description of a pattern is that it is a template for a solution. In programming, the number of different designs needed to accomplish a task is theoretically limited. So instead of re-creating the wheel on every programming project, there should be a way to reuse solutions for similar projects. Patterns are not language specific, but are more of a general technique used to accomplish any given task.

How does this relate to DotNetNuke? Well, one of the new advancements in Visual Studio 2005 and the .NET framework is the use of a pattern called the **Provider design pattern**. This pattern, which closely resembles the AbstractFactory pattern (GOF), allows for a pluggable architecture. This gives the developer the ability to decide on different ways to accomplish the same task without being tied down to a particular architecture. This new pattern has been incorporated into the current DotNetNuke framework. For example, DotNetNuke, using the Provider design pattern, allows you to use the database of your choice as long as there is a provider designed for your database choice.

HTML Editor Provider

To give you a general overview of the process, as we have seen in previous chapters, modules plug into the DotNetNuke architecture using a `PortalModuleBase` class that all modules need to implement. An HTML provider works in a similar way.

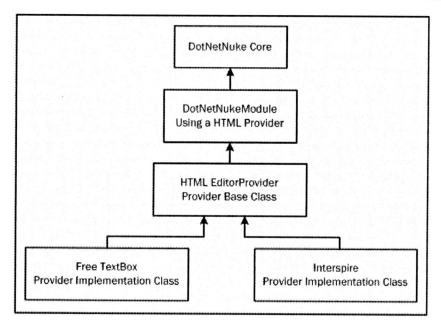

The HTMLEditorProvider base class is tied into each module that uses an HTML provider. This class defines a number of properties and methods that need to be implemented so that the HTML Editor functions properly. Each provider needs to implement these methods in order for them to be used in a DotNetNuke module. We will discuss this implementation in detail as we work our way through this chapter.

> In a default implementation, only one HTML Editor can be used at a time. The editor to be used is defined inside the web.config file.

While the FreeTextBox is a fantastic tool and (as the name implies) is free to distribute, you many want to use another WYSIWYG textbox. We will show you how to create the provider code necessary to include your HTML textbox into DotNetNuke.

For the purposes of this chapter, we have decided to use DevEdit by Interspire (http://www.interspire.com/devedit/). This control has some unique controls built into it, including forms, Flash inserts, and advanced table editing.

We will be using the free trial for our project. This is the complete product with all the features and the limitation of pop-up reminder ads. The package you download will contain all of the assemblies you will need as well as a .NET solution to give you the ability to inspect the DevEdit control outside the DotNetNuke project.

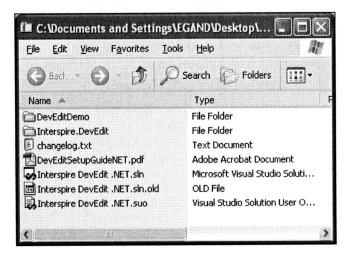

Setting Up the Providers Folder

Before you start to move any files, you first need to create the folder structure needed for your provider. Inside the DotNetNuke project, you will find a folder called `Providers`. This folder contains all the providers available in the portal. Open the `HtmlEditorProviders` folder. This is where we want the new provider to go. Create a folder called `DevEditProvider` inside the `HtmlEditorProviders` folder. The first thing you need to do is to copy some of the files that you downloaded from the Interspire website. Once unzipped, the necessary files can be found in the `devedit_aspnet_demo\DevEditDemo` folder. Copy the `de`, `images`, and `flash` folders from the download into the newly created folder.

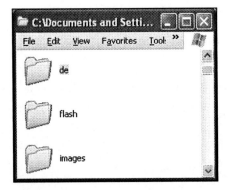

These folders contain the items needed by the control to work properly. Finally we will need to copy `Interspire.DevEdit.dll` to the `bin` directory of DotNetNuke. You will find this file in the `devedit_aspnet_demo\DevEditDemo\bin` folder of `devedit_aspnet_demo` that you downloaded.

Setting Up the Provider Project

The process used to create a Provider project will be similar to that for creating a project for custom modules. Again we will be setting up a private assembly (PA) project. To set up your private assembly, take the following steps:

1. Open up the DotNetNuke Providers Visual Studio.NET solution file (`C:\DotNetNuke\Solutions\DotNetNuke.Providers\DotNetNuk eProviders.sln`).

2. In the Solution Explorer, right-click on the DotNetNuke solution (not the project) and select Add | New Project:

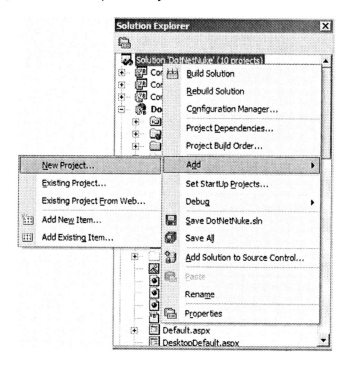

3. In project types, make sure that Visual Basic Projects is highlighted, and select Class Library as the project type. The controls will be running in the DotNetNuke virtual directory, so we do not create a web project as this would create an additional virtual directory that we do not need.

4. The location of your project should be under your `Providers\HTMLEdi torProviders\DevEditProvider` folder, which is located under `C:\DotNetNuke`.

5. The name of your project should follow the `Provider.ProviderTypeName` convention. This will help avoid name collisions with other providers. Our project will be named `Provider.DevEditHtmlEditorProvider`.

This will result in a new project added to the DotNetNuke solution. You'll need to modify a few properties to allow for debugging the project within the DotNetNuke solution.

1. Delete the `Class1.vb` file that was created with the project.

2. Right-click on our private assembly project and select Properties.

3. In the `Common Properties` folder, under the General section remove the Root Namespace (since we will be running this under the `DotNetNuke` namespace, we do not want this to default to the name of our assembly).

4. Click OK to save your settings.

To be able to use all of the objects available to you in DotNetNuke, you need to add a reference to the DotNetNuke project.

1. Right-click on the reference folder located below the private assembly project just created, and select Add Reference.

2. Select the Projects tab.

3. Double-click on the DotNetNuke project to place it in the Selected Components box.

4. Click OK to add the reference.

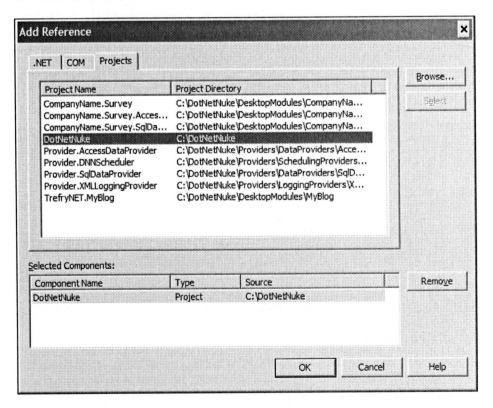

When we run a project as a private assembly in DotNetNuke, the DLL for the module should be located in the DotNetNuke bin directory. This is where DotNetNuke will look for the assembly when it tries to load your module. To accomplish this, there is a BuildSupport project inside each of the solutions. The BuildSupport project is responsible for taking the DLL created by your project and adding it to the DotNetNuke solution's bin folder.

To allow the BuildSupport project to add your DLL, you need to add a reference to the DotNetNuke project.

1. Right-click on the Reference folder located below the private assembly project you just created and select Add Reference:

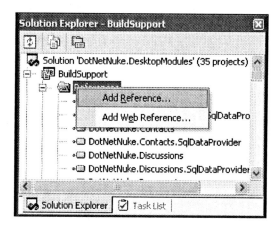

2. Select the Projects tab.
3. Double-click on the Provider.DevEditHtmlEditorProvider project to place it in the Selected Components box.
4. Click OK to add the reference.

After this, you need to add a reference to the Interspire.DevEdit.dll placed in the DotNetNuke\bin directory:

1. Right-click on the Reference folder located below the private assembly project you just created and select Add Reference.
2. Click on the Browse button and locate the Interspire.DevEdit.dll in the DotNetNuke\bin folder.
3. Double-click on the DotNetNuke project to place it in the Selected Components box.
4. Click OK to add the reference.

Before moving on, make sure that you can build the solution without any errors. After building the solution, you should see something similar to this in your output window:

```
--------------------- Done ---------------------
```

```
Build: 54 succeeded, 0 failed, 0 skipped
```

The number you have in succeeded may be different, but make sure that there is zero in failed. If there are any errors, fix them before moving on.

Creating the Provider

Here we want to create the class that will be responsible for controlling our HTML Editor. Within the DotNetNuke solution, right-click on the Provider.DevEditHt mlEditorProvider project and select Add Class. Name the class DevEditHtmlEd itorProvider and click OK. With the class created, we now add some imports to help with the class as well as surround it with a custom namespace:

```
Imports System.IO
Imports System.Web
Imports System.Configuration
Imports DotNetNuke
Imports Interspire
Imports System.Web.UI.Page
Imports System.Web.UI.WebControls
Imports DotNetNuke.Entities.Portals
Imports DotNetNuke.Common
Imports DotNetNuke.Framework.Providers

Namespace Interspire.HtmlEditor
        Public Class DevEditHtmlEditorProvider
```

This class will need to inherit from the HtmlEditorProvider base class.

```
        Inherits DotNetNuke.Modules.HTMLEditorProvider.HtmlEditorProvider
```

HTMLEditorProvider is the base class that all HTML Editor providers must implement in order to work with DotNetNuke. This file can be found in the DotNetNuke\Providers \HTMLEditor folder of the DotNetNuke project. It is declared as a MustInherit class, which means that it cannot be instantiated by itself and can only be used as a base class. The base class has several MustOverride properties and methods that we will need to override in our provider class. We will cover these as we implement them.

Returning to our DevEditHtmlEditorProvider class, we will first declare some class-level variables. To be able to implement the control, you will need to create an instance of the DevEdit control to work with.

```
    Dim cntlDevEdit As New Interspire.DevEdit.DevEdit
```

This is followed by variables to hold our provider. A constant will declare the provider type, which in this case will be htmlEditor.

```
    Private Const ProviderType As String = "htmlEditor"
```

Using this variable, we collect the configuration information that we will be placing in the web.config file.

```
Private _providerConfiguration As ProviderConfiguration = _
    ProviderConfiguration.GetProviderConfiguration(ProviderType)
```

Finally, we declare a variable to hold the path to the provider assembly that we will be creating.

```
Private _providerPath As String
```

Next, we create the constructor for our provider. We start by creating a variable that will hold our portal settings. This is available to us through the base class, which itself inherits from the Framework.UserControlBase class.

```
Public Sub New()

Dim _portalSettings As PortalSettings = _
DotNetNuke.Entities.Portals.PortalController.GetCurrentPortalSettings
```

We then collect our provider information along with its attributes by making a call to the web.config file. This works the same way as the Data provider, which looks for the default provider set inside the web.config file. We use this information to fill the _providerPath variable we declared earlier.

```
Dim objProvider As Provider = _
CType(_providerConfiguration.Providers(_providerConfiguration.Default
Provider), Provider)

_providerPath = objProvider.Attributes("providerPath")

End Sub
```

The provider path is then made available through a ReadOnly property as shown below:

```
Public ReadOnly Property ProviderPath() As String
            Get
                Return _providerPath
            End Get
End Property
```

Now before we move on to the next method in our class, we will take a slight detour into the TextEditor.ascs.vb file. This is the control that will be placed on your module when you want to use a text editor. You can find this file in the DotNetNuke\Controls folder. We will not be discussing this control, just what is called when the control is loaded. In the Page_Init section, you will find the following code:

```
RichText = RichText.Instance
RichText.ControlID = Me.ID
RichText.Initialize()
```

The first two lines call the Instance function in the HtmlEditor base class and set the controlID of our current control respectively, but it is important to bring your attention to the third line. Once an instance is created and the ID of the control is set, the `Initialize` method is called from our provider class. This method is declared in our base class as `MustOverride` and therefore must be implemented in the provider class using the `Overrides` keyword. The first order of business is to initialize the control variable that we declared above.

```
Public Overrides Sub Initialize()
        cntlDevEdit = New Interspire.DevEdit.DevEdit
```

We then grab our portal settings and pull our provider information from `web.config`.

```
Dim _portalSettings As PortalSettings = _
DotNetNuke.Entities.Portals.PortalController.GetCurrentPortalSettings

Dim objProvider As Provider = _
CType(_providerConfiguration.Providers(_providerConfiguration.Default
Provider), Provider)
```

We can then initialize properties that are specific to the HTML control that is being used. We can either hardcode them in our class as shown by the `FlashPath` property, or allow our users to modify this information by adding information to an attribute in the `web.config` as shown by the `ImagePath` property.

```
cntlDevEdit.SpellingButton = False

cntlDevEdit.DevEditPath = _
"Providers/HtmlEditorProviders/DevEditProvider/de"

cntlDevEdit.ImagePath = _
HttpUtility.UrlDecode(objProvider.Attributes("imagePath")).ToString

cntlDevEdit.FlashPath = "/DevFlash"
End Sub
```

To finish up the provider, we need to implement the remaining `MustOverride` methods and properties from the base class. We have already overridden the `Initialize` method, and so we only need to override the `AddToolbar` method. Since we will not be adding any extra toolbars to our provider, we just need to create the empty shell.

```
Public Overrides Sub AddToolbar()

End Sub
```

There are seven properties we must override: `HtmEditorControl`, `AdditionalToolbars`, `ControlID`, `RootImageDirectory`, `Text`, `Width`, and `Height`. We place these at the bottom of our class file.

We will need to declare a variable to hold the root directory for our images.

```
Private _RootImageDirectory As String
```

We then create a `ReadOnly` property for the `DevEdit` control we declared above. This will allow us to retrieve the instance of the control later on.

```
Public Overrides ReadOnly Property HtmlEditorControl() As _
    System.Web.UI.Control
```

```
Get
    Return cntlDevEdit
End Get
End Property
```

We then use the control to populate our Text, ControlID, Width, and Height properties.

```
Public Overrides Property Text() As String
    Get
        Text = cntlDevEdit.Text
    End Get
    Set(ByVal Value As String)
        cntlDevEdit.Text = Value
    End Set
End Property

Public Overrides Property ControlID() As String
    Get
        ControlID = cntlDevEdit.ID
    End Get
    Set(ByVal Value As String)
        cntlDevEdit.ID = Value
    End Set
End Property

Public Overrides Property Width() As _
    System.Web.UI.WebControls.Unit
    Get
        'Width = _width
        Width = cntlDevEdit.Width
    End Get
    Set(ByVal Value As System.Web.UI.WebControls.Unit)
        '_Width = Value
        cntlDevEdit.Width = Value
    End Set
End Property

Public Overrides Property Height() As _
    System.Web.UI.WebControls.Unit
    Get
        'Height = _Height
        Height = cntlDevEdit.Height
    End Get
    Set(ByVal Value As System.Web.UI.WebControls.Unit)
        '_Height = Value
        cntlDevEdit.Height = Value
    End Set
End Property
```

We then create a shell for our AdditonalToolbars property, and use the portal settings to set the RootImageDirectory property.

```
Public Overrides Property AdditionalToolbars() As ArrayList
    Get

    End Get
    Set(ByVal Value As ArrayList)
```

```
                    End Set
            End Property

            Public Overrides Property RootImageDirectory() As String
                Get

                    If _RootImageDirectory = "" Then
                            Dim _portalSettings As PortalSettings =
        DotNetNuke.Entities.Portals.PortalController.GetCurrentPortalSettings

                            RootImageDirectory =
        _portalSettings.HomeDirectory.Substring(_portalSettings.HomeDirectory
        .IndexOf("/Portals/"))
                        Else
                            RootImageDirectory = _RootImageDirectory
                        End If

                End Get
                Set(ByVal Value As String)
                    _RootImageDirectory = Value
                End Set
            End Property
```

This concludes our provider class. Build your project and confirm that no errors are
present. Next, we will configure our web.config to use our new provider.

Adding Your Provider to the web.config File

The final piece needed to utilize our new HTML Editor with DotNetNuke is to modify
the htmlEditor section of the web.config file. The first thing you need to do is to add a
section below the Ftb3HtmlEditorProvider section. This will add an additional
provider to the htmlEditor provider collection. We will do this using the <add> tag,
which should be placed after the ending tag of the element for the FreeTextBox provider.
In addition, we also want to change the defaultProvider attribute of the htmlEditor
element to specify the DevEditHtmlEditorProvider provider as the default provider:

```
<htmlEditor defaultProvider="DevEditHtmlEditorProvider">
    <providers>
      <clear />
        <add name="Ftb3HtmlEditorProvider"
         type="DotNetNuke.HtmlEditor.Ftb3HtmlEditorProvider,
         DotNetNuke.Ftb3HtmlEditorProvider"
         providerPath=
         "~\Providers\HtmlEditorProviders\Ftb3HtmlEditorProvider\"
        />

        <add name = "DevEditHtmlEditorProvider"
         type = "Interspire.HtmlEditor.DevEditHtmlEditorProvider,
            Provider.DevEditHtmlEditorProvider"
         providerPath =
            "~\Providers\HtmlEditorProviders\DevEditProvider\"
         imagePath=
         "~\Providers\HtmlEditorProviders\DevEditProvider\de\DevImages"
         />
    </providers>
</htmlEditor>
```

If you now run the portal, sign on as host or admin, and click edit on the HTML/Text module context menu, you will see that it is now using the Interspire HTML Editor:

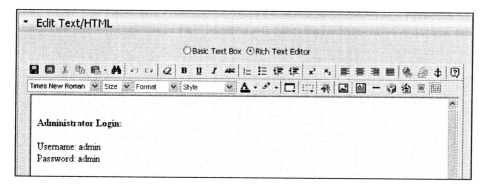

Other HTML Editor Providers for DotNetNuke

As the popularity of DotNetNuke grows, so will the number of providers available for use in the framework. You have already seen how you can create your own provider, but there are also other HTML Editors (in addition to the FreeTextBox) that have already been incorporated into DotNetNuke. One of the better examples of this is the CuteEditor.NET from CuteSoft (`http://www.CuteSoft.net`).

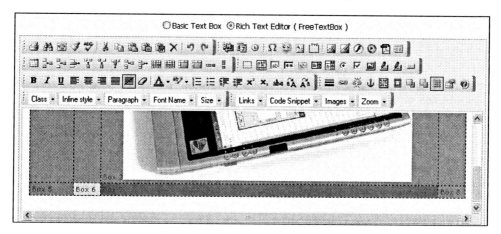

CuteEditor.NET is an advanced online web-based ASP.NET WYSIWYG control. The CuteEditor toolbar is completely configurable and it is also effortless to implement. CuteEditor is not free, but has some advanced features that you might want to implement for the portal.

So if you would like to use something other than the FreeTextBox but do not want to create your own provider, there are other solutions.

Summary

This chapter has given you a general overview of the Provider design pattern and walked you through creating one for use in the DotNetNuke framework. Even though we focused this chapter on a provider for the HTML Editor, you should be able to take this and adapt it for use with any of the providers that come with DotNetNuke.

Index

H

I

L

M

W

X

Y

Printed in the United States
26450LVS00001B/105-126